BROWN

THE HISTORY OF AN IDEA

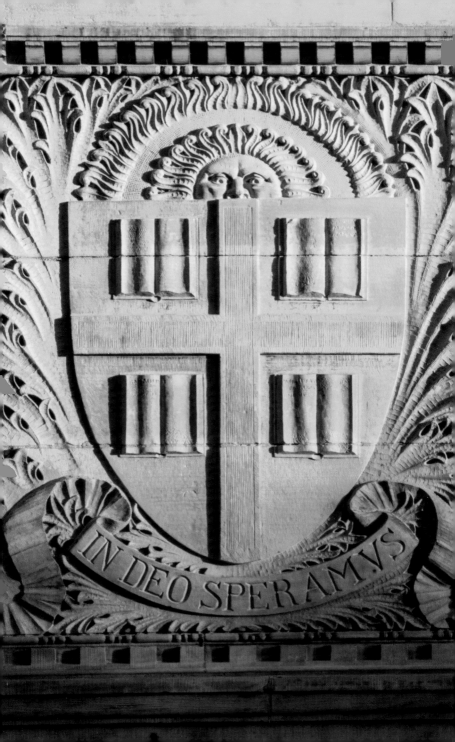

IN DEO SPERAMVS

BROWN

THE HISTORY OF AN IDEA

Ted Widmer

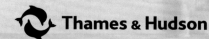
Thames & Hudson

*In my father I observed mildness of temper, and unchange-
able resolution in the things which he had determined on
after due deliberation; and no vainglory in those things
which men call honors; and a love of labor and persever-
ance; and a readiness to listen to whoever had anything to
propose for the common weal; and undeviating firmness in
giving to every man his deserts; and a knowledge derived
from experience of the right times for vigorous action and
for relaxation. . . . I observed too his habit of careful
inquiry in all matters of deliberation, and his persistency;
and that he never stopped his investigation through being
satisfied with first appearances; and that his disposition was
to keep his friends, and not to be soon tired of them, nor yet
to be extravagant in his affection; and to be satisfied on all
occasions, and cheerful; and to foresee things a long way off,
and to provide for the smallest details without display; and
to check immediately popular applause and all flattery;
and to be ever watchful over the things which were necessary for the administration of the empire. . . .*

—MARCUS AURELIUS,
Meditations

Be slow to speak and swift to hear; be angry only when absolutely necessary, and then you will not be likely to exceed due bounds. Despise the narrow, contracted principle which actuates the selfish, and only think you deserve the character of men when you affectionately love and glow with ardor to promote the happiness of all mankind.

—PRESIDENT JAMES MANNING,
CHARGE TO THE GRADUATING
CLASS OF 1773

CONTENTS

The Governor and Company of his Majesty's English Colony of
Rhode Island and Providence Plantations in America in their General
Assembly held at Newport within & for said Colony on the first monday
of August Anno Domini One Thousand seven hundred & sixty three
and in the third year of the reign of his Majesty George the third of
Great Britain France & Ireland King. To all to whom these
presents shall come, Greeting.

Whereas Institutions for liberal Education are highly beneficial
to Society, by forming the rising Generation to Virtue Knowledge & useful Literature, and thus preserving in a Community a Succession of Men qualified for
discharging the Offices of life with Usefulness & Reputation, they have therefore
justly merited and received the public Attention & Encouragement of every wise
and polite & well regulated State. And whereas a public School or Seminary
erected for this purpose within this Colony to which the Youth may freely resort
for Education in the vernacular & learned Languages, and in the liberal Arts
and Sciences, would be for the Advantage & honor of this Government. And
whereas the honorable Stephen Hopkins Esqr, the Honorable John Gardner Esqr,
the honble Samuel Ward Esqr, the honble William Ellery Esqr, James Honyman,
Abraham Redwood, Francis Willet, Simon Pease, Danl Jenks, Jno Tillinghast, Nicolas
Tillinghast, Joseph Russel, Dr Scott, Joseph Clark, James Helme Esquire, Col. Elisha
Reynolds, Col Jonas Lyndon, Col Benjn Hall, Col. Job Bennet, Mr. James David Chesborough,
Joseph Jacob, Nathl Coggeshall, Ephraim Bowen, William Ellery Junr, Gideon Wanton
Revd Messr Othniel Campbell, Edwd Upham, Jno Hunt, William Vinal, John Maxson, Gar-
diner Thurston, Ezra Stiles, Martin Brown, Thos Habberton, Thos Moffat M.D. George Hazard, Joshua
Clark Esqr, Saml Nightingale, Sherjashub Bourn Esqr, Mesr Nicolas Brown, Thomas
Eyres, Elnathan Hammond, Wm Rogers, Jno Tanner, Ezekiel Burrough, Henry Paxton,
&c &c

appear as Undertakers in this valuable Design: and thereupon a Petition hath
been preferred to this Assembly, praying that full Liberty & Power may be granted
unto them to found, endow, order & govern a College or University within this
Colony; and for the more effectual Encouragement & Execution of this design to incorporate them into one Body politic to be known in the law, with the powers,
privileges & Franchises necessary to the purposes aforesaid. Now therefore
KNOW YE that being willing to encourage and patronize such an advantageous
& useful Institution, We the said GOVERNOR and COMPANY in General Assembly
convened, do for ourselves and our Successors, in & by Virtue of the powers & authority
within the Jurisdiction of this Colony to us by the Royal Charter committed, enact,
grant ordain constitute and declare, and it is hereby enacted granted ordained
constituted and declared that the said Stephen Hopkins, John Gardner &c &c

FOREWORD

I N 1765, A YEAR AFTER ITS FOUNDING, William Rogers enrolled as the first student in the newly formed College of Rhode Island, an institution established for the purpose of preparing men for "discharging the offices of life with usefulness and reputation." James Manning, a Baptist minister who served as the new college's first president and sole professor, ran the college from his parsonage and meeting house in the town of Warren, Rhode Island. The college, although small and poor, was distinguished by an unusually open-minded and pragmatic approach to education. In a forward-looking departure from common practice, the college's charter declared that students from all religious backgrounds could be admitted. To better prepare students for their lives of usefulness, the charter described an education that was to be both rigorous and practical, teaching students in "the vernacular and learned languages, and in the liberal arts and sciences."

This book by historian Ted Widmer tells the story of how, over a quarter of a millennium, Brown was transformed from the College of Rhode Island to the modern university that it is today. It is a selective history, focusing on a few time periods, events, and people that influenced the course of Brown's development. Through the careful choice of subject matter, the book elucidates Brown's evolution and captures the spirit that has characterized Brown since its beginning. Ted shows us that despite the pronounced changes that have occurred over 250 years, Brown retains its core values: a deep commitment to academic excellence, a fierce dedication to intellectual independence, and a belief that education and scholarly inquiry are vital to the advancement of society.

OPPOSITE: Charter drafted by Ezra Stiles in 1764.

This book also illustrates that, from its outset, Brown was very much an American institution. Indeed, Brown's experience reflects both the best and worst of American society from the colonial era to the present. Ted describes our early and deep ties to the Atlantic slave trade, now recognized in a Slavery Memorial that was dedicated in September 2014. The memorial was installed close to University Hall, the college's original building, which was constructed in part by slave labor. The book also shows how Brown was engaged with and, at times, contributed to the political and social upheavals that swept through the country over this 250-year period, many of which resulted in positive changes at Brown: the addition of women and members of racial and ethnic minority groups to our student body and the faculty; the development of a deep commitment to making education accessible to students from all economic backgrounds; and the emergence of Brown as a global institution. Throughout all of this, Brown's educational priorities have been shaped by a sense of constructive irreverence that springs from the DNA of Rhode Island.

Two hundred and fifty years ago, did Brown's founders have a clear understanding of all that their new college would achieve? I doubt it. As I write, I am in Hong Kong for a celebration of the 250th anniversary of Brown's founding, which several hundred alumni and parents of Brown students will attend. Despite their commitment to accepting a diverse student body, Brown's founders were unlikely to have imagined that the Brown community would someday extend around the world. Despite their commitment to academic excellence, they could not have comprehended the contributions that Brown faculty would make in the then unknown fields of computer science, particle physics, and brain science. And, despite their desire to prepare students for lives of meaning and purpose, they could not have foreseen that, for example, one day two Brown alumni, a Korean American physician named Jim Yong Kim and a female economist named Janet Yellen, would lead the World Bank and the U.S. Federal Reserve, respectively—and not only because those institutions did not exist in 1764.

I invite you to read this book, not only to learn about Brown's past, but also to spark your imagination as to what Brown's future might be. Although it is impossible to predict the specific accomplishments that lie ahead, we can be confident that Brown's bold and independent spirit will continue.

CHRISTINA H. PAXSON
Nineteenth President, Brown University

BROWN

THE HISTORY OF AN IDEA

VAN WICKLE GATE, BROWN UNIVERSITY, PROVIDENCE, R.I.

CHAPTER I

BROWN BEGINS

Páspisha. *It is Sunne-rise.*

—ROGER WILLIAMS,
A Key into the Language of America, 1643.[*]

SUNRISE

A CURIOUS UNDERGRADUATE, raised on too much Harry Potter, might be forgiven for pausing before the Van Wickle Gates, beguiled. Here, surely, are mysteries worthy of decipherment. But where to begin? There are sculpted owls, suggesting that this might be an ancient Greek shrine to Athena. There are lamps, globes, and hourglasses resting atop old books and parchments, as if to remind the casual passerby not to tarry too long, when there is so much knowledge waiting to be discovered. There are city and state seals, as in the Middle Ages, when every castle and cathedral needed to proclaim where it was and how it fit into Creation. An anchor confirms that we are in Rhode Island, a place that long derived its living from the sea and its faith from the Good Book, which affirms that hope is "an anchor of the soul" (Heb. 6:19). A nearby

---

[*] Here and at the head of subsequent chapters, the wording as expressed in the language of the Narragansett Indians was recorded by Roger Williams (see endnote 1).

pictograph of men by a canoe tells the story of the flight from persecution that first brought Europeans to this place, where they were welcomed by the Narragansett, who had lived here for millennia.

Finally, above it all, a sunrise. The seal of Brown University offers a promising first impression. Near the top, the sun, refulgent, scans the horizon with far-seeing eyes.[2] Just below, four books present themselves, open, to the curious reader. Beneath, the Latin phrase *In Deo Speramus*, "In God We Hope"—a bit less omniscient than "In God We Trust," and consonant with the modest motto of Rhode Island: Hope.

All of these elements—enlightenment, knowledge, and hope—were palpably in the air in 1764, the date emblazoned at the bottom of the seal, when the university came into existence. And some modesty as well, befitting an institution whose entire student body, in its first year, consisted of a lone fourteen-year-old. Brown's sun has risen to a very high meridian since then. Indeed, an attempt to measure the sun, in 1769, showed how ambitious the founders were, and helped to settle the college on this hill, closer to heaven. But if that pioneering student could see the modern university, a quarter of a millennium later, he would not be entirely disoriented. For Brown retains a healthy connection to the clamorous time and place of its birth.

It was fortunate in each. Rhode Island had been devoted to freedom of conscience since the first settlers arrived, and it offered a natural home to askers of hard questions, banished from other places for doing just that. Likewise, the Baptists who sought a new college were naturally averse to authority and eager to build something better than what had come before (by which they meant Harvard and Yale, preservers of a status quo that the founders were none too impressed by). Given this DNA, how could Brown be ordinary?

1764 was a charged year in American history, the very moment that an argument over British taxes began to lead the colonists on the path that would culminate in independence. To a degree, that path was charted on College Hill. In that year, Governor Stephen Hopkins, one of Brown's original Corporation members, began to write a series of searing newspaper essays that would form his manifesto, *The Rights of Colonies Examined* (1765). It opened with the statement, "Liberty is the greatest blessing that men enjoy, and slavery the heaviest curse that human nature is capable of."[3] That statement revealed considerable blindness about slavery, already enriching many Rhode Island families, including his own. In the same year, his brother, Esek Hopkins, led a voyage to Africa, well documented in Brown's *Slavery and Justice* report. His vessel, the *Sally*, acquired 169 slaves in Africa; 109 died on the Middle Crossing. For all the talk of liberty, Rhode Islanders were in the forefront of the North American slave trade, carrying more than 100,000 Africans into bondage.[4]

This contradiction would take centuries to resolve, and indeed, it remains a work in progress. But in 1764 it seemed the entire world was beginning anew, and the moment was right to launch a new educational enterprise. The British and their American allies had just won a sweeping victory over the French, codified in the 1763 Treaty of Paris, which opened up new worlds to the ambitious Anglo-Americans. Once and for all, the problem of encirclement disappeared, and with less to fear from the French and their native allies, Americans felt free to explore. By the tens of thousands, they poured into northern New England, upstate New York, and the western regions of the middle and southern colonies, past the once impregnable barrier of the Appalachians. Sometimes they even ventured into the fertile basin of the Ohio River, over the objections of the British, who did not seem entirely in control of the spoils they had just won. A staggering increase in population ensued, as immigrants flooded in from the British Isles. A contemporary observer, Hector St. John de Crèvecoeur, was amazed by the "the prodigious number of houses rearing up, fields cultivating, that great extent of industry open'd up to a bold indefatigable enterprising people."[5]

At the same time, the British Crown was trying urgently to restrict and regulate American economic activity, immediately after galvanizing it by defeating the French. Accordingly, feelings were running raw on the eve of Brown's creation. The Sugar Act of 1764, an indirect tax on the colonies, touched Rhode Island to the quick, producing a vivid document of protest, the Rhode Island Remonstrance, that argued passionately against the new measure. In spite of its small size, the colony was at the center of an increasingly bitter argument in 1764.[6] Brown University was one result of a growing American tendency to talk back—the United States of America was another.

RHODE ISLAND

IN RHODE ISLAND, things were moving very fast in the year of Brown's birth. In the aftermath of Britain's victory, Newport and Providence were growing rapidly (New England's population rose 59 percent between 1760 and 1780[7]). The docks teemed with new arrivals, particularly from the British Isles, who brought with them a feeling that history was accelerating—with a quickening of economic activity, an inclination to start new ventures, and a sense that America was destined to become a theater of greatness.

Exorbitant self-promotion was already a feature of American writing, and there were few groups of settlers who did not claim, to some degree, divine favor for their schemes. But even the most cynical observer might come away impressed by the natural setting of Narragansett Bay. Since it first attracted notice from Europeans, this place had struck observers as different from the rest of New England: warmer than the cold Atlantic waters of Massachusetts Bay, oriented toward the South, gentler in its topography, and naturally receptive to visitors. In 1524, Giovanni da Verrazzano, charmed by the bay and its landscapes, had called it *Refugio*, a place to escape the oppressions of the world.

That prophecy had turned out well. From its founding in 1636 as a refuge for outcasts from Massachusetts, Rhode Island had grown considerably in wealth and sophistication. For much of the colonial period, it had been fashionable to insult Rhode Island for its failure to conform to the straitlaced standards of the Puritans. Cotton Mather, the legendary bluenose, had dismissed the colony as "the *latrina* of New England," adding to his moral superiority by using the Latin term, when "sewer" would have done just as well. The phrase was apt, he surely felt, because the wrong kind of people had been flowing toward his southern neighbor for some time.

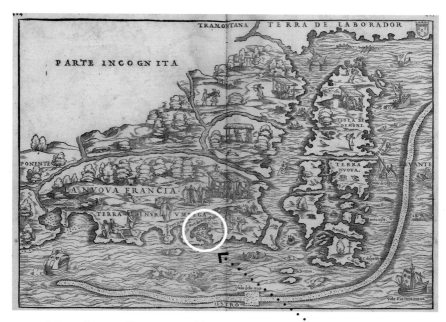

A sixteenth-century Venetian map of New England, showing the "Port du Refuge," or port of refuge, that Verrazzano found at what is now Narragansett Bay.

From the perspective of Boston and Harvard, especially, Rhode Island's shortcomings were obvious. It was not simply that the colony accepted just about anyone who chose to settle there and was becoming a kind of Babel, full of people rejected by the world's civilized societies. Even more annoyingly, the tiny colony was trying to turn its chaos into a virtue by celebrating, all too irreverently, a freedom that Massachusetts went to great pains to suppress: the right to worship in a manner of one's own choosing. The original Rhode Islander, Roger Williams, had been banished for asking too many questions—about the separation of church and state, about how the Indians were treated, about nearly every assumption underpinning the cold logic of Boston (Cotton Mather would compare him to a windmill, madly spinning). A flight into the wilderness followed, as Williams found his way through the forests and the Indian encampments, where he took shelter, before emerging on the eastern bank of the Seekonk River, at the

The compass and sundial used by Roger Williams in his flight through the wilderness.
RHi X17 1147. Compass and Sundial owned by Roger Williams. Providence, RI. c.1630. Brass.
Courtesy the Rhode Island Historical Society.

head of Narragansett Bay, in the spring of 1636. There he lived briefly, until Plymouth officials requested that he leave their jurisdiction—they considered the Seekonk their western boundary. So Williams did what pioneers always do—he kept going, and crossed over to the other side, in a canoe.

This was Narragansett land, and when Williams arrived, he came not as a conqueror, but as a supplicant, hoping to live in peace with the Native Americans, whom he befriended. Rhode Island's founding moment—captured in the pictograph of the Van Wickle Gates—was meeker than that of the other colonies and less predicated on the sense of moral superiority that suffused so many of the other foundation myths. To put it bluntly, Williams had nowhere else to go; but one understands why he felt that a "special providence" had guided his steps to the place he soon named for it, in gratitude. The Indians received him generously and gave him land, including the parcel Brown sits upon, as part of the original "Providence Plantations." When it came time to set up his own colony, he refused to establish an official church, or to demand conformity in any way except obedience to the law. He wrote simply, "I desired it might be for a shelter for persons distressed of conscience."[8] Once again, Narragansett Bay offered a refuge.

The royal charter of 1663 that finally brought a measure of legitimacy to Rhode Island was clear that all citizens possessed freedom of conscience—what Williams called "soul liberty." As a result, Rhode Island attracted a wide variety of seekers and, unavoidably, a few scofflaws and scapegraces as well. The charter predicted that a "livelie experiment" would ensue, and that certainly turned out to be true. Inevitably, there were problems uniting these iconoclasts, but over

A piece of "Slate Rock," which Roger Williams landed upon when he founded Rhode Island in 1636.

time the charter proved durable, and Rhode Island's freedoms survived. Despite the greater size of Massachusetts (and Connecticut, squeezing Rhode Island from the other side), the Rhode Island idea proved attractive, flavoring American history to no small degree. What we take for granted today—the religious freedom enshrined in the First Amendment, the Four Freedoms, and the Universal Declaration of Human Rights—owes something to the communities gathered around Narragansett Bay in the seventeenth century, working out their ideas about tolerance and coexistence. At a time when "democracy" was anything but a compliment, the little colony was developing democratic features, well in advance of the others. It even dared to use the word—"the forme of Government" was proudly declared to be "Democraticall."[9]

At times, this cacophony of free thought undermined the standing order, and some of the less well-known writings of Roger Williams show him desperately trying to get his fellow citizens to pull together. Rhode Islanders tended to be less organized at the kinds of efforts Massachusetts considered important—synods to enforce religious orthodoxy or military expeditions to quell Native Americans. Indeed, Williams didn't especially want to quell anyone, unless Rhode Island was directly threatened. He was a gifted speaker of native languages, and his first book, *A Key into the Language of America* (1643), offered a detailed look at the life and folkways of the Narragansett, whose spirituality and self-government he admired.[10] In many ways, this extraordinary book created a template for all that would follow. It revealed a highly sentient observer, speaking in the language of the Narragansett, learning from his new surroundings, and arguing (before a London readership) that he had found a special place where a higher conversation was possible. He claimed, somewhat radically, that all peoples were made "of one bloode." He studied nature closely, two centuries before Thoreau, and asserted the indigenous right to the land—one of the ways in which he had enraged the authorities in Boston. Reflecting on the consensual way in which he asked for permission to live among them, he wrote, "Rhode Island was purchased by love."[11]

A KEY into the
LANGUAGE
OF
AMERICA:
OR,

An help to the *Language* of the *Natives*
in that part of AMERICA, called
NEW-ENGLAND.

Together, with briefe *Observations* of the Cu-
stomes, Manners and Worships, *&c.* of the
aforesaid *Natives*, in Peace and Warre,
in Life and Death.

On all which are added Spirituall *Observations,*
Generall and Particular by the *Authour*, of
chiefe and speciall use (upon all occasions,) to
all the *English* Inhabiting those parts;
yet pleasant and profitable to
the view of all men :

BY ROGER WILLIAMS
of *Providence* in *New-England*.

LONDON,
Printed by *Gregory Dexter*, 1643.

Roger Williams, *A Key into the Language of America*, 1643.

In other words, many of the features that would ultimately distinguish Brown University—a strong attachment to free speech, an irreverence toward orthodox thinking, and an essential tolerance—were present from the start in the way that Rhode Islanders thought about the world. With time, the Rhode Island idea took root. The 1663 charter also gave Rhode Island a high degree of self-rule, perfectly suited to its intractability. Brown's distinguished historian Gordon Wood has written that royal authority was weaker in Rhode Island than anywhere else.[12] An English commentator said, "King and Parliament have as much influence there as in the wilds of Tartary."[13] Massachusetts authorities blinked their eyes in amazement at the things that were permitted to go on in "the licentious Republic," the "sinke hole of New England," and "the Island of Error," using these and other epithets for the place whose name they preferred not to say.[14]

This natural independence extended to every walk of life, including Rhode Island's financial dealings, in which local entrepreneurs displayed a notable preference for loose credit, debtor protection, and, occasionally, outright piracy. Indeed, famous pirates like Thomas Tew originated in Rhode Island, and the term was often useful in trying to describe what, exactly, passed for "business" in Rhode Island. In 1763, on the eve of Brown's founding, a governor of Massachusetts complained bitterly about Rhode Island's unregulated economy: "These practices will never be put an end to till Rhode Island is reduced to the subjection of the British Empire; of which at present it is no more a part than the Bahama Islands were when they were inhabited by Buccaneers."[15]

In this way, too, they were ahead of their more scrupulous neighbors, for as Gordon Wood has observed, Rhode Island's version of barely regulated capitalism was closer to what the American economy would become. As he wrote, "It is not surprising that the most liberal, the most entrepreneurial, and the most 'modern' of the eighteenth-century colonies—Rhode Island, where nearly everyone seemed to be participating in trade—was also the colony that developed the most far-reaching terms for the relief of insolvent debtors."[16] By the middle decades of the eighteenth century, the little colony was a beehive of entrepreneurial activity. With barely any hinterland of their own to draw goods from, Rhode Islanders turned to the sea. From Newport, first, and then from Providence, merchant vessels plied the waters of the Atlantic and the Caribbean, trading goods and bringing back new and different kinds of cargoes, including a bustling commerce in African slaves. Rhode Island vessels played a leading role in the trade—at times, 90 percent of the voyages that originated from North America.[17] In the early decades of the eighteenth century, slave-based plantations also spread across the fertile land of southern Rhode Island, in the so-called Narragansett Country. Approximately 12 percent of Rhode Island's population was African American, a higher percentage than anywhere else in New England, and that figure rose to nearly 40 percent in parts of the Narragansett Country. There they developed a robust cultural identity.[18]

These troubling contradictions only deepened as Rhode Islanders increased their trading activity in the eighteenth century. A painting from about 1758 by John Greenwood, *Sea Captains Carousing in Surinam*, revealed the dissolute nature of Rhode Island's business in the Caribbean. It takes some time to peer through the soot of the tavern depicted, but Esek Hopkins is one of a number of men drinking around a table, to the point of vomiting, while enslaved African Americans linger uncomfortably in the background, and animals run unfettered.[19]

Understandably, the British who sought to regulate the American economy found Rhode Islanders difficult to deal with. They barely settled their debts to each other; it was that much more difficult to get them to pay taxes to the king. There was also a thriving underground economy. Narragansett Bay, with its coves and islands, offered a natural haven for smugglers, a fact that was well known to the British, who were stepping up their attempts to collect taxes in the year of Brown's founding. Others as well were trying to collect from Rhode Islanders: Harvard College had significant land holdings in southern Rhode Island in the eighteenth century, until it finally gave them up, vexed by the difficulty of collecting rents from Rhode Islanders who insisted

John Greenwood's *Sea Captains Carousing in Surinam*, circa 1753–1758.

on paying in quasi-legal currencies from the Caribbean, or depreciated bits of coinage, or, in one case, with a very large cheese.[20]

Clearly, the Rhode Island model had glaring imperfections. But by 1764, the colony's many critics had to admit that its founders and their descendants had built a thriving, polyglot society. In particular, the colony had offered a safety valve to those who had trouble living within the strictures of Rhode Island's neighbors. When Benjamin Franklin's older brother James, a talented young printer, grew tired with the jails and censors of Boston, he started all over again in Newport, where he established Rhode Island's first printing press and newspaper, the *Rhode Island Gazette*. When the Irish philosopher George Berkeley came to America for a few years in the early 1730s, he chose Middletown, Rhode Island, as his seat. There he introduced a number of improvements to the sleepy provincial culture, bringing a circle of literary and artistic friends who began to talk about ideas in a way that Rhode Islanders had never heard—Palladian architecture, fine portraiture, and free will. Berkeley planned to build a college in Bermuda, a dream that never came to pass, but the aspiration to enshrine this kind of intellectual conversation in a more permanent setting lingered after his departure. He felt, specifically, that America needed a "Utopian Seminary," because Harvard and Yale existed "to little or no purpose."[21] A new idea was beginning to form.

Rhode Island's growing wealth was palpable in the decades that followed Berkeley's sojourn. Splendid buildings began to rise, in Newport especially, where sophistication developed more quickly than in Providence. The Old Colony House, the symbol of Rhode Island's growing economic and political might, was completed in 1741; the Redwood Library, which still radiates Berkeley's intellectual aspirations, was built by friends of his in 1748.[22] Perhaps the most impressive building of all remains Touro Synagogue, the oldest synagogue standing in the United States. When Newport's significant Jewish population needed a house of worship, they turned to the Redwood's talented architect, Peter Harrison. Harrison, Quaker by birth but Episcopalian by persuasion, rendered a design free of charge. That building, set off at an angle from the street so that it might face Jerusalem, perfectly captures the cosmopolitan air that Rhode Islanders liked to breathe.[23]

The small colony of iconoclasts was a natural haven for Jews fleeing the insults of the Old World. They may have come to Newport from Barbados as early as 1658 (the evidence is elusive), but in any

The Redwood Library and Athenaeum in 1768, considerably more magnificent than the tiny campus in Warren.

Touro Synagogue.

event they were well established by the end of the seventeenth century.
They added to Newport's reputation as an open-minded city, tied by
business and family to the other important ports of the Atlantic world.
They embodied some of the paradoxes of this heterodox community—champions of religious freedom, contributors to Newport's
growing splendor, and also, at times, slave traders themselves. Nor
should it be forgotten that George Berkeley himself, the embodiment
of Newport's worldliness, purchased slaves during his Rhode Island
idyll. But despite these inconsistencies, the seaport at the mouth of
Narragansett Bay was a thriving entrepôt on the eve of independence,
open to new ideas and new kinds of people.[24]

The colony's emerging democracy also included outspoken
women leaders. To be sure, their sphere was limited by the traditions
of the time, but they were permitted to speak their minds to an
unusual degree for colonial America. When Anne Hutchinson was
expelled from Boston in 1638, she came to Rhode Island at the invitation of Roger Williams. Women were full participants in the religious
meetings held at Providence, to the distress of the Massachusetts
authorities (John Winthrop, studying the matter, feared "the Devil

was not idle"). One settler refused to permit his wife to attend as often as she liked, and after a formal debate on whether the settlers should follow liberty of conscience or the scriptural advice that wives should obey their husbands, he was formally censured.[25] A century later, Rhode Island's official printer became Ann Franklin, the widow of James Franklin, and the sister-in-law of Benjamin. After James died in 1735 she published the colony's public documents and launched an important newspaper, the *Newport Mercury*, in 1758. In Providence, a remarkable mother and daughter, Sarah and Mary Katherine Goddard, helped to launch Providence's first newspaper and printing press, which made that community all the more inviting to Rhode Island College when it finally settled there.[26]

The Quakers who began to come to Rhode Island in large numbers in the 1650s also encouraged a tradition of women preaching, and the doctrine of the "inner light" was well suited to permit individual thinking to flourish, in defiance of organized church structures. In many ways, Quaker ideas about revealed religion were congenial to the various types of dissenters congregated around the Bay. A historian of the Quakers has called Anne Hutchinson's Antinomians "Quakers in everything but name."[27] One of the most celebrated Quaker martyrs, Mary Dyer, lived happily in Rhode Island before returning to Boston, where she was executed in 1660. Rhode Island would continue to send leading Quaker women into the world, including Jemima Wilkinson (who experienced an epiphany in 1776 that led her to change her name to "The Public Universal Friend") and Elizabeth Buffum Chace, a crusader for women's rights in the nineteenth century.

For much of the eighteenth century, Providence lagged behind the scintillating progress of Newport, but as the French and Indian War ended, that town too was poised for rapid growth. Besides the Hopkins family, another clan had achieved local distinction, descended from an early settler named Chad Brown. He had arrived in Rhode Island in 1638, leaving Boston "for conscience sake," according to his grave marker in the North Burial Ground, which includes a rising sun not unlike that of the Brown seal.[28]

Chad Brown's headstone in the North Burial Ground, showing the same rising sun that peeks through the clouds on the Brown University seal.

Chad Brown quickly made a mark as a leading figure, surveying land, and deciding to walk "in the Baptists way." Soon he was the "first Settler Pastor" of the infant Baptist church, the first in America.[29] He must have been something of a political genius if he could bring consensus to the original settlers, so quick to protest oppression, but slower to agree on anything. Roger Williams praised Brown for bringing "the aftercomers and the first twelve to a oneness by arbitration."[30] Serendipitously, the original parcel of land Chad Brown purchased included what would become the main campus of Brown University, although his descendants would have to go to some trouble to buy it back (having briefly discarded it in their many wheelings and dealings).[31]

Chad Brown's great-grandson, James Brown, first put out to sea in 1727, traveling to Martinique.[32] That was the beginning of what became an extensive global network of interests over the eighteenth century, including the African slave trade, extensive commerce in the Caribbean, the beginnings of the China trade, and a huge array of local concerns. Four of the sons who were born to James—Joseph, John, Nicholas, and Moses—were particularly astute businessmen, and each in his way would be instrumental in establishing the new college. As Charles Rappleye pointed out in *Sons of Providence*, two of those brothers, John and Moses, were diametrically opposed on the question of slavery—John was an ardent defender and slave trader, Moses, a leading abolitionist.[33] Yet they remained close to each other. A growing body of research has confirmed that all institutions of higher education in America in the eighteenth century were in some degree dependent upon slavery—permitting slavery to flourish in open view, seeking funds from wealthy slave-owning patrons, or economically tied to investments that derived from slavery. But the knowledge that other universities share certain burdens from the past should never permit Brown and Rhode Island to neglect the special role that slavery played in this very local marketplace 250 years ago. It was pervasive, touching not only the commercial world in which the Browns acted so freely, but also the intellectual milieu that Brown University would emerge from and even the most respected ministers of the colony.[34]

Like Newport, Providence was also cultivating a taste for culture, especially as fortunes accumulated, and ships went farther and faster. Inventories of wills reveal that libraries were growing larger, including those of the Brown family. If the Enlightenment was a distant phenomenon, still its influence was felt in Providence, and the Brown family included light among their various enterprises (they made spermaceti candles).[35] The Providence Library Company, an ancestor to the Athenaeum, was founded in 1753, revealing a growing hunger for books. In 1762, the town's first newspaper, the *Providence Gazette*, was issued by the Goddard family. Five years later, a young disciple of Benjamin Franklin's named John Carter arrived, eventually took over the paper, married into the Brown family, and became the grandfather of John Carter Brown. Next to his house on Meeting Street he placed a crude bust of Shakespeare's head, as a totem of the literary excellence he was striving for, with his handbills and newspapers. That was perhaps ambitious, but Carter's work lifted the city further, and his many publications added to the growing din coming out of Providence on the eve of the Revolution. As for Stephen Hopkins, as he mulled over the growing crisis with Britain, it was significant that he was writing and publishing his thoughts on the hill that rose to the east of Providence.

But even with these heightened efforts, Rhode Island was vulnerable to Boston's catcalls as long as it lacked an institution of higher learning. The colony's schools, rudimentary at best, taught lessons from books that contained embarrassing inaccuracies—including, in one instance, a geography that insisted Rhode Island was in the West Indies.[36] If Rhode Islanders were proud of their religious freedom, it was also true that they lacked a system to train new ministers, or conduct scientific experiments, or contemplate the Enlightenment theories and discoveries that seemed to arrive with every ship that sailed across the Atlantic. A college was needed, to defend the Rhode Island idea against its many critics, and to prove that religious freedom and intellectual elegance were not incompatible.

Few Rhode Islanders were more attached to the colony's ideals than Ezra Stiles, a Congregational minister in Newport. Although a man of the cloth, he had a scientific bent, and he dedicated his life to accumulating knowledge when that, too, was the charge of a minister (his best biographer, Edmund S. Morgan, called him "a monstrous warehouse of knowledge").[37] Among Stiles's many activities, he cultivated silkworms, conducted a long-term experiment to take the world's temperature (still of interest in our time of climate change), measured celestial bodies, carried out demographic studies of local Native American groups, and conversed extensively with fellow intellectuals—not only around the Atlantic world but even in Siberia (he wanted to know with scientific precision how cold it was).[38] He also supported schemes to educate African Americans (though he owned a slave named "Newport,"

Ezra Stiles, painted by Nathaniel Smibert, 1756.

whom he later liberated).[39] A charming chapter in Morgan's biography, "A Library of Unwritten Books," records the many unfinished projects Stiles undertook—a salutary warning to us all. Stiles was interested in a broad swath of religious traditions and believed deeply in the principle of promoting tolerance among the faiths. Impressively, he taught himself Hebrew, and when he left Newport to become president of Yale University, he added Hebrew letters to the Yale seal, where they remain to this day.

Stiles also played an important role in shaping what would become Brown University. In 1761, and possibly as early as 1759, he started drafting a bill to incorporate a college, open to all denominations.[40] He did not bring the effort to its conclusion, but his restlessness strongly implied that Rhode Island was ready for an institution of higher learning.

With the end of hostilities in the French and Indian War, the idea of a college was beckoning to more than a few interested parties. Colleges were beginning to dot the landscape of colonial America. For many decades, the field had been reserved to Harvard (1636), William and Mary (1693), and Yale (1701). But in the middle decades of the eighteenth century, new colleges began to proliferate, including the College of New Jersey (1746), which became Princeton in 1896; King's College (1754), which became Columbia in 1784; and the College of Philadelphia (1755), which became the University of Pennsylvania in 1779.[41]

ENTER THE BAPTISTS

SURPRISINGLY, THE DEFINITIVE IMPETUS to create Brown came from outside Rhode Island. On October 12, 1762, a group of Baptist leaders met in Philadelphia and advocated organizing a college. The pastor of the local Baptist church, Morgan Edwards, later claimed to be the "prime mover" of the plan. A Welshman who had only been in America a year, Edwards played a versatile role in the creation of Rhode Island College, helping to raise a charter and funds, serving on the Corporation for twenty-five years, and giving the first commencement sermon in 1769.[42]

To understand why the Baptists would want a college of their own, and why they would feel some apprehension about entering the field of higher education, it is helpful to reflect on this important American denomination. The history of the belief that Christians should baptize and rebaptize themselves is hardly unique to the United States. European Baptists and Anabaptists of various persuasions had appeared and disappeared in the long annals of Christendom, but the belief in adult immersion began to accelerate in the decades preceding the great migration of the English toward New England in the 1620s and 1630s.[43] Soon after Roger Williams arrived in Rhode Island, he began to experiment along those lines, encouraged by a new arrival, Katharine Marbury Scott, the sister of Anne Hutchinson. After being rebaptized around 1639, Williams rebaptized ten others, and a movement was started.[44] But Williams, typically quick to challenge orthodoxy, soon grew impatient with the new Baptist doctrine that he had helped to launch, and reverted to something even more primordial—a church in which only he and his wife were communicants.

Despite some difficulty agreeing on doctrine, and some differences between the disorganized churches of Narragansett Bay, a movement began, in which Rhode Islanders showed their usual obstinacy toward the official policies of Massachusetts. After an early leader of the Baptists, Obadiah Holmes, was whipped by the authorities in Boston, he turned to his assailant and said mockingly, "You have struck me as with roses."[45]

From those modest beginnings, a much larger movement spread across the colonies. Baptists continued to practice their faith in Rhode Island, where more than half of New England's Baptists could be found, and nearby as well, in lonely pockets of Massachusetts where religious practices could not always be supervised. In the 1660s, a group of Welsh dissenters founded a Baptist community in Swansea, just to the east of Providence. This ancient congregation was another ancestor of sorts, and in the eighteenth century would help to found the parent church of Rhode Island College, in Warren.[46] Baptists flourished in other places that permitted freedom of religion—in

Pennsylvania and in New Jersey (partly settled by former Rhode Islanders)—and eventually in the South, then dominated by the Anglican church.[47]

But their growth inevitably brought tension, as Baptists bristled against what they felt to be unfair taxes and other forms of persecution. In Massachusetts, they were routinely assessed for their contribution to the Congregational Church, and in Anglican Virginia, they were occasionally jailed. Brown's historian of religion, William McLoughlin, felt that Baptist battles against "the Standing Order" of official state-sanctioned churches were an important precursor to the American Revolution. Indeed, it was Baptist objections to unfair religious taxation that led Thomas Jefferson and James Madison to write their great documents building a wall of separation between church and state in the 1780s.[48] To "disestablish," or fight against the orthodox church establishment, was always high on the Baptist agenda, and in some ways their language of the 1760s paralleled the language heard on college campuses in the 1960s.

Earlier, in the 1730s and 1740s, the religious upheavals known collectively as the Great Awakening were not always aligned with the Baptists—they were not always aligned with *anything*—but, in general, they advanced Baptist fortunes.[49] In an era when Americans were hungry for spiritual revival and eager to hear the itinerant preachers who increasingly canvassed the colonies, the Baptists did well. They had always been outliers to the official religions of the colonies, and the outsider culture of the Awakening spoke to their followers. Even if the new believers were not always pure Baptists—some called themselves "Separates," much as Roger Williams had—a huge number of Americans were now speaking a new religious language, based on a quest for authenticity more than book learning.

Contemporaneous accounts convey some of the excitement. The setting was often outdoors, because the official churches closed their doors to the "New Lights," as the adherents of the Awakening were called (the Awakening itself was the "New-light-stir"). There was a lot of noise—Baptists were known to "whoop" in "odd tones," according to one source.[50] Preachers added to the noise, often delivering their sermons in a "holy whine," a kind of sing-song delivery. An eyewitness to a Baptist ceremony recorded that there were "multitudes, some roaring on the ground, some wringing their hands, some in ecstacies, some praying, some weeping; and others so outrageous cursing and swearing that it was thought they were really possessed of the devil."

To the individual undergoing these transformations, it was one of the most powerful experiences of a lifetime, as if a lifetime of darkness were suddenly being replaced by an infusion of light. Many of them, grasping to explain it, resorted to solar imagery. Isaac Backus, a Baptist who would play an important role in Brown's founding, had a powerful conversion experience of his own and wrote, "The Lord God is a Sun . . . [and] when any Soul is brought to behold his Glories, the eternal rays of Light and Love Shine down particularly upon him to remove his darkness." A rising sun was a vivid symbol of spiritual rebirth, not only to Baptists but also to the "New Lights" who flocked to the Great Awakening, and Brown's symbol may owe something to these olden ways.[51]

Americans thrilled to the sound of these new voices, who spoke with more feeling than those trained in the orthodox institutions (Harvard and Yale). Entire tracts were devoted to the danger of listening to the priggish ministers sent out dutifully by those places, who spoke memorized lessons rather than from the heart. In many settings, especially in the hills and valleys away from the seaboard, people preferred ministers who paid no attention to "the Learning in Fashion." Isaac Backus, who would serve on the Brown Corporation for decades, disliked it when elitists used "real or pretended knowledge . . . to keep others in ignorance, and to excite a high opinion of themselves, instead of laboring to enlighten and benefit others."[52]

This hostility to pretension is a bit hard to understand, given how primitive the first American universities were. But they were hierarchical, as so much of life still was, despite the largeness of opportunity in the New World. Students were required, as a president of Yale said, to "show due Respect and Distance to those who are in Senior and Superiour Classes." In the case of Yale, the distance was literal—students had to remove their caps at varying distances from their instructors—five rods for a tutor, eight rods for a faculty member, and ten rods for the president.[53] Some urged a broad approach to learning— Jonathan Edwards thought a college should be "the university of things," meaning that all topics were studied together, to form a unified body of knowledge.[54] But in practice, they were often more parochial than that.

While the Great Awakening's upheavals were spiritual, first and foremost, they included a political conviction that American society could be rebuilt along lines that were more inclusive and democratic. Those thoughts went together, in fact: to strive for an America that was more fraternal was in its way identical to the search for a deeper form of piety.

As the Baptists grew in number and respectability, they faced a conundrum. They wanted to establish themselves, train young men into the ministry, and answer the charge that they weren't as well educated as the more established denominations. To know the Bible in the old languages was admirable, a path to a deeper grasp of its truths, yet in all of America, only seven or eight Baptist ministers could read Greek.[55] At the same time, they recoiled from the prospect of offering the world more prigs. How could they create a different kind of college?

Isaac Backus later wrote a letter, explaining why Brown had been founded. For too long, he complained, critics of Baptists had argued "that none but ignorant and illiterate men have embraced those sentiments. . . . And as the Baptists have met with a great deal of abuse from those who are called learned men in our land, they have been not a little prejudiced against learning itself."[56]

To create a college unlike the others—that was the answer. And so, well before Brown was founded, voices were being raised that a college might be created that would avoid excessive hierarchy and keep learning fresh and authentic. To begin, it would be necessary to define "a College in which education might be promoted and superior learning obtained, free from any sectarian religious tests."[57]

The first Baptist efforts were modest: in New Jersey a school called Hopewell Academy was launched in 1756, to train young men for Princeton. This humble experiment only lasted until 1767, but it was an essential training ground for what would become Brown University, since it graduated Brown's first president, James Manning, and a number of early faculty members and friends.[58]

The pace quickened in October 1762, when Morgan Edwards proposed the college plan, and the Philadelphia Association seized the initiative. As the leading Baptists surveyed the landscape and considered the most favorable location for the new college, they briefly considered South Carolina, but ultimately settled upon the idea of Rhode Island College. Even if the faith had spread to the south and west, it had originated in Rhode Island, and Baptists were still well represented there—including in the legislature. Morgan Edwards wrote that the colony was "chiefly in the hands of the baptists, and therefore the likeliest place to have a baptist college established by law." Ezra Stiles calculated that in 1760 there were 22,000 Baptists in New England, 80 percent of whom lived in Rhode Island. He also estimated that Rhode Island had 11,000 "Nothingarians," or people whose religion was too vague or too absent to put in any category.[59]

The colony had not yet chartered a college, despite its rapidly growing sophistication. To be Rhode Island's college, as its original name implied, would plant the Baptist flag firmly in a sympathetic place and bring in support from the colony's political and economic elite. Baptists were well represented in both camps. The Brown family, rapidly rising in eminence, was only one of many examples—a Baptist family, with roots going back to Roger Williams, eagerly expanding their interests, and willing to go to great lengths to bring a sympathetic institution of higher learning to the shores of Narragansett Bay. In Baptist lore, a minister was supposed to feel "the providential call" before accepting his destiny. Now, by approaching Providence, that legend would soon acquire a double meaning.[60]

FOUNDING

THE IDEA TOOK A BIG STEP TOWARD REALITY in July 1763, when the Philadelphia Association sent a young man to Rhode Island to test the waters. James Manning, a recent graduate from Princeton with an educational bent, was specifically told to ask the leading Baptists of

Rhode Island whether a "seminary of polite literature" might find favor there.[61]

The response was encouraging from the start. Manning met the leading lights of Newport and explained the proposal to them. They responded enthusiastically, calling for a charter to be drawn up naming Rhode Island College and designing its general characteristics. That was an important job, and it fell to the right person: Ezra Stiles.[62] At exactly that moment, Stiles was developing his interest in Hebrew, for he attended the dedication of the new Touro Synagogue, also in 1763. Stiles worked quickly, and after consulting William Ellery, later a signer of the Declaration of Independence, he had a draft ready within two weeks.

Stiles modeled the new charter after that of Yale, his alma mater, but he injected some of his broad catholicity and specifically his belief, true to Rhode Island's heritage, that religion should not be forced. It may be an exaggeration to call the document "an educational Declaration of Independence," as one historian called it, but it breathed the progressive air of its time.[63] The charter still bears rereading, not only for its eloquence, but for its optimism, openness, and avoidance of any one creed's particularities. Stiles insisted that "into this liberal and catholic institution shall never be admitted any religious tests. But on the contrary, all the members hereof shall forever enjoy full, free, absolute and uninterrupted liberty of conscience." He did not mention the Baptists by name in the lines describing the general purpose of the college, or even the ministry. Instead, "Youth of all religious denominations of Protestants shall and may be freely admitted to the equal advantages, emoluments, and honors of the College."

One word stood out from the draft that was unusual—the new college would emphasize "vernacular" as well as classical languages—it would speak in the present tense. In the lines that are reread most often, Stiles defined a purpose of the college that has resonated through the centuries: it would form "the rising generation to virtue, knowledge and useful literature" and preserve "a succession of men duly qualified for discharging the offices of life with usefulness and reputation."

Although Stiles had done his work well and emphasized an air of

tolerance throughout the document, his draft excited some denominational scuffling. The latter part of the document, which outlined the
governing bodies of the college, distressed the Baptists, who wanted
more control than Stiles gave them. The first copy of the charter was
presented to the Rhode Island General Assembly at Newport in
August 1763, and the Baptists protested it, asking for a delay. Instead,
they proposed a new structure that reserved far more places in the
governing bodies for them, and offered more seats to Rhode Island's
Quakers and Anglicans as well.[64] Stiles and his fellow Congregationalists
were dismayed, but the Baptists were a force to contend with in the
Assembly and drove their revised charter through at a meeting in East
Greenwich, held in February 1764.[65]

The result was that Rhode Island College was founded as an
institution with some Baptist affiliation, yet still open, as Stiles
intended it to be, to all. On September 6, 1770, in its first meeting in
Providence, the Corporation clarified that "children of Jews" could be
admitted and "enjoy the freedom of their own Religion, without any
Constraint or Imposition whatsoever." The first known Jew would not
graduate from Brown until 1894, but it was commendable that this
policy was clarified at the start.[66] When University Hall was built in
1770, pine boards were donated by the Jewish community at Newport.

Although the text survives, the original charter itself was damaged
in the 1938 hurricane that ravaged Rhode Island. The manuscript of the
first draft tendered by Ezra Stiles rests secure in the John Hay Library,
and that document still emanates the broad tenets that would define
Rhode Island College. It was proudly Baptist—indeed, the first Baptist
college in the British Empire.[67] But the principles of inclusivity shared
by Rhode Island and the Baptists themselves would always militate
against too fine a standard of doctrinal purity.

In other words, Rhode Island College had been founded in the
right place. The decade in which it was founded, on the other hand,
was going to bring major challenges. The political conflict with the
Crown deepened, and Rhode Island played a leading role in sharpening that struggle. That was only one of a hundred problems confront-
ing the new college, beginning with the simple question of its location.

It made sense to place it in Newport or Providence, the two biggest towns of the colony. Each was thriving and boasted a large library and an interested citizenry. But James Manning needed a position as a minister to pay his salary, and the Baptist positions were filled in the two towns. So instead he went to Warren, a small town between Bristol and Providence, where Baptists had been congregating. He arrived in April 1764 and immediately opened a school for boys (for some time, that school would be significantly larger than the college). In November, the Baptists organized a new church in Warren and invited Manning to lead it. That month, the Corporation held its first meeting, and Stephen Hopkins was elected the Chancellor.

In its earliest incarnation, Rhode Island College was more influenced by Newport than Providence. Nicholas Brown was a member of the Corporation, but fourteen of the twenty-eight came from the larger city at the mouth of Narragansett Bay. Nearly a year later, in September 1765, the Corporation met again to appoint Manning president and "Professor of Languages and other branches of learning." At this same meeting, the original seal of Rhode Island College was designed. It included busts of King George III and his wife, Queen Charlotte, in profile—elements that were purged in a redesign after the Revolutionary War.[68]

In spite of the seal, and all the people clamoring to be on the Corporation, there was not much to the actual college in the early years. According to Morgan Edwards, who had first proposed the idea, it was "friendless and moneyless and therefore forlorn."[69] But that would not have made much of a motto, and so these Rhode Islanders relied, once again, upon hope. The campus was merely a "Colleg Chamber" (as the tradesman's bill described it) in the parsonage—a single

The original seal of 1765.

room. The original library was simply a drawer inside a pine table that held some publications.[70] But slowly, they built something. The first student, William Rogers, arrived in 1765, a fourteen-year-old boy from Newport. Nine months later, another student arrived—Manning's young brother-in-law, Richard Stites, from New Jersey. By 1766 there were five students, and four more in 1768. In 1767, Manning took a small but significant step to give Rhode Island College a bit more heft—with his gift of an old book, Valentin Schindler's 1612 *Lexicon Pentaglotton Hebraicum, Chaldaicum, Syriacum, Talmudico-Rabbinicum & Arabicum*. That book and those that followed would eventually cohere into a genuine library. It was a worthy beginning: a dictionary helping people to understand each other from the different linguistic traditions of the Holy Land.[71]

Still, the college remained desperately poor. Morgan Edwards was deputized to raise money, and in 1767 he went on a long trip to England and Ireland that brought in some donations, including ten pounds from Benjamin Franklin, then in London representing the colonies in their struggle. But the fact that Americans were asserting their prerogatives did not increase the desire of wealthy Englishmen to support them, especially if the demands came from an obstreperous colony and a perplexing denomination. So another fundraiser, Hezekiah Smith, was sent prospecting in 1769 and 1770, to South Carolina and Georgia, where he raised money from the people who had it—slaveholders.[72] Rhode Island offered some support with a lottery held in 1767 to build a house in Warren, a sign that the college was beginning to outgrow its tiny campus. New staff were brought in, including a talented graduate of Hopewell Academy named David Howell, who came as a tutor in 1767, then became professor of natural philosophy in 1769.

Ad Serenissimum Principem

DN. HENRICVM-JVLIVM,

PRÆSVLEM HALBERSTADIENSIVM,

Ducem Brunonivicensium & Lune-burgensium,

ET

Ad Illustriss. Generosissimumq. Principem,

DN. FRIDERICVM-HVLDERICVM,

HENRICI-JVLII F. DVCEM BRVNONIVICEN-
SIVM ET LVNEBVRGENSIVM,

Dominos Clementissimos,

PROOEMIUM.

T sapientissimum patrem, & filium paternarum virtutum certissimum æmulum, eadem oratione, una in re, uno fine de omnibus proposito, mihi utriusque laudum æquè studiosissimo compellare, uti toto animo libet, ita rectissimis de caussis licere, cùm ipse mecum statuo, tum æquos & harum rerum intelligentes censores, judicaturos arbitror. Neque enim aliquis improbabit, si duorum conjunctissimorum (quid autem patre & filio, ante omnes in optimis, naturâ conjunctius ? laudes complectar una lucubratione, præsertim si id absque omni adulationis specie faciam: quod ego enorme, & vitæ mortalium privatim, & publicè pestilens vitium odi & execror maximè. Nec potero apud vos, neque facilè apud alium quempiam, in illam suspicionem incurrere, qui cum de pluribus vestris virtutibus multa habeam dicere, non nisi unum vestrum beneficium, aut aliquam saltem singularis beneficii partem prædicabo: cujus mentione oblectemini ambo, & gratuletur mutuo alter alteri: imò gratulemini Academiæ vestræ Juliæ, & omnibus, in quos redundant vestra hujus generis beneficia. Occasionem sumo ex hoc libro, qui jam Orbi terrarum videndus, cognoscendus, censendusque primùm proponitur, natus maximam partem in Academia hac ipsa, profuturus primùm hoc loco vestris clientibus, sive beneficiariis: non tam enim qui hìc docent, quàm quotquot huc discendi gratia undique confluunt; ita meritò appellentur, & censeantur: profuturus deinde passim gentium, futuris item sæculis. Hujus generis laudum prima, adeoq; summa ipsa est, quòd beneficentissimus Dux JULIUS, Academiam ex fundamento condidit, filius patris beneficum ratum habet, & amplificat, nepos patris, avique vestigiis insistit, neutro, neq; ulla in re alia, neq; in hac futurus inferior. Quorum autem

* 3

ABOVE AND OPPOSITE: The first book in the library, Valentin Schindler's 1612 *Lexicon Pentaglotton Hebraicum, Chaldaicum, Syriacum, Talmudico-Rabbinicum & Arabicum.*

Cane used by
Morgan Edwards.

A culmination of sorts occurred on September 7, 1769,
the first commencement, and as it turned out, the only one
ever held in Warren. A large crowd assembled in the Baptist
Church to attend the proceedings, which began at ten in the
morning and consumed an entire day. Isaac Backus left a
lively account in his diary. A gesture toward democracy was
made by listing the candidates alphabetically and not, as
Harvard did, by order of their wealth and social distinction.[73]
There were expressions of patriotism in a time of rapidly rising
tension (Backus noted that "the President and all the
Candidates were dressed in American Manufactures"—
locally made clothing) and a spirited debate was held, in which
two seniors argued over the question of American independence (the student who took the negative, arguing against it,
was James Varnum, who would soon be an American officer
in the coming war). Backus wrote, with satisfaction: "Great
numbers were present, and those who were acquainted with
such affairs generally allowed that both the exercises of the
schollars and the decent behaviour of the assembly exceeded
their expectation."[74]

Near nightfall the prime mover, Morgan Edwards,
preached from Philippians 3.8, "Yea doubtless, and I count
all things but loss for the excellency of the knowledge of
Christ Jesus my Lord: for whom I have suffered the loss of
all things, and do count them but dung, that I may win

Christ." According to Backus, Edwards praised the liberal arts and sciences and concluded with an image of a sunrise, in keeping with the future seal of Brown University. His point was that a deeper knowledge of Jesus (symbolized by the sun) enhances all knowledge, but also, that there was room in the firmament of educational institutions for a new kind of college. As Backus recorded it in his diary: " 'When the sun is below the horizon, the Stars excell in glory; but when his orb irradiates our hemisphere, their glory dwindles, fades away, and disappears.' May this lesson be ever remembered and ever be duly regarded by this first Class, as well as all who may succeed them in Rhode Island College!"[75]

Only seven years had elapsed since the 1762 motion that proposed a new college, and five years since the charter was approved by the Rhode Island General Assembly. It was the fulfillment of a great many people's hopes, from Ezra Stiles, who had long dreamed of an ecumenical college for Rhode Island, to the Baptists, to the leaders of Providence and Newport, who dared to imagine a place for Rhode Island in the developing realm of American higher education.

TRANSITS

IN A THIRD FLOOR ALCOVE of the John Hay Library, a small three-foot telescope sits, surveying the campus. That is appropriate, for the work of the telescope in 1769 did a great deal to create the campus. As it turned out, the 1769 commencement at Warren marked the end of an era. In the same month, September, the Corporation opened up a momentous question by proposing that the infant college move from its seat in Warren. It is difficult to know all the reasons for the move, but the college was growing more quickly than the town, which was small and remote. It may have been uncongenial in other ways as well—a historian of the early years noted that in 1769, "to curb profanity and other evil practices, the town ordered two pillories, one of which at least was set up on the sidewalk so that no one could miss it."[76]

While a number of locations for the college were proposed—another place in Bristol County, or East Greenwich—the question soon turned into a contest between Rhode Island's two principal towns. For some time, the rivalry between Newport and Providence had flavored local politics, with clan-based struggles over legislation pitting Providence and Newport families against one another.

Over the fall and winter of 1769, the battle raged. In November, a local observer listed the criteria for selection. The site should be in a place where the air was clean and "not subject to epidemical disorders," and it should be in a location that was morally uplifting, if it was possible to find one in Rhode Island. He added that it should be a place of tolerance, in the Rhode Island spirit, open to a variety of denominations. It should have good transportation. And it should be a place of diversion and diversity, "so that the students may become acquainted with men as well as books, that when their academical studies are finished, they may not be finished blockheads."[77]

At first, the odds were in Newport's favor. Roughly twice the size of Providence (with a population of 8,000, compared with 4,000), it was a bustling entrepôt of culture and commerce, closer to the broad Atlantic, the source of the trade that brought the latest books, ideas, and luxury items to upwardly mobile Rhode Islanders. Indeed, in Newport's glory years of the mid-eighteenth century, its foreign trade exceeded New York's. It possessed a warm spirit and a warm climate as well—as the historian Carl Bridenbaugh wrote, its weather was "one coat" warmer than Boston's, and perhaps a shirt warmer than Providence's. Its intellectuals were impressive—not only Ezra Stiles, but also Samuel Hopkins, a prominent disciple of Jonathan Edwards (and an important opponent of slavery). Newport's culture of tolerance rivaled that of any other place in America. Its culture of knowledge was impressive as well, and the Redwood Library and Athenaeum held a significant collection of books and art, far more magnificent than anything in Providence. The latter place was still known for some religious looseness. A wandering Harvard graduate, Jacob Bailey, sniffed: "the inhabitants of this place, in general, are very immoral, licentious, and profane, and exceeding famous for contempt of the Sabbath."[78]

But Providence was coming up very quickly at precisely this moment. Whether one studies the old court records, the architectural legacy, or fictional accounts such as H. P. Lovecraft's *The Case of Charles Dexter Ward*, one senses a city teeming with energy, new wealth, and ideas. Indeed, the American Revolution would soon confirm that Providence, not Newport, was Rhode Island's center of resistance to the British Crown.

Providence was also emerging as a place of writing and publishing. Its library was not insignificant, and it too had a cluster of intellectuals—rising men of science as well as business (often a thin line separated the one from the other). If there was a single academic discipline in which the Brown family had excelled during its rise to power, it was mathematics—their business records contain extraordinary cipher books in which they did their prodigious accounting.[79] Joseph Brown, in particular, was experimenting along scientific lines, trying to cheat nature of her secrets. With his deep knowledge of the relatively new subject of electricity, he must have struck some of his townsfolk as a kind of wizard. In many ways, the four brothers were avatars of modernity, learning to build with new materials such as iron and glass, and bringing the latest technical knowledge of machinery and motive power. It is noteworthy that the Browns, unlike Newport's grandees, were at this time expanding their business into manufacturing (they launched their pig-iron works at Hope Furnace in 1765).[80] Providence also had more Baptists than Newport. Significantly, it had the tacit support of the college president, Manning, who apparently directed traffic throughout the contest, advising the friends of Providence on how to approach the Corporation.

Many were involved, but the ultimate triumph of Providence was very much a Brown family enterprise. Their multi-pronged strategy took full advantage of the fact that there were four Brown brothers, quadrupling their resources. A key stratagem was to secure the site. Here the Browns were very successful, offering a unique property that overlooked the city from their ancient demesne. John and Moses Brown efficiently created a campus from a four-acre tract they purchased from Oliver Bowen and another they offered from the old family homestead (ironically, the site for the Baptist college was on a street then known as Presbyterian Lane).[81] Joseph Brown, an architect, would design the college edifice. John Brown would lay the cornerstone. Nicholas would pay for much of it.[82] Throughout they displayed extraordinary generosity—and also a shrewd sense of what it would mean to Providence, and by extension, to them: "Building the college here will be the means of bringing great quantities of money into the place, and thereby greatly increasing the markets for all kinds of the Countrys produce, and consequently increasing the value of all estates to which this town is a market." [83]

But the contest revolved around more than just money. It also brought out each city's desire to display its intellectual acumen. Once again, the sun was involved. As the contest began in earnest, a question was asked: "In the infant state of a college where there is but a small library and probably no mathematical or philosophical apparatus & no professors in the learned sciences, in that case it would be certainly the most eligible to have it fixed in a town where those disadvantages might in some measure be remedied." In other words, which city could do more to support science?[84]

In fact, that question had just been answered. By coincidence, the transit of Venus took place at nearly the exact moment the question of where to locate Rhode Island College was to be arbitrated. Edmund Halley, the great British astronomer, had predicted before his death in 1742 that Venus would cross the face of the sun in 1761 and 1769. For the latter visit, amateur astronomers around the world offered to make observations and, by measuring the length of the transit, calculate the distance and size of the sun. It was a remarkable moment for the British Empire (on which, in theory, the sun never set). Colony by colony, as the day was experienced around the world, the transit of

Venus offered a chance for amateur scientists to prove their relevance to London and Paris.

In Providence, nearly two and a half centuries later, it is still possible to measure the impact of the experiment held on June 3, 1769. Local streets (Planet and Transit) bear tribute to this impressive act of self-betterment by a group of colonists, eager to impress London and ready for more sway over their own affairs. Indeed, the transit of Venus almost seems to have been sent by the heavens to give Providence a chance to show just how badly it wanted the college. In Newport, there was also a serious effort, involving Ezra Stiles and his friends, but it suffered from a few miscalculations. In Providence, the teamwork was impressive. Joseph Brown, more scientific than his brothers, dispensed money liberally (he ordered the telescope from London) and donated a month of his time getting ready for the big day.

A key ally was Benjamin West, a bookseller and mathematician, who hoped that a deeper knowledge of astronomy would help him prove the existence of God.

> From these observations we expect to discover the distance of the Earth, the Planets and Comets, from the Sun; and consequently their magnitudes and quantity of matter will be known, and also their proportion of light and heat. . . . From a knowledge of these things, methinks we shall have such a demonstration of the existence of a G O D, who made and governs all things, that even the reformed atheist must tremble when he reflects on his past conduct.[85]

If nothing else, the Providence team was ambitious. Other partners included Stephen Hopkins, Moses Brown, Jabez Bowen, Joseph Nash, and John Burrough. On June 3, the weather was clear and sunny. The measurement came off perfectly. And if they did not prove God's existence, they certainly proved their own, to all who would listen. This gave added weight to the Providence gambit to bring Rhode Island College to the hill where they made the observations. And indeed, this same team would do much to set the tone for Rhode Island College— Hopkins was the Chancellor, Bowen would also become Chancellor,

Joseph Brown and Benjamin West would become professors, and Moses Brown served on the Corporation.[86]

The meeting that finally decided the issue was held February 8, 1770, at Warren. Stephen Hopkins made the closing argument for Providence, and the Browns were out in force, lobbying and helping to sweeten the financial offer. The amounts raised by Newport and Providence were similar—but also hard to measure, for each side was indulging in creative math, counting pledges and hints of pledges to come.[87] Isaac Backus wrote in his diary, "Both sides shewed such indecent heats and hard reflections as I never saw before among men of so much sense as they, and hope I never shall again."[88] But finally it came down to a vote, and Providence prevailed, 21–14. It would never be the same city again. The Browns had done their work well.

Frustrated, the Newport team tried to advance a charter for a new college of its own, which would have brought two colleges into Rhode Island. But Stephen Hopkins and his friends still exerted a great deal of control in the assembly, and the effort died.[89] A very large question had been decided. Rhode Island's oldest university would rest eternally on the steep hill rising to the east of Providence and its busy wharves.

It is worth pausing to consider that fact. There was some symmetry to it, a historical rhyme that must have pleased the Browns—the college would now rest atop the hill, not yet named after the college, in a place where their ships could be surveyed, coming and going, on the ancestral land acquired by their first ancestor in Rhode Island. All of the principal Brown family residences were nearby, or would be soon.[90]

The location was unlike any previously chosen by an American college. Not one of the colleges that preceded Brown rested on an elevation to match it, and only three were in locations that might be described as urban, Harvard (though Cambridge was still a tranquil village outside Boston), King's (Columbia), and the future University of Pennsylvania. Some effort was required to climb the hill, which modern technology has not managed to eliminate, but the Baptists would likely have seen that as a test of character, a physical challenge before the mental exercise could begin. It should be noted, as well, that the Gospel of Luke comforts us with a promise of better landscaping to come: "Every valley shall be filled, and every mountain and hill shall be brought low; and the crooked shall be made straight, and the rough ways *shall be* made smooth" (Luke 3:5).

While complaints were registered about the "inaccessible mountain" that had been chosen, there were also many reasons to be grateful. Ever since ancient Athens, hilltops have been places where human beings dare to think like the gods. The Acropolis, of course, is built atop a steep elevation. Nearby is another rocky outcropping, the Areopagus—the place of jurisprudence for the Greeks, and the inspiration for John Milton's great defense of free speech, the *Areopagitica*. In Biblical narrative, some of the most profound moments of Judeo-Christian revelation have taken place atop high elevations—including Moses receiving the tablets and Jesus delivering the Sermon on the Mount. Borrowing from the latter idea, John Winthrop wrote a famous sermon of his own in 1630, urging that the settlement of New England be a kind of moral example to the world—a "city upon a hill," in his famous phrase. More than most universities, Brown truly sits atop a hill, able to contemplate the splendors as well as the imperfections of the world, blessed with a home that furnishes each on a daily basis. Morgan Edwards remarked, "Surely this spot was made for a seat of the muses!"[91]

The Browns wasted no time in seeing the project through to completion. That meant erecting a building, the so-called College Edifice, as University Hall was known for many years. It was the physical embodiment of the college from the moment it was built, and it too was closely linked to the Browns. Its architect was Joseph Brown, not long removed from the success of measuring the transit of Venus. Loosely modeled on Princeton's Nassau Hall, its size and shape may have owed something to James Manning and the college's New Jersey origins. John Brown laid the cornerstone on May 14, 1770.[92] But other Rhode Islanders contributed as well, from a wide range of backgrounds. Money and supplies were donated from around the colony, and recent research has confirmed that as many as four enslaved African Americans helped to lay the foundation for an institution that was not yet ready to receive them.[93]

Even before the first shovelfuls of dirt were turned, Rhode Island College existed in Providence, for classes were already being given in the spring of 1770, in the building a student diary described as "the New-Brick School House," still standing at 24 Meeting Street. It was in this building that the plan was laid for the ultimate location of the new college atop the hill that would bear its name, and instruction would continue there through 1771. This schoolhouse would host a great deal of later history as well, as a school for African Americans (in the nineteenth century) and for children with special needs (in the twentieth). In a sense, this was the second campus, after Warren, before the College Edifice was ready. A unique shrine to the history of education in Rhode Island, it fulfilled many of James Manning's hopes that Rhode Island's children would begin to receive a better education as part of the momentum created by the new college.[94]

REVOLUTION

If building UNIVERSITY HALL atop College Hill was a serious achievement, it was an achievement almost immediately imperiled by the American Revolution. Early tremors were felt keenly in Rhode Island—particularly the *Gaspée* incident of June 9, 1772, in which the leading merchants of Providence, including John Brown, organized a raiding party on a stranded British vessel near the entrance to the harbor—and events in and around Boston were within a day's ride. The new college would survive the test of the war, but at great cost.

For a few years after the move, the college flourished. It grew accustomed to the city, and the city to it. Commencements were held in a meetinghouse downtown, since "no other building in town could accommodate the throngs of interested listeners," and the commencement procession was an important ritual in these final years of British rule. The college president played his role well; an observer wrote that "the white wig of President Manning was of the largest dimensions worn in this country."[95] A letter Manning wrote in early 1772 brimmed with pride at the prospects: "The College edifice is erected on a most beautiful eminence, in the neighborhood of Providence, commanding

The second campus, 24 Meeting Street.

a most charming and variegated prospect; a large, neat, brick building, and so far completed as to receive the students, who now reside there, the number of whom is twenty-two."[96]

Other writings, expressing the point of view of the students, were no less sanguine. An undergraduate named Solomon Drowne of the class of 1773 kept a meticulous journal of his education, full of fascinating entries that show the college rising up around him. On June 8, 1772, the day before the *Gaspée* incident, he described the first time his class recited a lesson (from the *Education of Cyrus* by Xenophon) to President Manning in University Hall (specifically, the northeast room of the first story). Later that same year, in August, he wrote proudly,

"This day our Class disputed for the first Time, the Question was, Whether it is Lawful to Lye to save a Nation from Distruction?"[97]

That question was soon put to the test, along with many others, in the years to follow. The *Gaspée* incident brought tensions with the British to a new height, from which they never receded. The class of 1775 petitioned not to have a normal commencement, feeling "deeply affected with the distress of our oppressed country which now, most unjustly, feels the baneful effects of military power." Grimly, Manning wrote, "Institutions of learning will doubtless partake in the common calamities of our country, as arms have ever proved unfriendly to the more refined and liberal arts and sciences; yet we are resolved to continue College orders here as usual." The class of 1776 was the first to graduate from the new Baptist meetinghouse, designed to be both a place of worship "and also for holding commencement in."[98]

That meetinghouse is worth a moment of contemplation. Though not strictly a part of the campus, it partook of the same remarkable burst of energy that brought the college to its hill, and saw the architecture of Joseph Brown reach its pinnacle. Fresh from victory over Newport, Providence's ambition soared to new altitudes. To this day, it can be measured by the remarkable structure that began to appear at the foot of the hill, not long after University Hall was completed. For the record, the Baptist Meetinghouse is 185 feet tall, a skyscraper in every sense. After centuries of hiding their modest churches, or being told that they could not ring bells, the Baptists answered with a kind of cathedral. The generous belfry contained a bell, with a wonderfully populist inscription, that rang out to the faithful: "For freedom of conscience the town was first planted / Persuasion not force was used by the people / This church is the eldest and has not recanted / Enjoying and granting bell, temple and steeple."[99]

The steeple, the first seen on a Baptist church in Rhode Island, nearly commits the un-Baptist sin of pride as it thrusts higher and higher, nearly to the level of University Hall itself, reinventing itself several times along the way before tapering into a delicate weathervane that seems to point to the future. Though highly functional (the building's capacious first floor can seat 1,200, nearly a third of the city at the time it was built), this meetinghouse still celebrates the sophistication and daring that brought Rhode Island College here.

The job of building the meetinghouse—the biggest project in New England at the time—was quickened by the availability of Boston carpenters, thrown out of work by the Boston Tea Party and the Crown's repressive countermeasures. Soon it was apparent that the American Revolution would place Providence's ambitions on hold for some time. After the 1776 commencement, none was held from 1777 to 1782.[100]

During the long and grueling struggle for independence, Rhode Island College was asked to make many sacrifices. From the beginning, students and young alumni bravely joined the cause, and the entire campus was requisitioned, first to become a barracks for American militias (1776–80), and then to become a military hospital for the French troops of General de Rochambeau (1780–82).[101] The main building lent itself well to caring for and treating soldiers, and the college's vantage point gave it a commanding view of the Bay and the approaches to Providence. Newport was occupied by the British on July 18, 1776, and never fully recovered. Many of the merchants lost their business, and a considerable number of Jews left town, never to return, taking something of the cosmopolitan spirit with them. Providence remained safe, validating the decision of 1770.

In the summer of 1778, Rhode Island became a theater of war, and in the final days of August, the Battle of Rhode Island was fought in the northern part of Aquidneck Island. Somewhat inconclusive, the episode was important for proving the merit of the African American soldiers who fought with the Continentals. That they were on the battlefield at all was largely due to an alumnus of Rhode Island College, James Varnum, who had recommended the policy to George Washington.[102] In that battle, and in many others, the recent alumni of Rhode Island College played a valorous role. The early rolls of the college are filled with the names of those who served in one capacity or another. William Rogers, the first student ever, was a chaplain at Valley Forge, well acquainted with Washington; later he was a professor of oratory at the University of Pennsylvania, an abolitionist, and a prison reformer. The second student, Richard Stites, died in 1776, from wounds suffered at the Battle of Long Island. James Varnum, also a graduate of the primordial class of 1769, became a general, a delegate to the Continental Congress, and ultimately a judge in the Northwest Territory. Another chaplain at Valley Forge was Ebenezer David of the class of 1772, who survived that terrible winter only to die of typhus in March 1778.[103] Solomon Drowne of the class of 1773 was a surgeon with the Continental Army. Esek Hopkins (1775) the younger, a lieutenant in the Navy,

Detail of map.

was captured by the British, became a prisoner of war, and died in 1777.[104] The rolls also include a young graduate, William Edwards (1776), who became a colonel in the British army. That he was the son of Morgan Edwards, who had done so much to launch Rhode Island College, confirms how painful the war must have been for many families.[105]

In spite of all that bravery, the Revolution, which gave new life to the United States, nearly extinguished it at Rhode Island College. Newport, an early source of contributions, had been decimated by the British occupation. Around Narragansett Bay, there were signs of the trauma of war, including in Warren, where the original campus had been destroyed by the invaders in 1778.[106] With the fighting over, and the French departed, University Hall needed a thorough cleaning and, in some ways, a new start. Manning never stopped dunning possible donors for funds, including the king of France, and an interesting

ABOVE AND OPPOSITE: Perhaps the most beautiful map of Narragansett Bay ever designed was drawn by a British military surveyor, Charles Blaskowitz, and published in London in 1777, during the British occupation of Rhode Island. The new campus of Rhode Island College is included.

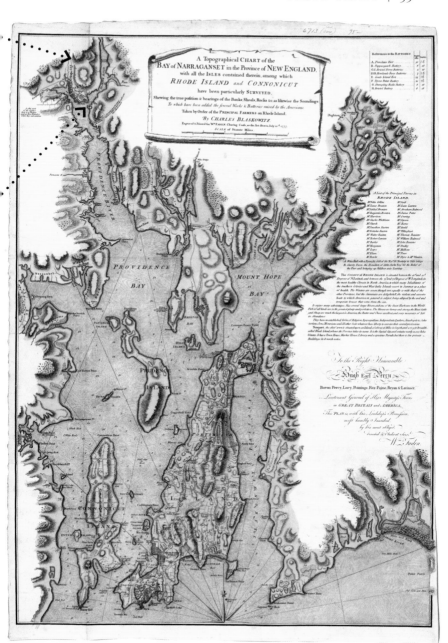

letter to a wealthy Welsh Baptist named Thomas Llewellyn in 1783 revealed him to be dangling naming rights:

> Cambridge College [Harvard] was so fortunate as to attract the attention of a Hollis, New Haven of a Yale, and New Hampshire of a Dartmouth, who have given their names to those seats of learning. We should think ourselves no less happy in the patronage of a Llewellyn. Llewellyn College appears well when written, and sounds no less agreeably when spoken.[107]

Rhode Islanders continued to do what they had always done, proclaim the separation of church and state. Many of the leading thinkers linked to the college, such as Isaac Backus, tried to turn the Revolution into an attempt to legislate "religious liberty" into a national priority, but that was one liberty that would take a little time to ripen.[108] When the Constitution was first drafted in 1787, it provided no protection for religious liberties, one of the reasons that Rhode Island held out longer than any other state before ratifying it. It was not until Congress proposed the Bill of Rights, including the First Amendment's guarantee of "the free exercise of religion," that Rhode Island's doubts began to subside. Indeed, when George Washington became president in April 1789, Rhode Island was still holding out, from concerns related to its expected loss of power (small states had more power to veto legislation under the Articles of Confederation), its desire for loose credit, and its general independence. Rhode Island's ratification in May 1790 was difficult to arrange and required considerable statecraft on the part of the leaders of Providence, including the leaders of the college. In celebration, President Washington himself paid a visit on August 18, 1790. Isaac Backus described the great day in his diary: "the president and many others took a Walk on the College Green, to visit the Illumination of that Edifice, which was done by the Students, and made a most splendid appearance." (Washington's visit is still commemorated at commencement, by lighting electric candles in each of the 146 windows of University Hall.) On the next day, the students escorted Washington (and Jefferson) back to the campus, where he was addressed by

Manning, and in reply expressed "ardent wishes that Heaven may prosper the literary Institution under your care." At commencement two weeks later, he was awarded the honorary degree of LL.D.[109]

In the final decade of the eighteenth century, Rhode Island College finally settled into something like a routine. Many of the great questions had been asked and answered—whether Rhode Island should have a college, in which city, and the extent of Baptist involvement. Along the way, Americans had negotiated even larger questions: whether or not they needed to be an independent nation, and if so, how they would govern themselves. Some momentous questions remained—none larger than the pernicious legacy of slavery, which fatally undermined most of the democratic premises of the ongoing experiment in self-government. But the college was up and running, and with every passing year, more solvent.

Throughout the turbulence, the leaders of the new institution had distinguished themselves with their patience and probity. The broad principles of the charter had served the college well, and students were coming from farther away to breathe its open air. As they left the college, they brought distinction to their alma mater, joining the ministry, fighting for their country, and in many cases, returning to teach. A casual look at the topics of student theses and commencement speeches reveals an undergraduate body teeming with curiosity, ranging from current events ("Is it for the Interest of the United States to assist the French Revolution against its Enemies in the present War?") to practical issues concerning everyday life on campus ("Whether the Use of Spiritous Liquors is advantageous to Mankind?") to philosophical questions relating to the near future ("Is Marriage conducive to Happiness?").[110]

Perhaps, on occasion, the students displayed too keen an attachment to their personal freedom. In Rhode Island, that principle had been sacrosanct for some time, but diaries and letters of the 1790s also reveal a typical undergraduate devotion to avoiding the rules, complaining about instructors, drinking too much, sleeping late, and lampooning the university administration. One letter from 1799 reveals a certain lack of respect for authority: "The Old Brick [University Hall]

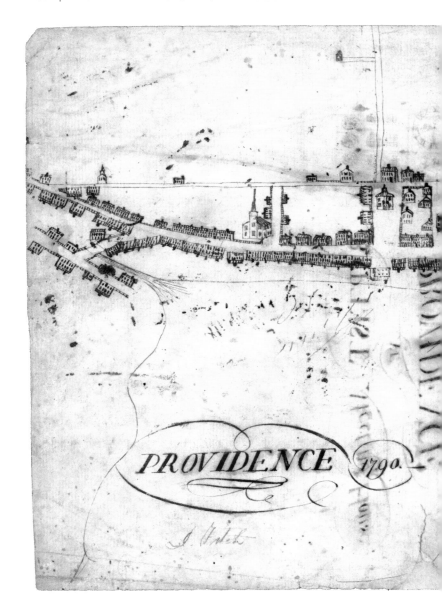

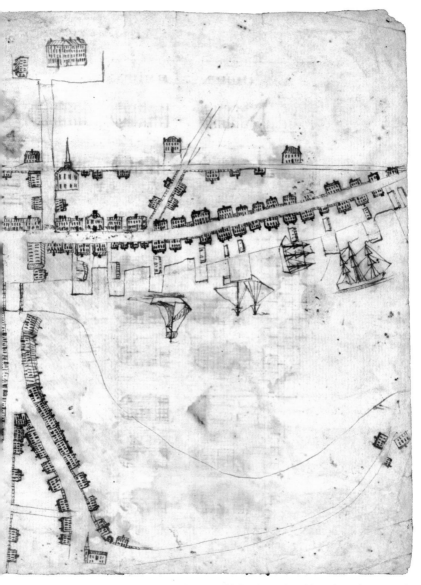

University Hall is distinctly visible in the earliest map of
Providence, drawn by John Fitch in 1790.

resounds very frequently with the breaking of glass bottles against Tutor T's door, if he can be called a Tutor. We have given him the epithet of Weazle."[111]

That tone notwithstanding, education was flourishing on College Hill. Strikingly, the first five professorial appointments were in science, including such men of great distinction as Benjamin Waterhouse, one of the first experts on natural history in the United States, and Benjamin West, who had helped to observe the transit of Venus.[112]

There would be no end of challenges. But Rhode Island College had become strong enough to survive the death of its founder, James Manning, who perished in 1791. Lamentations were loud and heartfelt. The obsequies were held in the College Edifice he had helped to build, and indeed, that was his great monument. Its progress from aspiration to reality had been largely due to his own energy in the field ("He was formed for Enterprize," the *Providence Gazette* eulogized). That field was sometimes literal, for Manning shaped the infant campus with his hands as well as his mind, wielding a scythe when necessary and building tidy stone walls (still visible in the early prints) to ameliorate its appearance. Though born outside of Rhode Island, he embodied many of its tolerant qualities, preaching to different denominations when necessary ("see what it is to be catholic like me," he boasted to a friend). In 1773, he urged students to "challenge the glorious prerogative of thinking for yourselves in religious matters, and generously grant to others without a grudge what you yourselves deem the dearest of all blessings." Just before he died, he called for the establishment of free public schools in Rhode Island.[113]

Another setback occurred in 1789, when Rhode Island College was rebuffed in its attempt to join Phi Beta Kappa, as it was surely entitled to do, especially with its growing science faculty. But neighboring institutions were allowed to weigh in, and Harvard's chapter insisted that standards were simply too low in Rhode Island for any institution to be admissible. A later Brown historian surmised, "It is not improbable that the inherited antipathy to the colony founded by Roger Williams and his associates, all of whom were despised and rejected of Massachusetts, may have largely influenced the action of the Harvard chapter." It might be argued that Rhode Island College's capacity to annoy Harvard, from so modest a campus, at such a safe distance, was an impressive achievement in its own right. Brown's candidacy was finally approved—in 1829.[114]

In this and other ways, the college was making its mark upon the world. If Rhode Island had been founded as "a lively experiment"— the memorable phrase used in the 1663 charter—its college lived up to the phrase. It had faced real adversity—intrastate and interstate feuding, the lack of resources, cessation of activity due to war, and insecurity relating to Rhode Island's fiscal and political troubles. But it had conquered all of them, led by a capable first president, a loyal Corporation, and a growing body of students and alumni. The idea had become fact.

At the end of one century, and the commencement of another, Rhode Island College was already fulfilling its destiny. With a winning combination of irreverence and seriousness of purpose, the plucky college could look back with considerable pride on the period that it had come through. From their perch, the students could see a country growing very fast. And they sensed that they were bound by geography and history to play a large role in its future. The college had been started by a denomination that was by nature antiauthoritarian, in a polyglot place that brooked little interference in its affairs and which had been founded by one of the great iconoclasts of American history. To be worthy heirs of Roger Williams and the Baptists who called for a new kind of education, they would have to think and act for themselves. After all, the first generation had never lacked ambition. They set their hope—that intoxicating word—atop a very steep hill. We have been walking up it ever since.

CHAPTER 2

BROWN, BAPTIZED

Wuskáukamuck. *New ground.*

—ROGER WILLIAMS,
A Key into the Language of America, 1643.

NAMING RIGHTS

THE NINETEENTH CENTURY opened promisingly for Rhode Island College, perched on its Athenian elevation and graduating ever-larger numbers of alumni, who spread Rhode Island principles as they made their way in the world. The hotly contested election of 1800 delivered a new kind of president, Thomas Jefferson, who thrilled Baptists with his crisp statements in favor of religious liberty. Some overexcited theologians even saw the election as "conclusive evidence, that the prophecies contained in sacred writ, will be fulfilled, and that their final accomplishment is near at hand."[1] If that prediction fell short of its mark, a letter the new president wrote to a group of Baptists in Danbury, Connecticut, offered a ringing endorsement of the "wall of separation" between church and state that Roger Williams had built a century and a half earlier. Over the nineteenth century, the United States would follow the path blazed by its smallest state in matters of religious freedom, but it would take time. Massachusetts clung to its state-supported church until 1833, and Connecticut withheld legal rights for Jews until 1843.[2]

· A S.W. view of the COLLEGE in Providence, together with the PRESIDENT'S HOUSE & GARDENS.

A southwest view shows the College Edifice and the president's house and gardens. Based on a drawing by David Leonard, of the class of 1792, it was originally engraved by Samuel Hill, circa 1795. This reproduction was produced in 1949 by the Meriden Gravure Company.

Rhode Island College was still a very small school, occupying a single building. When James Manning died in 1791, there were only twenty-two students. The library was a motley collection of 250 cast-off books, "mostly worthless . . . 'being such as our friends could best spare.'" The combined scientific resources of the college consisted of "a pair of globes, two microscopes, and an electrical machine." Money was tight, and the Baptist associations that had showed such interest in founding a college were showing conspicuously less in maintaining it.[3]

But year after year, the college sank its roots deeper into the soil. In the wake of James Manning, the presidential chair was successively occupied by two graduates, Jonathan Maxcy (from the class of 1787) and Asa Messer (from the class of 1790). More students came in, from a wider periphery (the 1800 catalog recorded 107 students). The library steadily approached respectability. And the financial outlook, perilous for so long, began to improve at last. In 1800, after nearly two decades of lobbying, the federal government finally discharged its debt for the damage caused by man and horse to University Hall during the American Revolution. The amount received was far less than hoped, but still a tidy sum at $2,779.13.

A great leap forward came in 1804. For some time, the Corporation had been guarding the ultimate naming right in its possession—the right to name the college itself. As noted earlier, James Manning had once offered it to a wealthy Briton, Thomas Llewellyn, but in 1803 the Corporation made it official, and voted "that the donation of $5000 Dollars, if made to this College within one Year from the late Commencement, shall entitle the donor to name the College."

It is likely they already had someone in mind, for the appeal was soon answered by someone very close to home—a Corporation member (the treasurer), an alumnus, and a Baptist, born and bred within the bosom of the college. Who was this ur-Brunonian?

A year later, on September 6, 1804, this letter was read into the Corporation's records:

Gentlemen—

It is not unknown to you that I have long had an attachment to this Institution as the place where my deceased Brother Moses and myself received our Education—This attachment derives additional strength from the recollection that my late Hond. [honored] Father was among the earliest & most zealous patrons of the College: & is confirmed by my regard to the Cause of Literature in general—Under these impressions I hereby make a Donation of Five Thousand Dollars to Rhode Island College to remain to perpetuity as a fund for the establishment of a Professorship of *Oratory* & *Belles Letters*—The Money will be paid next Commencement, and is to be vested in such funds as the Corporation shall direct for its Augmentation to a sufficiency in your judgment to produce a competent annual Salary for the within mentioned Professorship—

I am very respectfully Gentlemen with my best wishes for the prosperity of the College

Your obedt: friend

Nicho Brown[4]

At the same meeting, the Corporation voted, "That this College be called and known in all future time by the Name of Brown University in Providence in the State of Rhode Island, and Providence Plantations." With that, the Baptist college was rebaptized. It was doubly noteworthy, for the word "university" was as new to the equation as "Brown" and signaled a growing ambition for the new century.

"Nicho" was Nicholas Brown Jr., whose father was one of the famous four brothers who had done so much to bring the college to Providence. Less public than the others, the senior Nicholas may have been more effective for that reason. A different sort of captain from his freewheeling brother John, he was a financial wizard who ably steered through the economic squalls that accompanied the creation of the United States, reinvesting in one profitable business line after another. In particular, he excelled at the accounting skills that were essential in a rapidly accelerating economy—the account books, lovingly preserved, reveal an empire, rising one cash entry at a time.[5]

Nicholas Brown Jr. was born in 1769, the year before the move to Providence, and grew up in the shadow of the great edifice, with which he was roughly coeval. He attended Rhode Island College after the revolutionary excitement had subsided, graduating in 1786. Throughout his long life, he served his alma mater in nearly every way conceivable, advising presidents behind the scene, facilitating land purchases and new construction, and easing the flow of capital into the college's meager coffers. All in all, he served as a trustee or fellow from 1791, when he was 22 years old, to his death in 1841, a neat half-century.[6] In this time, he gave most of the major land and buildings to the college,

Nicholas Brown Jr., painted by Chester Harding, 1836.

and roughly $160,000. His son and namesake grew so alarmed over this philanthropy that he wrote a letter to his uncle begging that his father be institutionalized before he could give any more money away.[7] But the father obviously knew what he was doing. He reportedly shared the college's open-minded spirit—though he was a Baptist, "no sectarian attachments were suffered to fetter the exercise of his truly liberal and catholic spirit."[8] His epitaph, on an Egyptian obelisk in the North Burial Ground, proclaimed him "an eminent merchant, the friend of the friendless, the patron of learning, the benefactor of the insane and the liberal promoter of every good design."

To name Brown University after an American family was another way in which the small college was carving its own path in the world. Many American institutions bore prominent names, but they were often named after wealthy Britons of the seventeenth century, or after sovereigns: Harvard, Yale, William and Mary, to name a few. What distinguished Brown from the start was the single-minded interest of one family, still present and accounted for as the college grew from one generation to the next. If the Browns had not quite been the driving force behind the creation of the Rhode Island College, they had engineered its move to Providence, and its sustenance since then. They would be present throughout the growth of the eponymous university, leading with quite a few carrots, and the occasional stick as well. It is difficult to think of another institution of higher learning in the United States with as close a connection to a living, breathing American family. In the other college towns, no one actually knew John Harvard, or Elihu Yale, or William and/or Mary. But in Providence, it was difficult to throw a rock without hitting a member of this industrious tribe. That, too, rooted Brown University.

FRUIT OF THE LOOM

IF MEMBERS OF THE FAMILY had supported an impressive number of enterprises in the founding era, their coattails grew even longer in the nineteenth century. Without much territory to develop, Rhode Island had historically been unable to develop its own products to trade, which

Slater Mill, circa 1870.

made the success of the Browns something of a miracle, spinning gossamer out of a wide variety of threads. But soon a different kind of spinning began to take place in Rhode Island, in the textile trade, with ramifications that would be felt around the world. They would be felt on campus as well, and the ingenuity of Brown faculty, students, and Corporation members would play a significant role in the start-up. To an astonishing degree, a colony with no natural products to sell the world was turning into a place that could fabricate just about anything.

At the end of the eighteenth century and the dawn of the nineteenth, Rhode Island was beginning the greatest economic transformation in its history, as local commercial interests awakened to America's version of the Industrial Revolution, launched in nearby Pawtucket when Slater Mill began its operations. That enterprise had been financed and planned by Moses Brown, tinkering with similar projects until he could recruit someone with the late-eighteenth-century equivalent of a killer app—the knowledge of how to build the machinery to spin cloth, powered by waterwheels in turn propelled by churning rivers. In a classic tale of industrial espionage, a young

Englishman named Samuel Slater memorized the workings of a sophisticated device in England, then rebuilt it along the Blackstone River in Pawtucket, not far north of the first encampment of Roger Williams. On December 20, 1790, the system was in place, only a year after Slater's arrival in America.[9]

Once more, Rhode Islanders were at the curious nexus of intellectual freedom and subterfuge, as they were when their aggressive privateering on the high seas accelerated the conflict with Great Britain. Again, these efforts were financed by a member of the Brown family.[10] Soon, the lonely landscapes of Rhode Island's inland river valleys would teem with manufacturing villages—small clusters of houses around mills harnessing waterpower to drive the new machinery of textile production. Many of these new places were named after the same families who were sending their sons to Brown: Allendale, Lippitt, and Saylesville, to name only a few. The Brown family was not idle, either—John Brown was a sponsor of a canal linking the growing industrial centers of Providence and Worcester.[11] Larger factories would be built in Lowell, Massachusetts, in the 1820s, but at the beginning, Rhode Island surprised the rest of the United States with its quick and adaptive approach to the challenge of industrial production.

Over the nineteenth century, an impressive number of technological advances would come out of greater Providence, as the challenges of mechanization were worked out on a smaller scale before they were imitated nationally (often by Rhode Islanders investing in the West, as the Browns themselves did). The first patent issued to an American woman was given to Samuel Slater's wife, Hannah Wilkinson Slater, who invented a kind of thread, and significant numbers of other scientific breakthroughs occurred close to Brown, as the energy supplied by Rhode Island's rivulets was converted to massive industrial output. Suddenly, a people whose idea of industry had been to flee the tax collector found themselves in the forefront of a wave of productivity that would carry Rhode Island for a century and more. At first, the business was textiles (cotton, then woolens). The first census of manufactures, in 1810, found that there were already 26 mills in Rhode Island. By 1815, there were 169 mills within a thirty-mile radius of Providence, with 135,000 spindles in action.[12] By the time the Civil War began, Rhode Island had by far the biggest concentration of textile factories in the United States, when measured per capita.[13]

Soon the mills were spinning off a wide range of industrial products. As part of the insatiable search for new sources of energy, Providence became a leading city in the development of steam power, and a Providence resident, George Corliss, was one of the nineteenth century's great steam pioneers.[14] Providence also led the way toward a new standard of machine tools, measured with exquisite accuracy to the thousandth of an inch. The firm of Brown and Sharpe achieved a mastery of precision with their calipers and other mechanical instruments that allowed other industries to grow in cities around the country.[15] And Rhode Island had plenty of local concerns that became nationally famous, including Fruit of the Loom, Nicholson File, Gorham Silver, and American Screw. To this day, a number of global firms, including Berkshire Hathaway and Textron, can trace their origins to obscure manufactories that sprang up in northern Rhode Island in the early decades of the nineteenth century.[16]

The Industrial Revolution helped Brown University in at least two ways. It brought new sources of wealth into the university community, and many of the names of the new industrial concerns would be immortalized on Brown structures. These included dormitories (Slater) and classroom buildings (Sayles) as well as more than a few residences of industrial magnates that were converted to administrative use (Nicholson House, Corliss House, and the Brown Faculty Club). In addition, Brown's curriculum began to reflect the economy's shift toward science and precision. Of course, science had been relevant since the transit of Venus in 1769, and the charter itself. But now, the spread of local industry brought a keener sense that science had immediate applications that were of public and pecuniary interest. Accordingly, the small Baptist seminary began to expand its offerings.

A significant change came in 1811, when the Corporation organized a medical school. Students had been learning medicine in Providence for some time, but now three professors were appointed,

Solomon Drowne, painted by
Charles Cromwell Ingham, 1863.

and the pace quickened.[17] Solomon Drowne (the alumnus whose diary did so much to illuminate campus life in the early 1770s) was to teach *materia medica* and botany; William Ingalls, anatomy and surgery; and William C. Bowen, chemistry.[18] Bowen allegedly died from inhaling toxins as he was trying to launch a bleaching industry, an indication that some faculty members were eager to capitalize on the new business possibilities so evident in Rhode Island. He was replaced by John DeWolf Jr., a former undergraduate, who helped launch the Philophysian Society, a student organization dedicated to debating chemistry and performing experiments. The medical school, in its first incarnation, only survived until 1828, but it graduated eighty-seven men, many of whom became teaching doctors.[19] It served the public well and brought medical topics not only before the college, but also before the city as a whole, through public lectures and vivid discussions. These teachers made their medical and botanical learning available in other ways too, including through botanical gardens, a specialty of Solomon Drowne's.[20] One historian wrote, "No one who turns over the pages of the minute-book of the Brown Medical Association, founded with the school in 1811 and active as late as 1825—a meeting-place for professors, students and local physicians— will question that a major stimulus was given to medical thought in Providence by the new institution."[21]

The changes wrought by the Industrial Revolution dovetailed with the university's growth in the nineteenth century, and quickened the pace of life on campus. A great many Brown alumni were its beneficiaries, either because they found jobs in the factories and supporting businesses of Providence and southern New England, or simply because they appreciated the broader benefits of inexpensive clothing, increased leisure time, and the development of a broad middle class that was in its own way tied to the changes in the American economy.

As with any great change, there were troubling repercussions. If Rhode Island had been complicit in the slave trade in the eighteenth century, it remained economically involved with slavery as its economy converted to the manufacture of cloth, often from cotton. As Moses Brown, who opposed slavery, began to invest in textiles, his brother John, who supported slavery, wrote a letter to goad him, arguing, "I can recollect no one place at present from whence the cotton can come, but from the labour of the slaves."[22] Southerners were important to Rhode Island mill owners; they mingled socially (Newport was beginning to attract wealthy southerners to its more bearable climate in the summer), they consulted on political matters, and they understood that they depended on each other in certain ways. These relationships were remarkably complex. To cite only one example, Rowland Gibson Hazard, a Rhode Islander with extensive business interests in the South, sold cloth to Southern plantations for the use of slaves, but he also worked to emancipate African Americans who had been illegally enslaved, and was considered an abolitionist. He did not attend Brown, but he endowed the Hazard Professorship of Physics.[23] In other cases, after the slave trade became illegal in the United States in 1808, former slave traders used their wealth to invest in the new industrial economy. James DeWolf, one of the most notorious, helped build the Arkwright Mill in Coventry.

Many Southerners were wary of the new industries—Thomas Jefferson had warned, "For the general operations of manufacture, let our work-shops remain in Europe."[24] Ironically, his administration had hastened these tendencies, for his trade embargo greatly frustrated New England merchants like the Browns and led them to invest in factories. The rapid growth of Providence and its mill villages was not an unmixed blessing. It introduced higher levels of poverty, as transient workers came and went, and immigrants willingly took up low-paying jobs. And it clearly brought on an early form of environmental degradation, though that concept was poorly understood. Unregulated by legislatures and towns, the new factories contaminated local rivers and waterways with impunity, and farmers and artisans often tried to damage the new mills that were damming rivers, killing fish, and putting the older trades out of work.[25] Moses Brown fought such episodes in Pawtucket, and a Brown alumnus, Joseph K. Angell of the class of 1813, became an important explicator of the legal issues relating to water rights.[26] A historian of Rhode Island in the nineteenth century described a rapidly deteriorating landscape:

> Slimy waste drained from tanneries and slaughterhouses into stagnant, odiferous pools; pigs fed from the refuse in distillery cellars and yards; factory workers were crowded into unsanitary, teeming tenements, and they worked long hours under hazardous conditions; congested areas suffered from inadequate drainage facilities and from impure water supplies; and recurrent outbreaks of yellow fever endangered life.[27]

In other ways as well, the rapid trend toward factories was troubling. In the earliest days of the Industrial Revolution, children were considered highly desirable employees, because their fingers were small and nimble and worked well with the machinery. Samuel Slater's first employees, a small group of boys and girls, were between the ages of seven and fourteen.[28] As the factories grew, so did the cities that supported them, to the distress of some observers, like Jefferson, who believed that America should remain a society of rural yeomanry. Those cities developed complex class structures of their own, workers poured in to the mills, and Rhode Island wrestled mightily with attendant problems of immigration, growth, and stratification. Significant race riots occurred in Providence in 1824 and 1831, pitting African Americans against other vulnerable groups, competing for the city's lowliest jobs.[29] In the most sensational crisis of the era, a scion of the city's mercantile elite, Thomas Wilson Dorr, led an effort to reform the state's outdated voting requirements, which excluded most urban Rhode Islanders by requiring that they own $134 worth of real estate.

Dorr's movement proceeded through normal political means at first, but when that approach was thwarted, he and his supporters tried to seize power through force in 1842. Dorr was opposed by nearly everyone in the city's educational and industrial hierarchy, including his father, Sullivan Dorr, who sat on Brown's Corporation (their anguished correspondence serves as a healthy reminder that generation gaps have existed for some time).[30] Once again, Brown became a military barracks, as the troops assembled to put down the rebellion were quartered in the college "for several days."[31] At times, atop its steep elevation, Brown University could seem like an ivory tower, removed from the troubles spreading out below.

Yet that same location could also seem like a moral high ground. If Brown did not come to the rescue of the city's underprivileged in that extreme instance, its faculty and alumni were involved in a wide range of philanthropic activities, designed to mitigate the impact of an Industrial Revolution that was clearly not bringing equal benefits to all members of society. Throughout the Jacksonian era, which wrestled with American contradictions that were all too easy to discern, lectures were given on campus that explored these problems. In 1843, a chief justice of the Rhode Island Supreme Court, Job Durfee (of the class of 1813), warned his audience that technological progress was so powerful a force that democracy would have great difficulty keeping up with it. (Speaking of steam, he said, "Democracy is strong, but here is a power still stronger, that *will* have its course.")[32]

As already noted, the headstone of Nicholas Brown Jr. proclaimed him a "friend to the friendless," and many Brown graduates lived up to that inclusive phrase. As the number of Americans living at the margins increased, so did the institutions devoted to softening the hard edges of life, from public libraries to schools to a growing range of institutions. Butler Hospital, a mental institution, was opened in 1844, with significant funding from Nicholas Brown Jr. and other leaders from the university community. The Dexter Asylum, a lovely spread of greenery on the far side of College Hill, began to serve as a place for the dispossessed to live in 1828. It continues to serve a useful purpose as Brown's athletic complex (since 1957), but the massive stone wall that encloses it reminds the visitor of its less recreational origins.

To take full advantage of the economic possibilities offered by the Industrial Revolution while taking steps to mitigate its impact could be a difficult balancing act, but one alumnus offered a valuable example of how to act locally. Zachariah Allen (1795–1882) graduated in 1813 from Brown, after a college experience that was not entirely happy—his sober scientific experiments conflicted with the increasingly Dionysian tone of student life at Brown. As he recalled later, "Seats of learning are not always the abodes of wisdom, as I had occasion to observe when I was in college. Young men entertained false and pernicious ideas, one of which was that the use of spirituous liquors is favorable to genius and learning. The poet Horace was quoted as countenancing libations to Bacchus."[33]

This serious young man was in no danger of being ensnared. He pursued his scientific experiments both on campus and at home, and took advantage of Brown's Medical School to attend lectures and deepen his knowledge of physiology. Upon graduation, he became immersed in the early stages of the textile boom happening around Providence. A historian of that revolution has written that "Zachariah Allen represented the best qualities of the Rhode Island system."[34] Allen closely studied the technology of the new industries, and explored Rhode Island to find likely places to start new enterprises. One of them, still called Allendale, was a "solitary place" along the Woonasquatucket River, in what is now North Providence. He converted it into "an industrious little village," unusual by the standards of the day for its efforts to offer educational opportunities to the families living and working there. Allen particularly strove to create evening lectures, at a time of day when working families could hear them, and he helped launch a wide variety of public projects, ranging from urban parks (Roger Williams Park in Providence) to libraries (he helped found the Providence Athenaeum) to hospitals and mental health institutions (Butler Hospital). His sympathy did not extend to any form of violent social protest, of which Rhode

Island saw its share in the Jacksonian era. But the efficiencies that Allen introduced to factory work helped both labor and management at a time when they were still working out their thorny relationship, and he was widely lionized as an enlightened mill owner, whose concerns extended to the broader community. He particularly worked to increase mill safety, through inspections, fire prevention, better sprinkler systems, and higher insurance standards. In other ways, too, Allen's technical mastery addressed the disruptions facing a city growing extraordinarily quickly, such as the perpetual need for a dependable supply of clean water. His former home continues to nourish a wide community, as the Brown Faculty Club.[35]

GREEK REVIVAL

As they entered the nineteenth century with growing confidence, Americans sought to define their place in the world, and Brown University alumni were involved in such efforts from the beginning. Several played especially valuable roles in developing rules of international law. Jonathan Russell of the class of 1791 was one of the American commissioners at Ghent in 1814, when Britain and the United States agreed to resolve their nasty dispute; and Henry Wheaton of the class of 1802 has been called "the father of international law." The War of 1812 was dispiriting to many Americans who believed they had already won their war with Britain, particularly in New England, but several figures associated with Brown played important roles, including Usher Parsons, a surgeon who served with distinction under Oliver Hazard Perry and taught in the first incarnation of the medical school. Parsons, who lectured on historical topics as well as medical ones, claimed the great naval victory at Lake Erie was a part of Rhode Island history, because such a high percentage of the officers hailed from the state. Another doctor who would teach at the medical school, John DeWolf, even wrote a song defending Americans from impressment by the British.[36]

As they struggled to defend democracy in a world that for the most part remained antidemocratic, Americans looked for inspiration.

They found it in a distant time and place, along the shores of the Mediterranean, in the ancient Hellenic world. Greece, after all, was where democracy had originated, in the fifth century BC. Like Americans, the ancient Greeks had rejoiced in the potential of the human spirit, while tolerating slavery and war. The Greeks offered a foreign model that was not British—helpful when the United States was struggling against Britain in nearly every realm. A particular point of pride, felt locally, was the rise of a Greek independence movement in the 1820s, seeking to liberate the original proponents of democracy from their Ottoman overlords. No American played a more heroic part in that struggle than a young Brown graduate from the class of 1821, Samuel Gridley Howe. A marker on the Green honors his memory.[37]

For all these reasons, the study of antiquity was especially congenial on College Hill, where Greek and Latin had been part of the curriculum since the beginning. Well into the nineteenth century, incoming freshmen were expected to know Virgil, Cicero, the Greek Testament, Xenophon, Sallust, and Horace, for starters.[38] Indeed, College Hill began to look more and more Greek, as the principles of Greek architecture spread and left a deep imprint in Providence. As the architectural historian Talbot Hamlin observed, "It was in the smallest of the New England states, Rhode Island, that the Greek Revival was perhaps most successful and its monuments most notable."[39]

In the 1820s and 1830s, Rhode Island was enjoying the heady confluence of new wealth, local pride, and civic energy. With its Mediterranean geography of islands and inlets, it was easy to feel a similitude with the ancients. From private homes to factories, buildings began to sport porticos, columns, and other reminders of the glory that was Greece. Several buildings in Providence were especially Hellenic, including a columned arcade downtown, built in 1827–28, that brought a new sophistication to the city (it has been called America's first shopping mall). And just down College Street from the campus, the Providence Athenaeum was built in 1838, with strong support from members of the university community. Indeed, throughout the early decades of the Athenaeum, it was a significant complement to the college, greatly expanding the library options available and opening its doors to women as well as men. (Famously, the local poet, Sarah Helen Whitman, brought her lover, Edgar Allan Poe, there, but could not slow his descent into alcoholism, drug use, and madness.) To this day, a first glimpse of this temple to learning, guarding the approaches to Brown, serves as a reminder that intellectual sustenance awaits the patient traveler who persists in climbing toward the crest of the hill.

Like the city, Brown too adopted classical models, and as the campus grew, it grew more Greek. University Hall had served heroically as the entire campus since its erection in 1770, but the rising endowment and student body demanded that new structures be built. In 1823, Hope College was erected, its expenses defrayed by Nicholas Brown Jr., on land he donated.[40] It retained many of the traditional elements of American college architecture, but twelve years later, Manning Hall, Brown's third building, brought something new to campus, and the Greek Revival was suddenly in full bloom. Manning would house a growing college library and a chapel. In 1840, another Greek building appeared when Rhode Island Hall was dedicated for the use of Brown's expanding scientific disciplines.[41] Across Waterman Street, yet another Greek edifice was built in 1844 by the Rhode Island Historical Society to house Rhode Island's precious artifacts—the papers of Roger Williams and other founders who had first settled in these parts. That too gave a strong, local flavor to the campus, and fortified Brown's sense that it was carrying on a heritage of free speech, bequeathed by early defenders of intellectual freedom. Long known as "The Cabinet," it was integrated into the university campus in 1942.[42]

Oratory, another classical legacy, was flowing volubly on campus. Americans saw oratory as an essential skill, integral to the performance of democracy, as it had been for Pericles and Cicero. Long political careers in the nineteenth century, including those of Daniel Webster, Henry Clay, and John C. Calhoun, were founded upon the ability to mesmerize an audience with displays of learning, emotive power, and logic. Brown was proud of its oratorical prowess—it was to establish a chair in oratory that Nicholas Brown Jr. had given his large gift in 1804. One of the chair's occupants was a distinguished local orator, Tristam Burges, who taught oratory to a generation of Brown undergraduates. He was himself a former student, from the class of 1796, and had conquered a speech impediment to give the valedictory address. With fondness he remembered how well rhetoric, or "the divine art of persuasion," had been taught in the days of Manning and Maxcy, including the ordeal of speaking "surrounded by the entire collegiate assembly, awed by the continued and pervading spirit of the hour and the occasion."[43] Similarly, he forced his students to stand up and speak, arguing "a theoretical orator will succeed no better, if as well, in teaching eloquence, as a theoretical anatomist will in teaching surgery."[44]

Commencement speeches and debates were lively in the early days and often reflected on controversial political topics.[45] Something of a local legend, Burges used his prowess at speaking to enter local and then national politics. In Congress, he became briefly famous for a rebuke to a Virginia firebrand, John Randolph, that included the phrase, "divine providence takes care of his own universe."

That is how it felt on campus, as the pace of student-generated activity increased. With help from Burges and others, a number of oratorical organizations were founded in the waning years of the eighteenth century and the beginning of the nineteenth. Dedicated to debate and conviviality in equal measure, they had impressively Hellenic names, so much so that it was quite difficult to tell them apart. The Philermenian Society, the Philandrian Society, the Philendean Society, and the Philophusion Society all clamored for attention (the Philermenian actually received it, hosting fortnightly debates that attracted wide interest).[46] A chapter of Phi Beta Kappa was launched in 1830, a year after Harvard finally gave its approval.[47]

Brown also began to attract a different kind of Greek organization, as fraternities began to populate American campuses in the 1830s. That was only one of many manifestations that students were enjoying their time in college and saw it as a chance to pursue their education through all channels, including those that were disapproved by the administration. The college rules offer a fascinating window into how life was actually lived on campus, and suggest that all of those Greek names were cloaking some rather barbaric behavior. Indeed, the rules of 1803 reveal that order had been a problem for some time:

> No student shall keep any kind of fire-arms or gunpowder in his room, nor fire gunpowder in or near the College, in any manner whatsoever.
>
> If any scholar shall willfully insult any of the officers of government or instruction, if he shall strike them, or break their windows, he shall be immediately expelled.
>
> No student shall play on any musical instrument in the hours allotted for study, on the penalty of eight cents for every offense.
>
> All students are strictly forbidden to make indecent, unnecessary noises in the College at any time, either by running violently, hallooing, or rolling things in the entries or down the stairs.
>
> Every student is strictly forbidden to throw any thing against the College edifice, to attempt throwing any thing over it, or to throw water or any thing else from the College windows, or in the College entries.[48]

Assuming that these warnings were describing activities that were happening often enough to warrant interdiction, Brown must have been a noisy place. In addition to all of the proscribed noises, the College Edifice had a bell to ring students to class. And on any given day, students might be heard declaiming their orations. But below the surface, one can also detect some unruliness, as a letter of 1819 from the President, Asa Messer, to a parent, reveals:

> I hasten to state, That, some weeks since, our chapel and dining-hall doors were, during the darkness of night, burst in, and carried off; that the furniture was carried from the latter, and some of the seats, and even the Pulpit, from the former; that the gates and bars of the college yard, and the blinds of the college-house were carried off. The day after this had occurred, a notification, probably stuck up the day before, was found in the college-entry; and the features of it may be collected from the consideration that it was a notification of a meeting of "Hell fire rummaging club at half past twelve this night."[49]

A runic archaeological find that still speaks to the restlessness of the era: student graffiti on the southwest corner of University Hall. "W.P.B.J." was Walter Price Bartlett Judson of the class of 1818.

Another letter, written by Messer in 1824 to the presidents of Williams College and Union College, revealed a president living in some fear: "During our last spring and summer Terms unusual disorder prevailed among our students. They broke open the Library: they beat down the Pulpit: they prevented or disturbed for several weeks a regular recitation: they even assailed our house, in the night, and broke the windows."[50] As the college's friends grew concerned, they instinctively looked to University Hall for help. But it too was a target of practical jokes. One day a local farmer found his ox-sled and a load of wood sitting on its roof.[51]

President Messer was distracted not only by student rowdiness, but also by accusations that his personal religious beliefs were drifting toward more modern forms of worship than old-school Baptism. This charge—and one can assume it was prompted by some truth—led to his termination, but it violated the spirit of an institution that so often trumpeted its tolerance as a kind of saving grace. The so-called Era of Good Feelings was a time of steadily liberalizing approaches to religion, as personified by the long career of William Ellery Channing (born in Rhode Island), and Messer sympathized with Channing's brand of Unitarianism. He attended services in the nearby First Unitarian Church of Providence on Benefit Street, and suspicions of his apostasy deepened when he received a divinity degree from Harvard University in 1820.

The arrival of serious science on campus was also destabilizing traditional ideas about piety. A guest lecture on campus in 1825 ridiculed the old ideas that had organized colleges for centuries—classics and mathematics, in support of a general program of theology—and instead called for science, museums, herbaria, and anything else that would lead to a fact-based understanding of Creation. Messer was thus, in his way, in the forefront of something new. It is easy to see why some of the older Baptists were anxious—although that is not to condone the way in which he was criticized, behind his back, and ultimately removed. After he was hounded from office, a concerned trustee wrote, "God forbid that a Spanish Inquisition should ever stand on a soil sanctified by the bones of Roger Williams."[52]

WAYLAND

UNDER MESSER'S PRESIDENCY, Brown's students seem to have gone beyond constructive irreverence on to something more like assault with a deadly weapon. After Messer was pressured to leave office for his liberal views—not a luminous moment in the university's history— a disciplinarian was brought in, but one who nonetheless shared certain of Messer's views.

In spite of his young age (thirty), Francis Wayland was impressive from the start. The son of a minister and a minister himself, he had the proper Baptist credentials. As a child he had been strongly affected by his mother, Sarah Moore Wayland, who instilled in him a strong streak of egalitarianism and a protective instinct toward religious liberty:

> If I have ever cherished a genuine abhorrence for religious intolerance, the sentiment was first awakened by my mother's conversations. Nor was she merely an enemy of persecution for the

sake of religion. I have never known a more consistent lover of human liberty. For oppression of every kind she felt a true and noble disdain.

Wayland grew up peripatetically around New York State, in one instance attending an interracial school, highly unusual for its day. He later wrote that "the only thing that I remember of this school is, that no distinction was at the time made in respect to color."[53]

From the moment he arrived on campus, his presence was felt. Wayland was commanding in person, almost Greek himself. An early student recorded:

> President Wayland was at that time at the very culmination of his powers, both physical and intellectual. His massive and stalwart frame, not yet filled and rounded by the accretions of later years, his strongly marked features, having still the sharp outlines and severe grace of their first chiseling, his peerless eye, sending from beneath that olympian brow its lordly or its penetrating glances, he seemed, as he stood on the stage in that old chapel, the incarnation of majesty and power. . . . The effect was indescribable. No Athenian audience ever hung more tumultuously on the lips of the divine Demosthenes.[54]

It was one thing to speak, another to lead. First, Wayland set about restoring order. Although it took some effort, he succeeded in suppressing the daily insurrections, and he revived rules that required faculty members and tutors to live on campus, in close proximity to the students. This inconvenienced some of Brown's more distinguished faculty members, particularly in the medical school, with the regrettable result that the school was obliged to close soon after Wayland's arrival. That suppressed a promising initiative for over a century, and was all the more surprising for the fact that Wayland had trained in medicine as a young man. It is difficult not to agree with the historian Donald Fleming, who passed severe judgment on this otherwise very successful president: "Wayland must be charged with inflicting a grave wound on the University and on the city of Providence. No more doctrinaire impoverishment of the intellectual resources of the University has ever occurred."[55]

Undeterred, Wayland continued his reforms. He upgraded the appearance of the campus and was a very public presence, speaking and writing on a huge variety of topics.[56] He was an educational reformer even before his arrival, calling for learning to be "as free as the air we breathe."[57] He saw a first-rate education as a means to spread democracy, for the good of the whole. But he also had a clear sense of what was important to the individual, and why the relationship between teacher and student was essential to get right. In an 1830 address on education, he included this penetrating description of the kind of teacher he admired:

Francis Wayland, painted by George P. A. Healy, 1846.

> Let us never forget that the business of an instructor begins where the office of a book ends. It is the action of mind upon mind, exciting, awakening, showing by example the power of reasoning and the scope of generalization, and rendering it impossible that the pupil should not think.[58]

The students responded; James B. Angell of the class of 1849, later president of the University of Michigan, wrote, "We students in Brown believed that there was no better teaching in any college than in ours."[59]

Wayland also believed in a stronger relationship with the city that was growing up quickly around him, and he sought to promote it through his words as well as his works. In 1842, he wrote a treatise on education, *Thoughts on the Present Collegiate System in the United States*, that criticized most colleges as "isolated to a great extent from connexion with the community around [them]." No civil engineer could level College Hill, but Wayland could make the university more accessible to Providence in other ways, including his own service on countless committees to introduce reforms to the crowded city.

But he had an ambitious agenda beyond that. Brown's library records a dizzying 195 publications by Francis Wayland. In a letter he wrote to his sister in 1832, he compared himself to a dray horse: "I am in the harness from morning to night, and from one year to another. I am never turned out for recreation." Still, he exercised his body and mind, sawing wood, and writing prodigiously, on large topics as well as issues of passing concern. His major publications even dented the national consciousness, especially *The Elements of Moral Science* (1835), which sold in large numbers, was translated into Hawaiian and Armenian, and established Wayland as a national leader in moral philosophy.[60] In many ways, that book placed Wayland in a line extending back to Brown's origins, as a defender of the right to worship in the manner of one's choosing.

In 1849, Wayland shocked the community by resigning, to call attention to problems of low salaries and declining enrollments (from 196 in 1837 to 152 in 1849). The Corporation, suitably chagrined, implored him to stay, and he did, while at the same time issuing a comprehensive report to the Corporation in 1850. It was a bold document, pointing out the ways in which Brown and the entire American university system had failed to keep up with the times, and offering a way forward. Wayland was disturbed by the prevalence of old habits, including an overemphasis on Greek and Latin and a corresponding inattention to up-and-coming subjects of great value in the hurly-burly of the nineteenth century, including civil engineering, the sciences, and what he called "the Science of Teaching."

Obviously, Wayland had noticed the changes taking place all around him, in a city and state growing exponentially, thanks to the mechanical arts: "It is manifest to the most casual observer, that the movement of civilization is precisely in the line of the useful arts.

Steam, machinery and commerce have built up a class of society which formerly was only of secondary importance." [61] He also put it bluntly before the Corporation, that the college needed an infusion of funds, roughly $125,000, if it was to maintain its excellence.[62]

Wayland's report had a wide impact. The press praised "the New System" and applauded his democratic intentions to create a more practical course of study, with more relevance to the era, and more accessible to different members of society. Wayland hinted at the freedom with which future Brown students would approach the curriculum, by urging that "the various courses should be so arranged, that, in so far as it is practicable, every student might study what he chose, all that he chose, and nothing but what he chose." [63] He also recommended that a law school be created (a recommendation that never came to pass).[64] The Corporation raised the necessary funds, and student enrollment increased sharply, from 174 in 1850–51 to 252 in 1854–55. But this rapid growth also concealed some genuine concern that Brown was admitting just about anyone, and standards were in decline.[65]

His work finally done, Wayland submitted another resignation, this time for certain, in the summer of 1855. After a noisy era, one sound was a harbinger of calm. As the bell atop University Hall rang in a new academic year, just after his resignation, he said, "No one can conceive the unspeakable relief and freedom which I feel at this moment to hear that bell ring, and to know, for the first time in nearly twenty-nine years, that it calls me to no duty."[66]

During the three decades of Wayland's tenure, Brown grew into a larger, more organized institution. Commencement became a more formal event, less riotous (a newspaper in Wayland's first year had written, "It is earnestly hoped that those who attend the Commencement will go there for the purpose of HEARING, and not merely to display fine clothes, fine faces, and fine chat").[67] Brown had strengthened a sense of its own history as well. In 1842 an alumni association formed during commencement week, and a year later, it held a dinner at which a member of the class of 1799 gave a history of the college, and "a spirited song" about Brown was sung.[68]

Students began to act more constructively on their own behalf, conscious that they too had a role to play in shaping this enhanced institution. Their lives on campus grew richer. Student musical groups were forming, adding to the din; in 1837 a group called "The Brunonian Band" performed in Manning Hall.[69] In 1829, the first issue of a student magazine appeared. The *Brunonian* only lasted until 1831, but it was a significant new step, bringing poetry, commencement speeches, and topical essays to a wider audience—and the occasional surprise as well (for example, a student from South Carolina contributed an article on "Southern Slavery," in which he defended that institution).[70]

To be sure, the spirit of fun did not entirely disappear under Wayland. There were still quirky traditions, reminiscent of the earlier days, when an undercurrent of mischief underlay the surface appearance of academic repose. In 1908, Susan B. Ely recorded her memory of an old Brown ritual from the 1830s, in which the freshmen held a bonfire to burn their academic essays:

> The first thing I remember about college affairs was the burning of the essays by the students when I was about seven years old. It was probably at the end of the spring term of 1831. Commencement was then the first Wednesday in September. One morning I noticed two tall poles standing on the east side of Hope College with bundles of white paper tied on them. Soon I heard music, and running up the garden promptly climbed the fence to investigate. A procession of students, dressed in fantastic costumes, came around University Hall, not a lengthy procession like those of the present day, but quite as enthusiastic, and the music . . . was very inspiriting. They went by the old well up the back campus and halted; probably there were speeches. Then the papers were lighted, and made a very pretty bonfire.[71]

Organized sport was also becoming a part of the Brown experience, according to the diary of a student named William Latham. In the spring of 1827, well before baseball was officially invented, he was playing a game much like baseball. On March 27 he wrote, "We had a great play at ball to day noon." And on April 9, "We this morning . . . have been playing ball. . . . They do not have more than 6 or 7 on a side, so that a great deal of time is spent in runing after the ball, Neither do they throw so fair ball, They are affraid the fellow in the middle will hit it with his bat-stick."[72] Football, or something similar, was also in the mix—a member of the class of 1846, almost seventy years later, remembered: "We had games of foot ball organized in two minutes, engaged in by most of the students residing in the College Halls."[73] A boat club organized in 1848.[74]

By the time of Wayland's resignation, Brown had come a long way toward becoming a modern, multidisciplinary institution, eager to serve its community in thoughtful ways and to lead a national conversation. There is no doubt that the Brown of today begins to be recognizable in those extraordinary years of Wayland's presidency. When he arrived in 1827, it was a university in name, but not exactly in substance, with three professors and two buildings. When he departed in 1855, Brown University was a known commodity, of the kind he so admired, with eight professors, four buildings, and a library of 30,000 volumes.[75]

INTERLOCKING PARTS

BY MOST STANDARDS, the country was moving in Rhode Island's direction. The principle of religious freedom that had once been so divisive between Rhode Island and Massachusetts was widely accepted by midcentury, despite occasional bursts of know-nothingism. The industrial practices introduced at Slater Mill were imitated around the United States, often on a much greater scale, as other states embraced the new economy and all of its supporting props, from the railroad and the telegraph to the faster, easier systems of finance that Americans like to traffic in.

Brown had eased into the new century comfortably. The last of the four Brown brothers lingered well into the Jacksonian era—Moses Brown did not die until 1836, at nearly ninety-eight. Long into the

Union Station, Providence, was designed by Thomas Tefft
of the class of 1851 when he was a freshman.

presidency of Francis Wayland, one might have had a conversation
with an eyewitness to the founding of Brown in 1764.

But change had not been effortless. From 1800 to 1855, Americans
experienced a rate of growth that stunned the world. Cities were
metastasizing, especially in the North, and Providence was a substantial American place, bigger than Washington, Cleveland, Chicago, or
San Francisco. As train and telegraph lines spread like capillaries
through the industrial river valleys of northern Rhode Island, the
state's largest city extended its dominance of the local economy.
According to the 1860 census, Rhode Island had 174,620 people
(twenty years earlier it was only 97,210), and Providence had 50,666 of
them.[76] The faster the city grew, the more guidance and design it
needed and, here again, Brown alumni were ready to serve. A Brown
freshman, Thomas Tefft (class of 1851), furnished the design for

Providence's first great train station. The decision to place the major railroad route between Boston and New York City through Providence was a significant factor in stimulating the Rhode Island economy and heightening Brown's relevance to each city.[77]

In such a quickly evolving environment, Brown had to be nimble. Wayland's reforms helped the entire university community think about its larger purpose. While the narrow sectarian controversies of the eighteenth century were far in the past, Brown still occupied an important position within Rhode Island, asking the hard questions that sometimes needed to be asked of a society that was becoming wealthy quickly and unequally, with imperfect attention to the democratic principles Rhode Islanders held dear. Political participation was deepening by some measures—expanded suffrage, for example, after the Dorr Rebellion of 1842—but most definitions of American democracy still excluded women, people of color, and a substantial number of immigrants. Brown's practices were similar, in keeping with exclusions at nearly every university in the country.

Yet in the Wayland years the university was clearly trying to think about the central contradiction of American democracy—its reliance on a racially defined form of slavery. Wayland's own evolution spoke for many: as a young president, he wrote cautiously on the topic, making his disapproval clear, but also expressing his hope that the defenders and critics of slavery could at least talk to each other. He was joined in that moderate but ineffectual hope by many members of the university community. As the United States expanded vertiginously in the 1840s, it was clear that there was no resolution coming, and that expansion was in fact driving the parties further apart. That made life difficult for a college president, and a Baptist in particular (the Baptists split into Northern and Southern branches in 1845). There were always Southern students representing the views of their region, or sympathetic Northerners such as Brown alumnus William L. Marcy, the secretary of war during the Mexican War (1846-48), and secretary of state during the pro-Southern administration of Franklin Pierce (1853–57). Sometimes these issues could be debated—James B. Angell of the class of 1849 recorded that the Southern and Northern students discussed slavery over three weeks in their class on moral philosophy.[78] But by the 1850s, there was a clear hardening of feelings against slavery on campus, led by Wayland's increasingly hostile statements. Perhaps the most passionate abolitionist of them all, William Lloyd Garrison, was the son-in-law of George Benson, the business partner of Nicholas Brown Jr.

If the university benefited from the rise of new industries and the wealth that they created, some alumni also tried to mitigate the class stratification that was also part of the Jacksonian era, despite its much-trumpeted zeal for the common man. In their orations and essays, Brown students were asking questions about the reach and purpose of American democracy, and if they did not have clear answers, they at least did not shy from broaching the topic of democracy and its contradictions.

One Brown student came closer than most to the greatest study of that problem written to date, *Democracy in America*. When Alexis de Tocqueville, having returned to Paris from his travels in the United States, set about writing his magnum opus, he turned to a young Brown student for help. Francis J. Lippitt (class of 1830), only twenty-two years old at the time, was living in France and fluent in French. Tocqueville asked him to translate and explain a broad range of American documents, to help him understand the voluble people he had just visited. Somewhat bewildered by the "wilderness of books" he had acquired, Tocqueville needed a young person to explain America to him—and Lippitt's Brown education fitted him well for the challenge.

Sixty-three years later, at age eighty-nine, Lippitt remembered his part:

> Some time in 1834 I was called on by a stranger who informed me that he was desirous to have the assistance of an American gentleman "of education," and that I had been recommended to him by the American Legation. I accepted at once the terms he offered me, and I was to commence at once in his study at his father's hotel in the Faubourg St. Germain. His physique was not at all striking. He was slightly built, and his height did not exceed five

feet six inches. His age was apparently somewhere between twenty-five and thirty. There was certainly nothing about the contour of his head or the expression of his face that indicated him to be a man of more than ordinary intelligence. His manner was quiet and dignified, but somewhat cold. I afterwards learned that he had lately returned from the United States . . . and that he was a son of the Comte de Tocqueville.

A few words will describe the nature of my duties. Many shelves in his study were filled with books and pamphlets he had brought with him from America. What he desired of me was to write out summary statements of our political organizations, both State and Federal; and those books were chiefly statutes of the different States of the United States. . . .

He usually came in about 3 p.m. to read over the memoirs I had been preparing for him, and to get my oral explanation on certain points that interested him. Our interviews throughout were simply of questions on his part and answers on mine. You will easily believe that his questions indicated a most penetrating intellect. . . . From the ensemble of our questions I certainly did carry away with me an impression that his political views and sympathies were not favorable to democracy. I knew nothing of his intention to write a book until after my return to America in 1835.[79]

Lippitt was not the only versatile young Brown graduate who seized opportunity in the early nineteenth century. The Industrial Revolution had introduced the notion of interlocking parts, the well-made components of a device that work together. In his Phi Beta Kappa address of 1831, President Wayland celebrated something similar when he pointed out two "self-evident principles" underlying scientific discovery. First, in a good system, "the parts will resemble the whole," and, second, people are more likely to discover the parts they need if they understand "the spirit of the system."[80] Brown's "spirit" prompted discovery, but Wayland also sought to ensure that his country's ethical standards kept up with its rapid technological progress.[81]

Although Brown's undergraduates did not always express that hope in the same language as a theologian, several of them followed this line of reasoning, in their lives as well as their writings. It would be an exaggeration to say that there was already a Brown way of looking at the world, but a number of bold undergraduates, even from the outset of the nineteenth century, were ready to engage the world fully on their own terms. Many might be cited, but three stand out.

Adoniram Judson, of the class of 1807, the son of a Congregational minister, began to read the Bible at age three. He underwent a conversion after an unusual experience while traveling—in an inn, he could hear the sounds of a person in medical stress, and upon inquiring the next morning, learned that the traveler had died and that it was his best friend from Brown. Shaken, he decided to attend Andover Theological Seminary, where he began to pursue a dedicated course of study that would allow him to go overseas as a missionary. With three friends, he formed the first cohort sent out by the American Board of Commissioners for Foreign Missions, an organization that would send large numbers of young American missionaries around the world throughout the nineteenth century.

Judson and his wife, Ann, were sent to Calcutta, and during the long journey Judson studied the Baptist faith. Initially he did so with an eye toward refuting its claims, but they became persuasive to him, and he became a Baptist upon arrival. After the British East India Company expelled missionaries, he and his wife fled to Burma, where they established a long presence, translating the Bible into Burmese, printing tracts, and organizing schools. Despite their attempts to live in relative isolation from the West, they were frequently in peril and dragged into colonial conflicts. Judson was jailed as a spy from 1824–26, under grim conditions, during the First Anglo-Burmese War. Thanks to his wife, herself a gifted linguist, he was finally released, and served as a translator for the Burmese in their treaty negotiations. During his long service in Burma, often in complete isolation, he traveled deeply into the interior, befriending the Karen people in particular. Many remain Baptist to this day; indeed, Burma has the largest number of Baptists in the world after the United States and India.

Judson continued work for twenty-four years on his Bible translation, and finally finished it in 1834. In November 1845 he came back to Brown, where he renewed contacts and spoke with students. Four of his sons and a stepson ultimately came to Brown as students, and at least three alumni went to Burma as missionaries, probably because of Judson's special connection to his alma mater. Several different buildings on campus have been named after him. Another legacy is Judson Church on New York City's Washington Square. Named after his son Edward, class of 1863, a minister of the church, it subsequently became a bastion of support for the civil rights and antiwar movements of the 1960s.[82]

Certainly one of the most accomplished Brown graduates of the nineteenth century was the great education reformer Horace Mann (1796–1859), now honored by a house facing the campus. Although Mann never lived in that residence, Brown transformed him all the same. As a child in Franklin, Massachusetts, Mann was alienated by the dark portrayal of the world offered by a local minister, still in the throes of an extreme Calvinism. As was so often the case, Rhode Island offered a refuge, and Mann blossomed. He graduated as valedictorian in 1819, delivering an oration on "The Progressive Character of the Human Race," and never stopped acting on that assumption. After studying some law and returning to Brown as a tutor and librarian, he embarked on a long career as a reformer in Massachusetts. Elected to the legislature in 1827, he quickly gained notice for his energy and purpose, reforming a mental health institution in Worcester and helping revise the state's unwieldy statutes to better serve a rapidly changing population. Mann began to see education as the best means to deepen democracy, in no small part because his own childhood had been so unhappy and his own education so meager before

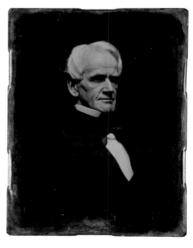

Horace Mann.

attending Brown. In 1837 he became the secretary of the new Massachusetts Board of Education, and for the next eleven years, he used that position as a pulpit of his own, expounding the gospel of universal education, with high standards and buttressed by teacher training, inspections, ample public funding, and other supports.

The improvement in Massachusetts public schools was so rapid and comprehensive that Mann became celebrated around the United States, and other states quickly acted to incorporate his reforms. Through his annual reports, he galvanized additional converts, writing lucidly and passionately about the value of education in a society that was in some danger of losing its democratic bearings. His twelfth such report, from 1848, painted an eloquent vision of free education as the remedy for the social disruptions caused by a rapidly modernizing society. As he argued, education is "the great equalizer," "the balance-wheel of the social machinery."[83]

Mann fought particularly hard to ensure the secular character of the schools, in a state that still revered the memory of its Puritan founders and did not disestablish the Congregational Church until 1833. Mann's advocacy of the separation of church and state may have been a small act of revenge against the preacher who terrified him in childhood, or it may have been a gesture toward the religious freedom Brown stood for, but in any event it helped to set the United States on a clear path toward free secular education for all citizens. One passage in particular from the twelfth report shows some evidence of Mann's Brown training: "If, then, a government would recognize and protect the rights of religious freedom, it must abstain from subjugating the capacities of its children to any legal standard of religious faith, with as great fidelity as it abstains from controlling the opinions of men."[84]

Mann was elected to Congress in 1848 to replace John Quincy Adams; like him, he was a strong voice against slavery. Near the end of his life, Mann was briefly the president of Antioch College in Ohio. His final speech to the students included the injunction, "Be ashamed to die until you have won some victory for humanity." He is buried in

Providence's North Burial Ground, alongside his first wife, Charlotte Messer, the daughter of Brown's third president. Appropriately, there are Horace Mann Schools named after him, all around the country.

Last, Samuel Gridley Howe (1801–76) deserves mention on any short list of Brown's colorful alumni from the early nineteenth century. He led a life that was nearly cinematic in scope—indeed, Daryl Zanuck nearly made a film about him in 1952.[85] An alumnus of the class of 1821, it was a small miracle that he graduated at all, for his entire time at Brown seems to have been dedicated to subverting authority. Like so many families from Massachusetts, the Howes looked to Rhode Island for relief, and Howe's father was convinced that Brown would offer a more liberal and less Federalist education than Harvard. Upon arrival, Howe joined a group of rebellious students who styled themselves "the Knights of the Long Table." They generally tortured their instructors, cavorted, and conceived pranks that became the stuff of legend. No parent wants to receive a letter like the one President Messer wrote to Howe's father in 1819: "Your son, since his return, has thrown a stone through the window of one of the Tutors, and has put into his bed a shovel of ashes; though the Tutor had given him no Provocation; nor did even know him." [86] On another occasion, he led the president's horse to the top story of University Hall, and in his daughter's words, long after the fact, "There was no keeping the twinkle out of his eye, as he told how funny the old horse looked, stretching his meek head out of the fourth story window, and whinnying mournfully to his amazed master passing below." [87]

Many years later, Howe came back to Providence and visited the elderly former president, to apologize for all of his "monkey shines," to use his own term. Messer received him with "a look of alarm" and interrupted Howe's apology to move away from him, saying "I'm afraid there will be a torpedo under my chair before I know it." [88]

Howe was rusticated for these offenses, but after some study and promises to behave better, he was readmitted. Following graduation, he studied medicine at Harvard, and then, inspired by the writings of Byron about the nascent Greek revolution, he decided to join the cause. Throughout a long sojourn in Greece, he was variously active as a fighter, surgeon, and polemicist. Nearly single-handedly, he promoted awareness of the Greek cause in the United States, and he returned home a genuine hero in an age that craved them. Howe raised considerable money for the Greeks and was a kind of relief administrator on the island of Aegina, running a community of refugees, called Washingtonia, as "governor, legislator, clerk, constable, and everything but patriarch."

In 1831, in an abrupt career change, Howe began to teach the blind, an enterprise to which he gave the rest of his life. Here too he was as effective a polemicist as he was a practitioner, and he effectively moved Americans to think about the sightless in new ways, especially after achieving a widely noted breakthrough with his student, Laura Bridgman. By wedding his equally famous wife, Julia Ward Howe, he married into Rhode Island royalty—or at least, to a descendant of two of Rhode Island's colonial governors, Richard and Samuel Ward of Newport. He continued to be an advocate for the rights of self-determination around the world, embracing at different times the Polish, the French, and, to a considerable degree, African Americans who were unfree in his own country. He was part of a group that provided material support to John Brown in advance of the raid on Harpers Ferry, though it should be noted that, after the raid, he was accused of cowardice for temporarily fleeing the country. He did not always advocate the self-determination of women, and his own marriage to a talented and independent woman was compromised by his unwillingness to let her prove her talents.[89]

But Howe's was a life of remarkable range. In 1859, his friend Theodore Parker wrote a mock epitaph for him, predicting he would die at seventy-seven (it turned out to be seventy-four) and celebrating the lifelong achievements of a Greek chief who fought to free the slaves, fight oppressors, make "the blind see, the dumb speak, / And the foolish understand, / As well as *he* could." Near the beginning of that exercise, his friend, himself in his final illness, recalled something of the old prankster who had been able to "disport" at a sympathetic college where he ultimately "became well versed / In the difficult dialect of / Brown University, / Its Arts, its Letters, its Philosophy."[90]

These Brown students shared an impatience with the status quo, a willingness to work outside of known systems, and a deep sense of empathy with the people they were trying to help. Of course, a mere desire to improve society was not always adequate, in an era when injustice was pervasive, particularly in relation to America's vexed racial politics. Some problems require solutions on an epic scale, and slavery was one of them. Well-meaning reformers had been trying for years, with little to show for their labors, and the situation was only getting worse in the late 1850s. In 1856, a year into retirement, Francis Wayland addressed a group of Yale alumni and said the country was fast approaching a "switching-off place" toward good or evil.[91] That was apocalyptic language for him and resembled the excitement with which Baptists and others had greeted the election of Thomas Jefferson in 1800. But America's racial problems had grown more serious in the intervening half century, and Wayland was right, the time for temporizing solutions had passed. To resolve America's contradictions would not be simple, but Brown students had shown a willingness to take on difficult challenges. The war that was coming would certainly qualify.

CHAPTER 3

BOOKENDS

Aukeeteaûmitch. *Planting time.*

—ROGER WILLIAMS,
A Key into the Language of America, 1643.

THIS BOOK BEGAN in front of the Van Wickle Gates and their beguiling mysteries—the rising sun, and the owls and lions that can spring to life before a tender intelligence. If that same young visitor were to turn around 180 degrees, she or he would encounter a pair of impressive libraries guarding the approaches to the university. Like bookends, they face each other across College Street and the city spreading below. They could not be more different architecturally, but each is a monument to an undergraduate whose life was transformed by Brown. Looking out from the gate to the right, a neoclassical shrine honors the great statesman John Hay, class of 1858. To the left, a fortress of metal, concrete, and glass remembers John D. Rockefeller Jr., of the class of 1897, and also recalls the bicentennial of 1964, when it was dedicated. Together, they frame not only the view, but a great deal of Brown's history, just as the two Johns themselves framed the experience of the late nineteenth century at Brown. Between their arrivals, forty years apart, the campus would be greatly enhanced by a cluster of new buildings, an enlarged student body, and the arrival, at last, of a women's college.

Western view of Brown University, 1861.

HAY

JOHN HAY'S ARRIVAL AT BROWN IN 1855 was hardly a foregone conclusion. A son of the Midwest, he had grown up in Salem, Indiana, and Warsaw, Illinois. But his family, solicitous for the future of a talented child, felt the tug eastward. Hay's grandfather, David Augustus Leonard, had graduated from Brown in 1792, as the class poet. Hay inherited a poet's way of looking at the world and a poet's name—he was baptized John Milton Hay, after the great English writer and champion of free speech (and not so incidentally, the friend of Roger Williams). Accordingly, at sixteen the young versifier was sent to Brown, where he could nurture his talents, sharpen his wits, and prepare for what life had to offer.

In his case, life was extraordinarily generous. In spite of arriving on campus as something of a country cousin, fresh from the prairie (his eyes, mouth and ears were full of "cinders and dust" from the train ride), Hay took to Brown. He made friends easily and soon was known for his ebullient wit. His breakthrough came one evening when he was called upon spontaneously to make a speech. As he stood up, utterly unprepared, a cynic yelled, "We don't want anything dry."

John Hay, Senior Class Portrait, 1858.

At that moment, Hay responded, "Hay that is green can never be dry." The joke was so natural and perfect that it ensured his success. Obviously, this was no hayseed.[1]

Hay embraced all that Providence had to offer as well. He joined the Baptist church in "the rigorous fashion of those days, by immersion in the Seekonk River, a hole having been cut in the ice for the purpose."[2] He frequented the Athenaeum, where he fell in with a crowd of local poets, all of whom seemed to be women. Their leader was a local eminence named Sarah Helen Whitman,[3] who, as noted earlier, had been engaged to Edgar Allan Poe during a chaotic series of drug-addled visits the author made to Providence in 1848. Providence was still atwitter, and Hay was drawn to Whitman, who became something of a mentor to the young writer. She evidently took her role as a literary person very seriously. Not only did she call herself "The Priestess," but also, according to a contemporary report, "She dressed always in white, and she appears to have sprinkled her garments with ether, instead of cologne or other perfume, which shed a fragrance suggestive of a neurotic condition in the wearer."[4]

Fortunately, Hay also found time to carouse outdoors with his friends. To a surprising degree, given the punctiliousness of his portraits and the seriousness of his future responsibilities, he was something of a hellion at Brown. He joined a fraternity, he stayed out late with friends, and he wrote and laughed effortlessly. An acquaintance describes him as a typical exuberant undergraduate, only more so:

> His enthusiasm was boundless, and his love for and appreciation
> of the beautiful in nature and in art was acutely developed. If he

was smitten with the charms of a pretty girl, he raved and walked the floor pouring out his sentiment in a flood of furious eloquence. He would apostrophize a beautiful sunset until the last glow had expired. I remember being called out of bed by him one night to witness a beautiful display of Northern Lights. The display was gorgeous, but the night was cold, and after stating my view of the situation, I retired to my room leaving him with chattering teeth and eloquent language addressing "Aurora B."[5]

Another legendary experience, long remembered by his classmates, was "the night when Johnny Hay took hasheesh," as a controlled experiment to see if it helped his poetry. We don't know the result of the experiment, but after graduating and leaving Providence, the future secretary of state alluded to it:

> If you loved Providence as I do, you would congratulate yourself hourly upon your lot. I turn my eyes eastward, like an Islamite, when I feel prayerful. The city of Wayland and Williams that smiles upon its beauty glassed in the still mirror of the Narragansett waves, is shrined in my memory as a far-off mystical Eden where the women were lovely and spirituelle, & the men were jolly and brave; where I used to haunt the rooms of the Athenaeum, made holy by the presence of the royal dead; where I used to pay furtive visits to Forbes' forbidden mysteries (peace to its ashes!), where I used to eat Hasheesh and dream dreams. My life will not be utterly desolate while memory is left me, & while I may recall the free pleasures of the Student-time.[6]

Obviously, Brown had left a deep imprint upon the young writer. He became the class poet, like his grandfather, and delivered an elegiac poem upon graduating in 1858. That augured the depression he would feel at leaving Brown; and sure enough, he was soon miserable, back in his small Illinois town, so far from great individuals like the Priestess. He wrote plaintive letters to her, lamenting the "Boeotian" atmosphere of his hometown (Boeotia is a remote province

Sarah Helen Whitman.

of Greece) and pining away for "Providence and civilization." According to this formula, Providence is Athens, and University Hall the Parthenon.

But the prairie was not quite as Boeotian as he thought, and the pace of life quickened for him, as his uncle found a job for him in a Springfield law office. It may have been the best job in history for a recent college graduate, for Hay soon became attached to a gangly lawyer he met there. Abraham Lincoln was a shrewd judge of talent, and like Alexis de Tocqueville, saw some value in keeping a young Brown alumnus nearby. He soon engaged Hay as his personal assistant, just as he was beginning the extraordinary rise that would

Edgar Allan Poe in Providence, November 13, 1848.

culminate in his election to the presidency in 1860. Hay rose with him, and they were together until the last day of Lincoln's life. Hay's frequent observations of Lincoln, penned with literary artistry and profound insight, constitute a major source of information concerning the sixteenth president.

For that reason alone, Hay would be important. But his versatility showed in other ways. Though young, he was a trusted political aide whose judgment made crises disappear and whose wit lightened the atmosphere for the beleaguered president. In 1864 Lincoln sent him as his representative to negotiate a possible peace with the Confederates (it failed). Though clearly busy, Hay still found time in that year to remember his alma mater, now a hundred years old and in need of a poem for the centennial. Hay obliged with something short but serviceable:

> *A hundred times the bells of Brown*
> *Have rung to sleep the idle summers,*
> *And still today clangs clamoring down*
> *A greeting to the welcome comers.* [7]

Following the trauma of the assassination, Hay rediscovered his interest in foreign lands and received an attractive assignment for a still-young poet—a posting to Paris, where he served as a junior diplomat. That was the beginning of a career that merged statecraft and literary expression with a remarkable dexterity. Hay moved from posting to posting like a goat clambering up an Alp—Madrid, Vienna, London. Far from hurting him, his Midwestern origins struck his friends as deeply American, and Hay retained a democratic ease throughout his life. His Brown training refined that ore and helped him develop a gifted way of expression, an insatiable curiosity, and an intellectual self-reliance that never failed him. He wrote important works of fiction, essays, state papers, and the essential biography of Lincoln. Like Lincoln, he married up—the daughter of a Cleveland railroad magnate—and as he grew wealthier and older, he became more conservative than Lincoln likely would have, criticizing the labor movement as it began to find its voice. But he always retained his charm. With a close circle of friends that included the historian Henry Adams and the explorer Clarence King, he joined an important Washington salon of writers in the shadows of the White House, then occupied by a series of late-nineteenth-century presidents who were decidedly un-Lincolnesque.

Finally, Hay got the job he wanted, and as secretary of state led the United States through a time of upheaval in its foreign relations, including the end of the Spanish-American War (which he called, too fliply, "a splendid little war"), the Open Door policy in China, and the

negotiations that would eventu-
ate in the Panama Canal.
Together, these dealings marked
the emergence of the United
States as a great player on the
world stage, and Hay was, as
usual, at the center of everything.
Though devoted to the growth of
the United States as a global
empire, he never lost his feeling
for what Lincoln called the "better angels," and in 1903 took a
public stand against the prosecu-
tion of Jews abroad, in a time of
growing ethnic unrest.[8] It would
be difficult to think of an
American who led a more varie-

John Hay as an elder statesman.

gated life, or who better personified the shift from a rural society to a
world power. When Hay died in 1905, he was buried in Cleveland, but
his most impressive monument is the John Hay Library, built in 1910.
Appropriately, it houses one of the greatest Lincoln collections in existence, purchased for Brown by none other than John D. Rockefeller Jr.

REBELLION

THE REASON WE VENERATE LINCOLN, of course, is that he led the
United States through the worst crisis in our history and articulated
our finest principles while doing so. The Civil War was deeply trau-
matic for Brown, as it was for every community in the country—
especially communities that were populated, as Brown's was, by young
men. In its earliest years, the tiny Brown campus was so near to the
skirmishes of the American Revolution that the enemy could be seen
from the rooftop of University Hall. During the Civil War, the battle-
fields were more distant, but the war touched home in every way.

For years, as we have seen, a surprising undercurrent of physical danger could be detected in undergraduate hijinks. In 1857, a duel was held between two students, arousing great attention in the local press, although no one was hurt. But those antics were overshadowed by the epic display of violence that began in spring of 1861. The Civil War engulfed the university, leaving few aspects of undergraduate life as they were. That the students were following political events closely is clear from undergraduate accounts—one student remembered going downtown to hear Abraham Lincoln speak, on February 28, 1860, the day after his triumph at the Cooper Union. Unimpressed, the student was put off by Lincoln's "grotesque and uncouth" manner and some of his western irreverence ("he made faces at the audience when asked questions not always pertinent"). A week later, on March 8, Lincoln spoke in Woonsocket, and ninety Brown students went to hear him, singing a drinking song along the way ("Here's to Abe Link, drink him down").[9]

A year later, Lincoln was president, trying to keep the country intact even as most of the South was seceding. Fort Sumter fell on April 12, and as the news filtered to Providence, emotions ran very high. On April 15, Lincoln issued his call for 75,000 volunteers, and Brown's seniors asked for permission to raise a large flag over University Hall. A lone voice dissented, from a Mississippian (John J. Ward, class of 1861), who asked that the flag of the Confederacy also be flown—his proposal was of course rejected.[10] A student who was there said, "having recorded his vote, he seceded."[11] Eventually, he found his way back to Mississippi, where he entered the Confederate army. Three years later, he died in service to his cause from a gunshot wound to his knee, followed by scrofula.

The flag was unfurled on April 17, before a large crowd, with speeches and intense expectations for the contest to come. It was coming up very quickly indeed. Regiments were forming around Rhode Island, and they began to leave from Fox Point the next day, to defend Washington. Once again, the roof of University Hall afforded a view of soldiers going to war. In May, a military company was formed at Brown. They were first called, with a bit of academic pretension, "The Wrath of Achilles," but wiser heads prevailed, and they changed their name to the University Cadets. Resplendent in their new self-designed uniforms, with dark blue shirts, light blue Zouave pants, and red caps, they paraded at the Class Day on June 13.[12] A little over a month later, the first real battle of the war took place outside Washington, at Bull Run, and Brown students, until recently worrying about their exams, were there. One of them, Leland Jenckes, class of 1861, was wounded and captured, and could not attend his own graduation in September because he was a Confederate prisoner of war.

An older alumnus, Sullivan Ballou, was not as fortunate. Ballou had conquered a number of obstacles in his life even before coming to Brown, including orphanhood. After his graduation in 1852, he forged an impressive career as a local leader. He was elected to the Rhode Island Assembly and became its speaker in due course. He joined the infant Republican Party, helping to promote the unlikely candidacy of Abraham Lincoln. After Lincoln's call for volunteers, Ballou immediately enlisted, and he was given the rank of major, third in command of the Second Rhode Island Infantry Regiment. At Bull Run he found himself in the thick of the action and was mortally wounded when a cannonball sheared off part of his right leg. The rest of the leg was amputated, and he was left to die on the battlefield, which he did a week later. Although he was buried by Union soldiers, the battlefield was soon occupied by troops from Georgia, who dug up the Union dead, decapitated them, and burned their bodies. Northern sensibilities were shocked by this act of desecration.

With considerable emotion, Ballou's remains were retrieved, returned to Rhode Island, and reburied in Swan Point Cemetery. After his death, a letter to his wife was found in his personal effects, hinting at the doom he felt on the eve of battle. Exquisitely written, it was delivered to her after his death. One can only imagine her feelings upon receiving it. One hundred twenty-nine years later, the reading of this letter caused a sensation during the televised history of the Civil War presented by Ken Burns, the most watched series in the history of public television when it aired in 1990. A few excerpts follow:

My dear Sarah,

.... If it is necessary that I should fall on the battlefield for my country, I am ready. I have no misgivings about, or lack of confidence in, the cause in which I am engaged, and my courage does not halt or falter. I know how strongly American Civilization now leans upon the triumph of the Government and how great a debt we owe to those who went before us through the blood and sufferings of the Revolution. And I am willing—perfectly willing—to lay down all my joys in this life, to help maintain this Government, and to pay that debt. But, my dear wife, when I know that with my own joys I lay down nearly all of yours, and replace them in this life with cares and sorrows—when, after having eaten for long years the bitter fruit of orphanage myself, I must offer it as their only sustenance to my dear little children—is it weak or dishonorable, while the banner of my purpose floats calmly and proudly in the breeze, that my unbounded love for you, my darling wife and children, should struggle in fierce, though useless, contest with my love of country?....

O Sarah! If the dead can come back to this earth and flit unseen around those they loved, I shall always be near you—in the garish days and the darkest nights ... amidst your happiest scenes and gloomiest hours—always, always, and if there be a soft breeze upon your cheek, it shall be my breath; or the cool air fans your throbbing temple, it shall be my spirit passing by. [13]

Bull Run extinguished the hopes of the entire country that the conflict might be short and decisive. Instead, it was to be a grueling war of attrition. But through those four long years, Rhode Island and the Brown community answered the call with honor and great sacrifice. The war never seemed all that far away—the Naval Academy moved to Newport from Annapolis during the war years, and Narragansett Bay was busy with troop transports and other logistical operations. The factories of Providence worked overtime fabricating uniforms, weapons, and tools for the troops. Sisters, wives, and mothers sewed garments, wrote letters, and helped to provide encouragement in every way they could. Moved by the suffering of veterans, wealthy

Brown alumni began to plan for a modern hospital in 1863, and five years later, Rhode Island Hospital opened its doors.[14]

A wide variety of Brown students and alumni served, including those who were too old, those who were too young, and those who would take some time to graduate after returning (they ranged from the class of 1825 to the class of 1874). Some came from the wealthy families of Providence (a grandson of Nicholas Brown's sister, Thomas Poynton Ives, class of 1854, was killed), but most came from the great rank and file of Rhode Island and its environs. There were occasional glimpses of the famous and near-famous, including the brothers-in-law of William Tecumseh Sherman (Thomas Ewing, class of 1856) and Stephen Douglas (James Madison Cutts, class of 1856).[15] John M. Thayer, class of 1841, became a Major General under Ulysses Grant, whom he admired greatly. During a speech he gave on campus in September 1863, Thayer predicted that Grant possessed the power and the will to "crush this infernal rebellion."

But talented Brown men were also serving on the other side. One of Robert E. Lee's mapmakers was a resourceful graduate named Albert H. Campbell, class of 1847. Confederate records are more difficult to verify, but nineteen Brown men had joined the Confederate ranks by July 30, 1861, and twenty-four would serve afterwards, as surgeons, engineers, and common foot soldiers.[16] One of them was Clarence Bate, class of 1858, who had caused the trouble with the duel in 1857. It speaks of the strangeness of the war to realize that his life was probably spared because of his Brown connection. During the war, he was nearly executed by federal authorities for opening a Confederate recruiting station, only to have President Lincoln intercede with a pardon at the last moment—a pardon most likely engineered by his undergraduate friend, John Hay.[17]

A similar strangeness might be found in the story of a hot-tempered Virginian named Martin Luther Laws, who probably served in a Confederate militia in 1861 before deserting, then entered Brown as an undergraduate while the war was still raging, in the fall of 1863. When a frightened freshman asked Laws to defend him from a hazing ritual, Laws pulled out a revolver to shoot the assailant. Fortunately, his hand was jostled, and as an account informs us, the bullet merely grazed the "olfactory protuberance" of the would-be hazer. Laws was sent away for a while but managed to graduate in 1864. In April 1865, it was over, and Brown students celebrated with an enormous bonfire on April 9, the night Robert E. Lee surrendered at Appomattox. All in all, an astonishing 417 Brown men served in the war, though it took some time to get right with the records. Remembering the war was nearly as important as fighting it, and a memorial plaque went up quickly, unveiled in Manning Hall on September 4, 1866. Then, with great care, a lavish memorial publication was issued in 1868, honoring 21 young men killed on the Union side, and still bristling with anger over the loss of so many young men.[18]

Over the next generation, the veterans would return to campus with a tragic wisdom that no professor could ever impart. With time, Brown would remember all of its young men who had fought, including those who fought for the Confederacy. Henry Burrage, class of 1861, the same young man who kept a journal of his student life in the spring of 1861, when the war was starting, and then compiled the memorial book of 1868, lived long enough to bring out a new edition in 1920, when passions had subsided. In that book, less ornate but more temperate, he included the names of everyone from Brown who had fought. By that time, he counted thirty-nine who had been killed. In his final version of the roll, Burrage broadened his definition of service to include not only those who fought, but also those who performed other kinds of patriotic duty—including Brown's former president, Francis Wayland, who worked to open a veterans home. That larger definition was appropriate, for the tragedy of the war had touched everyone in the Brown community, directly or indirectly.[19]

NOT IN KANSAS

THE CIVIL WAR LEFT MANY LEGACIES, on campus as well as off. Eventually, as the veterans drifted back, the old sights and sounds of college life returned to normal, and conversation turned to baseball games and boat races.[20] But it was clear that the nation had changed profoundly. The

IN·MEMORIAM·FRATRUM·SUORUM
QUI·PRO·LIBERTATE
ET·PRO·REIPUBLICAE·INTEGRITATE
IN·BELLO·CIVILI·CECIDERUNT
LITERARUM·STUDIOSI
IN·HAC·UNIVERSITATE·COMMORANTES
HANC·TABULAM·POSUERUNT.
MDCCCLXVI.

1840. COMMANDER HENRY STEARNS NEWCOMB.
1847. ASSISTANT SURGEON JOSHUA JAMES ELLIS.
1847. LIEUTENANT WALTER HERBERT JUDSON.
1848. SURGEON FAYETTE CLAPP.
1852. MAJOR SULLIVAN BALLOU.
1852.   MILES JOHNSON FLETCHER.
1852. LIEUTENANT COLONEL CHARLES BERTRAND RANDALL.
1854. COMMANDER THOMAS POYNTON IVES.
1855. BREVET BRIGADIER GENERAL LOUIS BELL.
1855. ASSISTANT SURGEON WILLIAM POTTER GRIER.
1857. LIEUTENANT and A.D.C. ROBERT HALE IVES.
1857. ASSISTANT PAYMASTER JOSHUA GORDON WOODBURY.
1858. CAPTAIN WILLIAM LOMBAERT KNEASS.
1860. CAPTAIN ALBERT GARDINER WASHBURN.
1861. CAPTAIN JAMES CLARK WILLIAMS.
1862. MAJOR WILLIAM IDE BROWN.
1863. LIEUTENANT HERVEY FITZ JACOBS.
1864. PRIVATE CHARLES LOUIS HARRINGTON.
1864. PRIVATE MATTHEW McARTHUR MEGGETT.
1864. PRIVATE EUGENE SANGER.
1867. LIEUTENANT JAMES PECK BROWN.

Civil War Memorial, Manning Hall.

experience of administering the war had greatly enlarged the federal government and changed the relationship of citizens to the state—including, of course, the huge numbers of recently emancipated African Americans, who had not been citizens at all. In the course of prosecuting the war, Congress had undertaken several ambitious projects that displayed an appetite for shaping the future along new lines. The transcontinental railroad was one of these, and its completion in 1869 signaled a new era of federated national purpose. Another was the Morrill Act of 1862, one of the more visionary pieces of legislation in American history. Named after a Vermont congressman, Justin Morrill, the act set aside money for each state to create public universities, to be funded from the sale of western lands apportioned to each state according to its population. The intent, which mirrored some of Francis Wayland's ideas, was to adapt universities to a modernizing age and increase the teaching of what was useful. Morrill's act specifically called for education in "agriculture and the mechanic arts," and he added military science as the bill was making its way through a wartime Congress.

The act also recognized a growing truth in the nineteenth century, which built upon Horace Mann's work with free schools—that education was not just a privilege, but a right, and that it benefited a democratic society to extend this right to as many people as possible. A large number of important universities owe their origin to the Morrill Act, ranging from state universities (including those in the South, where the Act was ultimately extended), historically black colleges, and technical schools such as MIT. Even an Ivy League school, Cornell, was created by the Morrill Act—its funding came from New York's wise selection of valuable timberland in Wisconsin.

At first glance, Brown was an unlikely place to study agriculture. It was a more urban college than most, becoming more so as Providence continued to grow. Indeed, in all of the United States, it would have been difficult to find a college less likely to suddenly devote its energies to crop rotation and livestock. But Brown needed new funding, and Rhode Island was eager for its share of the apportionment to come, which would amount to 120,000 acres of land scrip, to be applied toward a purchase somewhere out west. It was expected that this land, when sold, would bring in $150,000. Ten percent of that would go toward building an experimental farm, and the rest toward teaching all of the agricultural and mechanic arts, including chemistry, geology, botany, mineralogy, and math. In other words, it was possible to bend the grant, with some dexterity, toward a range of sciences, beyond agriculture. If done well, Brown might add to its endowment, increase the number of students, expand the curriculum, and develop a private-public partnership with the state and federal governments that would serve the institution well in the future.

Rhode Island designated Brown, the state's only university, as the official recipient of the expected funding. But over the years to come, what would seem a relatively straightforward administrative matter turned into an albatross for a succession of Brown presidents. The first task was to choose a suitable western parcel (since Rhode Island did not have any federal land of its own to give for this cause). Brown's president, Barnas Sears, and his agent (a Brown grad, Horace T. Love, class of 1836) went to Kansas with the intent of choosing land that would ultimately appreciate in value, when, as they hoped, the railroads of the future went through it. Brown was in some danger of deviating from its mission when it briefly entered the business of encouraging settlers to come to Kansas. A pamphlet was actually printed, under the university's auspices, promoting the living conditions there ("The climate of Kansas is delightful and healthy").[21] But there were problems. To begin, Love filed an imperfect claim for Brown's land in July 1863. Then, Brown's Corporation began to divide over the matter, with a strong minority opposing these Kansas schemes. Ultimately, President Sears would resign in 1867, ostensibly because of his health.

A number of complex financial and political arguments followed, in which Brown's claims were weakened, and the value of its expected income diminished. To make matters worse, Brown had not moved with dispatch to create a new line of courses in agricultural instruction. Ultimately, John Whipple Potter Jenks, the curator of an eclectic museum of natural history in Rhode Island Hall, allowed his arm to be twisted, and he began teaching a class on "agricultural zoology."[22] But it was clear that Brown was not about to reinvent itself as a serious center of agricultural education. A contemporary observer wrote of Jenks, "What he didn't know about agriculture would fill a library, but his colleagues knew even less." Evidently the course consisted of "interesting recollections" from Professor Jenks, and "drawing and identifying the parts of a cow."[23]

This sluggishness had some local effects. Rhode Island's General Assembly had a disproportionate number of farmers, and their impatience with Brown began to take a toll. In 1884, a large parcel of land in Providence (which now includes Brown's football stadium and, formerly, Marvel Gymnasium) was given to Brown by the Metcalf family. Brown's then president, Ezekiel Robinson, wondered if this land might be dedicated to an agricultural research station, in keeping with the spirit of the original Morrill Act, and asked the state Senate for $5,000 toward that end. But by that point, the Assembly had lost all patience and began proceedings to create a public university more truly dedicated to agriculture. The result was the founding of the University of Rhode Island, which opened at Kingston in 1890.

REALISM

THE CIVIL WAR LEFT SO MANY LEGACIES that it is difficult to enumerate them all. One result was the triumph of science. Before the war, Confederate elites had often proclaimed their fealty to airy notions of chivalry and honor (witheringly parodied by another Southerner, Mark Twain). In the aftermath of the war, it was clear that those ideals were not especially effective before the hard facts of Northern artillery, railroads, and Springfield rifles. Providence, too, was in the business of hard facts. The urgencies of war nurtured a number of industries vital to war production, including armaments and the textile industries that supplied uniforms and blankets to the Northern cause. Port traffic nearly doubled in the 1860s, and more and more immigrants came from Europe and Canada to work the machines. The growth in population and wealth continued for decades. In spite of the occasional hiccup of a contraction in an economy that was unregulated by the government, money poured into

Rhode Island coffers throughout the final third of the nineteenth century. The most ostentatious dwellings in the United States were built in Newport, and to this day houses like the Breakers, with its seventy rooms, stand as monuments to something rather distant from the egalitarianism that brought the first settlers to Rhode Island.

Providence, too, saw a frenzy of building in the late nineteenth century, and beautiful mansions were built in close proximity to the university, where the city's commercial elite could enjoy the same view of the city as the students. Many of them are now, in fact, part of the university—Corliss House, for example, was the home of America's leading steam engine designer, George Corliss, famous for powering the entire 1876 Centennial Exposition at Philadelphia with a single, overwhelming machine.

The campus was also growing rapidly, as money came in to nourish a university that had been starved for funds since its inception. Robinson Hall was dedicated in 1878 as the new college library, to house a collection that had been moved from building to building since its beginnings in University Hall. Slater Hall came a year later, to fill in the last slot on the front campus; mighty Sayles came two years after that, as Brown began to expand over the crest of the hill, to the east. Romanesque Wilson Hall, originally designed to house physics and mathematics, was dedicated in 1891; Lyman Gymnasium and Ladd Observatory also opened that year; Pembroke Hall for the Women's College emerged in 1897; an Engineering Building came to Lincoln Field in 1903; and in 1904, the growing campus received two memorable additions: the John Carter Brown Library, a jewel furnished by the Brown family, housing an extraordinary collection of rare Americana, and the Carrie Tower, an eccentric ninety-five-foot skyscraper that testifies to the love shared by Paul Bajnotti, of Turin, and his wife Carrie, the granddaughter of Nicholas Brown Jr. The motto emblazoned on the tower, "Love Is as Strong as Death," mixes terror and uplift in equal proportions.

In addition to new buildings, the Brown campus began to attract new kinds of students. Another tangible legacy of the Civil War was the expansion of educational opportunity for African Americans.

African American children playing in Providence, circa 1880.

It would be gratifying to say that this university, so open to students of different religions and hospitable to those without means, was equally generous in its approach to students of color. But for a long time, Brown alumni were in advance of Brown itself. Horace Mann's educational innovations would ultimately extend to African Americans. Edward Lillie Pierce of the class of 1850 did important work early in the Civil War when his unit, the 3rd Massachusetts Volunteers, was stationed near Fort Monroe in Virginia, at the mouth of the James River. Escaped slaves were arriving there in large numbers, well in advance of the Emancipation Proclamation, or any fixed policy of what to do with them. Pierce wrote a prescient article in *The Atlantic Monthly* of November 1861, titled "The Contrabands of War," that urged the integration of African Americans into the Union army, a key step toward citizenship and full membership in society.[24]

African Americans were never far from the campus. By the late nineteenth century, a black neighborhood had grown up around Congdon Street, a stone's throw away from the Carrie Tower. It was likely stretching credulity to claim, as a journalist did in 1888, that "in no other city in the Union will you find a colored community better off than in Providence, when it comes to money."[25] But still, the city was prosperous enough that it attracted talent and labor from other states, including African Americans seeking to flee the South in the aftermath of the Civil War and the beginnings of Jim Crow. The great opera singer Sissieretta Jones moved to Providence from Virginia at the age of seven, in 1876, and returned after her career had ended. Like many African Americans in Providence, she went to school in the old brick schoolhouse on Meeting Street, where the college classes had met in 1770, before University Hall was built.[26] But if African Americans lived and worked in close proximity to the university, they could not attend Brown as students until the 1870s. Elizabeth Buffum Chace recalled an incident that did not reflect well: "About the beginning of the war, a lad of rare excellence and attainments was refused an examination for admission, by the authorities of Brown University, on account of the color of his skin."[27]

But the Civil War adjusted racial attitudes in Northern universities, and slowly they began to reexamine their policies. It helped that progressive colleges such as Oberlin had admitted African Americans well before the war (Oberlin's first black graduate was a member of its class of 1844). Dartmouth took an African American student in 1824 (he did not graduate). Harvard graduated its first African American in 1870, and Yale likely did so in 1874 (the situation is complicated because the racial identity of some earlier students is not clearly known).[28] Princeton did not graduate an African American until 1951.

The records are not available to shed light on Brown's deliberations, but things improved in the mid-1870s, with the arrival of Inman Page and Gregory Washington Milford, members of the class of 1877, and another student, Gabriel Grisham, class of 1878, who arrived in 1874 but did not graduate. They were an impressive group, not only for breaking the color line at Brown, but also for their lives of service to the cause of education long after leaving campus. Page's story is especially memorable. He was born into slavery in Warrenton, Virginia, in 1853, but fled with his family during the Civil War and made it to Washington, DC. He attended local schools there, including the infant Howard University, and then transferred to Brown, where his gifts were impressive enough that he was chosen to be class orator at commencement.[29] His topic addressed "Intellectual Prospects of America," and he improved his own with the speech. The *Providence Journal* noted:

> Mr. Page is the first colored graduate from the University. . . . Mr. Page did not receive his position as class orator from a chivalrous recognition of his race by his white associates, although the choice is none the less creditable to them. He is an orator of rare ability, speaking with weight and sententiousness without effort at display and at times rising to a profound and impressive eloquence. The scope of the essay indicated grasp of thought and the language was often remarkable for elegance and power. There is no doubt but he fairly earned his honors.

Immediately after his speech, Page was recruited to teach in Natchez, Mississippi, the beginning of a lifelong career in education. He became the head of the Lincoln Institute in Jefferson City, Missouri, then in 1898 moved to Langston, Oklahoma, an all-black town, to lead the Colored Agricultural and Normal University (later Langston University). Over seventeen years he canvassed the state, increasing enrollment to over 600, raising buildings, and expanding courses in the agricultural and industrial sciences. Eventually called "the grand old man of education" in Oklahoma, he lived until 1935.[30]

That would all be impressive enough, but a single encounter from this life of service bears closer scrutiny. Page left an indelible impression on a talented young student in Oklahoma, Ralph Ellison, who went on to become a great novelist. Ellison himself, in a visit to Brown in 1979, talked about their encounter and how Page had never stopped teaching him. He confessed that it was difficult for him to even imagine the great old man as a young student at Brown ("To me he was always lofty and enigmatic, a figure of authority and penetrating vision"). His memories of Page were almost those of a biblical patriarch, and he remembered Page reading often from Paul's Letters to the Corinthians, inspiring awe with his commitment to education, character, and "the New England tradition of education" in Oklahoma. Language was no small part of that tradition, and Ellison affirmed,

"Just listening to him taught one the joy and magic of words."

Ellison then told an extraordinary story of a comic encounter that might have resulted in ending his own career as a writer. During a school chapel service, as he and Page were mounting the stairs to a stage, they bumped into each other, and Ellison, thinking a student had pushed him, pushed back. As they fell, they grabbed a rope, connected to a stage curtain, that pulled them onto the stage and deposited them, in a giant

Inman Page, class of 1877.

pratfall, before a stunned audience. Terrified and confused, Ellison ran out of the packed auditorium, sure that he would be instantly expelled for this supreme indignity. But amid the "chaos and disgrace" of that public fall, he heard Page "chuckling under his breath." Ellison ran away, terrified, but he never stopped hearing "that mysterious chuckle, a chuckle which was so incongruous that I could not be certain I had heard it." Out of that searing experience, and the mysterious chuckle, he forged a lifelong attachment to Page and a powerful creative imagination that led to *Invisible Man* (which recounted the incident) and a life of dedication to words. During his visit to Brown, Ellison summed up the influence of the educator: "It was a most pessimistic period for his people but he did his best, and therefore, thanks to Inman Page—and no matter how incongruously—I am here." In his eloquent closing thoughts, Ellison stared unblinkingly at the many failures of American history, but ended on an affirming note:

> perhaps if we learn more about our unwritten history, we won't be so vulnerable to the capriciousness of events as we are today.

And in the process of becoming more aware of ourselves we will recognize that one of the functions of our vernacular culture is that of preparing for the emergence of the unexpected, whether it takes the form of the disastrous or the marvelous. Such individuals as Dr. Page and his daughter worked, it seems to me, to such an end. Ultimately, theirs was an act of faith: faith in themselves, faith in the potentialities of their own people, and despite their social status as Negroes, faith in the potentialities of the democratic ideal. Coming so soon after the betrayal of the Reconstruction, theirs was a heroic effort. It is my good fortune that their heroism became my heritage, and thanks to Inman Page and Brown University, it is also now a part of the heritage of all Americans who would become conscious of who they are.[31]

An impressive number of Brown's early African American students went into similar lines of work. Including Page, Brown graduated five presidents of black colleges. One of the most distinguished was John Hope, class of 1894, after whom the illustrious historian John Hope Franklin was named. Hope became president of Morehouse College in Atlanta, the future alma mater of Martin Luther King Jr., and an important ally of W. E. B. Du Bois. Together, they fought to achieve genuine equality of opportunity, beyond the calming nostrums of Booker T. Washington. Like Page, John Hope had an impressive career at Brown, punctuated by a senior oration that foreshadowed his life's work. It included this paean: "Let us observe that to have been at Brown University is to have drunk in the unpretentious, unobtrusive, yet all pervading idea of liberty and brotherhood; and to have acquired a breadth of culture which means the erasure of all lines, be they of race, or sect, or class, and recognizes no claim other than that which highest manhood makes."[32]

Hope supported Du Bois as he planned the 1905 Niagara Movement, with its ringing endorsement of a broad platform of core human rights for African Americans, and he particularly argued for college education as a vehicle of progress. It is worth noting that many of these distinguished early African American alumni, including Page and Hope, spent part of their career at a Baptist college in Nashville,

Roger Williams University, founded by a Brown alumnus, Daniel W. Phillips (class of 1837). That university no longer exists, but its founding immediately after the Civil War shows that Brown alumni were ever moving forward, often showing Brown the way.

Brown was becoming more reflective of the United States in other ways as well. Increasingly, Brown students looking over the crest of the hill could see downtown buildings rising up to meet their gaze on equal footing. Providence was growing exponentially, in height as well as extent. The colonial and Greek Revival homes of College Hill were charming, and they spoke to the great effort of lifting Providence from its swampy origins along the Providence River and the Great Salt Cove. But now the city's energy was pulling it in new directions, toward the west and north, as a modern metropolis was coming into existence, with sprawling factories, billowing smokestacks, and the constant sound of trains, both intraurban (streetcars clanging their way up College Hill) and interurban (railroads going in all directions).

Another way in which these urban energies were released was through the rise of sports. Providence could boast a championship baseball team in the Providence Grays, who won the National League pennant in 1879 and 1884, and who, by defeating the New York Metropolitans of the American Association in the latter year, won what may have been the first World Series. At Brown, athletic competition was becoming an important element of student life, and a charming memoir of the period makes it sound as if the main Green was something close to a sandlot, with students using Manning Hall as a backstop for their frequent baseball games.[33] Brown students were also playing a role in the spread of sports to a national audience. The first curveball ever officially thrown may have been the one that a talented Brown pitcher (J. Lee Richmond of the class of 1880) threw in front of University Hall in 1878, to prove to his physics professor, Walter Greene, that "curved delivery" was no theory.[34] The first-baseman's mitt was likely invented by Fred Tenney of the class of 1894, who also devised several routine infield plays we now take for granted.

Also in 1878, Brown played its first intercollegiate football game, against Amherst, and years later, when the forward pass was

The Brown Bicycle Club, late 1880s.

introduced to rejuvenate the game, a Brown student played a role in its development (John Heisman of the class of 1891).[35] Brown's first baseball game, against Harvard, had taken place in 1864 (in his report on the game, Brown's indefatigable historian, Reuben Guild, felt a need to comment on the "different theological tendencies" of the two institutions.[36] A boat house for crew was erected in 1871, bringing Brown's footprint very near to the place where Roger Williams had first landed in what would become Rhode Island.[37] Brown would also play an important role in the spread of ice hockey in the United States, thanks to the efforts of some barnstorming young athletes in 1894.[38]

Between 1860 and 1890, Providence's population nearly trebled, from 50,666 to 132,146. By 1910, that figure would climb to 223,326, considerably above the current population. Providence was becoming a metropolis, a teeming beehive of activity, and a capital worthy of the name. In 1904, the majestic pile of the Rhode Island State House was completed by McKim, Mead and White. Its luminous white Georgia marble and classical lines suggested a purity that was elusive in local politics. Then as now, Rhode Island had a reputation for a certain freedom from ethical norms. A sensational muck-raking article of 1905, by Lincoln Steffens, proclaimed Rhode Island to be a state for sale to the highest bidder—lobbyists and corporations—and called the man who effectively managed the nation's economy, Senator Nelson Aldrich of Rhode Island, the "General Manager of the United States."[39]

But the economy hummed, and the factories purred, and they brought ever-newer inhabitants, including those who came from the southern, western, and eastern extremes of Europe. It took time, but Brown gradually began to shed some of its traditionally Anglo-Saxon orientation and admit students from different backgrounds.

That was only one way in which Brown began to change with the times. As Providence grew rapidly, Brown grew with it, and the value of living inside a dense urban setting was not lost on the faculty. Although it had long ago surrendered its medical school, the university offered increasingly sophisticated courses in science and public health. Charles Parsons, a son of one of the professors at Brown's first medical school, became a professor of physiology, and in the latter decades of the nineteenth century, Brown strove to develop new approaches to natural history, zoology, and other forms of science. Jenks's museum of natural history inside Rhode Island Hall offered passersby a chance to gaze at bits of shark, giraffe, Pomeranian, as well as at a Shetland pony that belonged to Queen Victoria and the nails from Roger Williams's coffin.[40] Brown attracted one of America's leading entomologists (A. S. Packard) as well as a professor of physics (Eli Whitney Blake Jr.), who suggested important modifications to the design of the telephone that Alexander Graham Bell was working on. Charles Chapin was particularly important, both to Brown

Telephone prototype designed by Eli Whitney Blake and John Peirce.

and to Providence. Chapin became a professor of physiology in 1882, and two years later he became the superintendent of health for Providence, a job that he filled until 1931. In that capacity, he did extraordinary service fighting infectious diseases, improving local hospitals, and generally bringing humane standards of disease treatment and prevention to a large city teeming with recent immigrants.[41]

Immigrants were an increasingly important political fact of American life, and universities ignored them at their peril. Fortunately, Brown did not. For a time, in the 1890s, it offered extension classes (in the peak year, 1892–93, 2,000 attended), and it scored a coup in 1906 when it persuaded a nationally renowned expert on class structure, Lester Frank Ward, to accept a position as chair of sociology.[42] A polymath, Ward had led a rich life before turning to teaching, publishing in botany and other scientific disciplines. After the Civil War, in which he was wounded, he had headed west, like so many young men seeking to clear their heads (Theodore Roosevelt would do the same). He joined the United States Geologic Survey, doing impressive work as a geologist and paleontologist as the survey participants worked to

Lester Frank Ward.

understand the magnificent new domains between the Mississippi and the Rockies. From the study of the phyla and strata of the plant and mineral worlds, Ward turned his attention to the messier topic of humankind. With the publication of *Dynamic Sociology* in 1883, he helped to define a new field, of growing relevance to an increasingly complex society, with more extremes of poverty and wealth than it cared to admit. At the time, most sociologists of repute, such as Herbert Spencer and William Graham Sumner, felt that society owed little to the poor and therefore should do little to intervene in the Darwinian struggle for survival. Ward felt differently. With a scientist's eye, he brought discipline to his work, and some passion as well. Ward argued that society needed to be more responsive to its problems. Life was not random, and social divisions did not develop without cause. Instead, they could be studied, interpreted, and ameliorated by those willing to devote themselves to the task. He wrote:

> Thus far, social progress has in a certain awkward manner taken care of itself, but in the near future it will have to be cared for. To do this, and maintain the dynamic condition against all the hostile forces which thicken with every new advance, is the real problem of Sociology considered as an applied science.

In other words, Ward was building the underpinnings for a new, progressive outlook, proactive rather than passive. He hated the phrase "laissez-faire" and the lazy assumptions that underlay it. The first sentences of *Dynamic Sociology* bristled with impatience, attacking "the essential sterility of all that has thus far been done in the domain of social science." The result was a new philosophy of activism that galvanized presidents from Theodore Roosevelt to Woodrow Wilson and Franklin D. Roosevelt, and led to new interventions on behalf of the vulnerable. In his writings, Ward also voiced early and important support for protection of the environment and for women's equality.[43]

PEMBROKE

By the late nineteenth century, more and more Rhode Islanders began to feel the same way. With its religious pluralism, Rhode Island had attracted outspoken female leaders from Anne Hutchinson onward. In the nineteenth century, Rhode Island's most prominent reformer was Elizabeth Buffum Chace. Born into a Quaker family in northern Rhode Island in 1806, she drew from her religious inheritance and the ancient Quaker commitment to social justice to develop a passionate opposition to slavery, before turning her sights toward the various forms of inequality she saw around her in Rhode Island after the war. Her vast energy led her across a broad landscape of causes, protecting the rights of poor women, children, prostitutes, prisoners, and industrial workers, until she signed on to the great battles of the second half of her life, advocating for the right of women to be educated and to vote. In an 1891 speech, she argued that women had so much ability that if they were permitted to run Rhode Island politics, they might make "a place fit for gods to dwell in."[44]

Brown had permitted young girls to be educated in the grammar school that operated just off campus, but it had never opened its classrooms to women, although that possibility had been glimpsed early in Brown's history. In 1796, a commencement orator daringly spoke "In Favor of Female Education," and a young woman even more daringly proved it possible: Heart Hopkins, the sister-in-law of President Jonathan Maxcy, took every class offered, although in private tutorials rather than classes.[45] At the first meeting of the Philandrian Society, in 1800, the question debated was, "Would it be good policy to allow females in the United States an Education equal to the males?"[46]

For a long time, Brown's official answer was no. But the question kept returning, because of the great irrefutable fact of talent, and a logic of educational justice that went back to Brown's founding. Even during the long decades when the doors were closed to women, they made their voices heard.

A close study of Chace's life indicates that Brown was radiating influence to the community beyond the tiny numbers of men who were permitted to attend. In Chace's youth, around 1825, a recent Brown graduate named George Prentice (class of 1823) came to her village to teach and brought a wealth of reading from the Brown library. Chace found herself reading recent fiction (the Waverley novels), poetry (Byron), new American writers such as James Fenimore Cooper, and sharing her love of learning with the other girls of the village.[47]

In addition to Chace, many of the most brilliant women of the era lived in or passed through Rhode Island. Julia Ward Howe, the author of "The Battle Hymn of the Republic," was a Roger Williams descendant who grew up in a family with many connections to Brown University. Throughout her long life, she tirelessly advocated women's rights.[48] Mary Peabody was an educational reformer in her own right, whose life intersected meaningfully with other contemporary reformers, including her husband, Horace Mann, and her sister, Elizabeth Peabody (one of the leading feminists of the era). Caroline Hazard, a talented student from Peace Dale, Rhode Island, was privately tutored by a Brown professor before embracing a number of reformist causes in adulthood; she ultimately became a transformative president of Wellesley College from 1899 to 1910, greatly advancing the cause of women's education.

Evidence from around the United States showed that women could succeed in any kind of classroom, at any level, whether learning alongside men or not. Coeducation had flourished at Oberlin College since 1837, the same year that Mount Holyoke opened (though only as a seminary at first), and Wheaton Female Seminary had opened in 1835, in nearby Norton, Massachusetts.[49] The movement for women's education accelerated with the Civil War. As in later wars, women contributed in important ways to the cause, serving on the home front, taking over responsibilities reserved for men, and joining ably in the total war effort.

In the decades after Appomattox, the momentum for change grew. Vassar was founded in 1861; Wellesley in 1870; Smith in 1871. In 1879, Frederick A. P. Barnard reported to Columbia University on the "Higher Education of Women," and argued that English efforts to create coordinate colleges at Queen's College in London and at Cambridge University had been successful.[50] Rhode Island began to hear similar arguments. An anonymous letter, signed only by "Amazon," appeared in the *Brunonian* in 1869, and eviscerated a male writer who had written a "ponderous" piece about marriage. Its conclusion still resonates:

> Logical arguments drawn out to gossamer fineness, have not been attempted. For what need has a woman of logic, when her unerring instinct guides her to the same conclusion which it takes a man hours of dull, plodding study to reach? Climb up the tedious

steps of your syllogisms, gentlemen, and when you get to the top you will find a woman there before you. She sees right through all of your arguments.[51]

After the war, women spoke more publicly, through new platforms—the Rhode Island Woman Suffrage Association, founded in 1868, and the Rhode Island Woman's Club, founded in 1876—and they raised the question of their own civic identity more urgently.[52] In 1874 five young women asked the faculty for permission to take the entrance examination, but were told that it was "inexpedient."[53] Such evasions and euphemisms were beginning to wear thin.

Inevitably, the question kept moving forward. In 1877, the educational picture brightened considerably when the coeducational Rhode Island School of Design was founded, deriving largely from the energies of local women who had organized Rhode Island's exhibit at the 1876 Philadelphia Centennial Exposition (the same one that was powered by the giant steam engine of George Corliss).

A lingering influence from the seventeenth century—Quakerism—was in the air as well. Elizabeth Buffum Chace cited the seventeenth-century Rhode Island martyr Mary Dyer as someone who spurred her to a life of activism.[54] Quaker meetings encouraged women as well as men to speak in public, at a time when that was rare for women, and Quakers held relatively progressive views on education as well. The Friends School adjacent to Brown (now called Moses Brown School) taught girls as well as boys, including Chace. In 1881, a local girl wrote to the venerable Quaker poet John Greenleaf Whittier, a Brown trustee, asking for his help. He waxed enthusiastic in his reply: "I shall do all in my power to open the doors of Brown University to women."[55] He continued in the mode of a prophet: "Of course the world is growing better; the Lord reigns; our old planet is wheeling slowly into further light. I despair of nothing good. All will come in due time that is really needed. All we have to do is work and wait." In a note to fellow trustee Richard Atwater, Whittier was more direct, writing, "Brown University cannot afford to hesitate much longer in a matter, like this, of simple justice."[56]

The time of waiting was drawing to an end. As Whittier knew, Rhode Island's own traditions argued for a broader view. Brown had always prided itself on its opposition to the forms of social exclusion that were easily found at Harvard and Yale. Whittier went to the nub of the matter in a note to another Quaker trustee: "I hope the time is not far distant when Brown University will be open to woman. The traditions of the noble old institution are all in favor of broad liberality and equality of rights and privileges."[57]

Furthermore, a new model was coming into view—that of the women's college created in close proximity to, and coordinated with, an all-male college. Tulane had opened its Sophie Newcomb Memorial College in 1887, and Columbia University launched Barnard College in 1889.[58] Ezekiel Robinson, president from 1872 to 1889, acknowledged that the "plea" for women's education was "not a weak one," but no action was taken until his successor, E. Benjamin Andrews (in office from 1889 to 1898), joined forces with Sarah Doyle, a longtime leader in female education, and turned Robinson's inconclusive intention into a personal crusade.[59] Andrews "fairly electrified the students" with his energy and commitment to the cause.[60] And Doyle, though she never attended college herself, was a formidable force within Providence—active in the Woman Suffrage Association, the head of the girls' department in the city's public high school, and comfortable within the corridors of City Hall (her brother, Thomas Doyle, was the long-term mayor).[61] Doyle believed that women "were capable of transcending those [domestic and maternal] constraints to shape a full life of independence." She understood that women had to organize and enlist support to achieve their goals. The city led the university on this question, rather than the other way around. The *Providence Journal*, often conservative, provided energetic leadership, pointing out that Rhode Island women were leaving the state to attend universities elsewhere.[62] Led by Doyle's restless energy (an admirer wrote, "she even looked dynamic when she was standing still"), influential women of Rhode Island gathered together to form a new civic association, the Rhode Island Society for the Collegiate Education of Women, or as some of its younger members called it, The Society with the Long Name.[63]

Mary Woolley and Anne Weeden, class of 1894, the first two female graduates of what would become Pembroke College.

The great day finally arrived on October 1, 1891. Two young women, Nettie Serena Goodale of Pawtucket and Elizabeth Peckham of Bristol, attended a French class, with President Andrews sitting discreetly in the background. Then, in the afternoon, four more arrived: Clara Comstock, Maude Bonner, Anne Weeden, and Mary Woolley, who would herself become a force for reform as the president of Mount Holyoke. At last, the dam had been breached.[64]

Fifty years later, Mary Woolley remembered the earliest days of the women's college with pride, but without undue sentimentality, revealing the purposefulness that these new arrivals brought to the challenge. They needed it when hair-splitting lawyers were trying to find ways to block their way (arguing that the word "youth" in the college charter could only apply to young men). They endured small rooms, moving between Benefit Street and temporary chambers here and there (including, on occasion, the President's office). And yet they displayed a remarkable esprit, not unlike the zeal with which the first Rhode Islanders celebrated the fact that they had been banished. Woolley recalled the origins:

> In thinking back to the early nineties, one adjective has rung persistently in my ears, the adjective *great*. That little college—small as it was in numbers; limited as it was in material possessions; with no "reputation" built upon achievement; no past; practically no future, as far as assurance from Brown University was concerned;—still that persistent adjective great.[65]

From that first day, events moved quickly; the student body grew from seven in 1891–92 to 157 in 1896–97. In 1893, two women took master's degrees. In 1894, Sarah Doyle received an honorary degree from Brown, the first for a woman, for her long service to teaching. In 1896, the Corporation approved the founding of the Women's College, and defined it as a department of the university. As President Andrews had recommended in his report, "no mere 'annex' is desired or intended. The College must be part and parcel of the University, giving women students the full university status."[66] Each year, the number of

Pembroke Hall.

alumnae increased, and a sense of community deepened. Mary Woolley's remembrance stressed that the greatness had come from three sources—a great conception whose time had come; great teachers who turned a college education into "a thrilling adventure"; and great leadership from a president who served all too briefly at the helm, but had "a vision of an University for *human beings*, not alone for men."[67]

Early versions of the name included "Women's College of Brown University" and "Women's College Adjunct to Brown University," "Women's College in Connection with Brown University" and "Women's College in Brown University" (obviously, the prepositions were giving them trouble).[68] But an important word began to predominate with the dedication of Pembroke Hall in 1897. The building was named after Cambridge University's Pembroke College, founded by a woman (Marie de St. Pol, Countess of Pembroke) and conveniently linked to Roger Williams, who studied there.[69]

That local women had raised sufficient funds for a building of their own was an impressive feat (and tweaked the Brown undergraduates who referred teasingly to "Deadbroke"). Many years later, in 1928, the entire Women's College would be rebaptized Pembroke College.

Speaking at the dedication of Pembroke Hall in 1897, Sarah Doyle said, "The women's sphere is one of infinite and indeterminate radius," and the building reflected that vision. A vivid advertisement for the value of a college education, the hall encompassed a gymnastic space, lunchroom, social spaces, a chapel, recitation rooms, and a library decorated with a frieze portraying education, beginning with a mother and her children and including "Genius, Sculpture, Architecture, Agriculture, Engineering, Navigation, Crafts, and Commerce."[70] An early brochure emphasized that physical culture was an important part of the experience: "Careful attention is given to Physical Culture. Exercises with dumb-bells and Indian clubs and in Swedish movements are required of all women students weekly during the second term of the year."[71] Contemporary accounts reveal the hall to be filled with the sounds of "rehearsals and debates, lunchroom clatter, gymnastics (marching, jumping and basketball played by boys' rules until Dean King decided in 1905 that these were too rough)." Sayles Gymnasium came next, in 1907, with athletic facilities (including bowling alleys), and year by year, the extracurricular offerings for women expanded, along with the number of students. By 1900, there were 152; by 1905, 203. At the same time, certain courses were omitted from the women's college that were easily available to the men, including (but not limited to)

Ethel Robinson, Pembroke's first African American graduate, from the 1905 class photograph.

classes relating to hygiene and physical education, political science, science, economics, engineering, and even Greek sculpture.[72]

Within a decade, it was clear that the new college was a roaring success. Women performed well—certainly in the classroom, where one professor said that they "did in four meetings what the boys did in five."[73] President Faunce may have remarked in 1903 that they had survived despite "no coddling whatever," but it seems doubtful that the idea of being coddled ever entered their minds.[74]

By all measures, Brown was thriving as it approached the twentieth century. President Andrews, in particular, had embodied a commitment to academic excellence of which the education of women was only the most striking example. During his decade in office, Brown advanced in every category that could be measured. His tenure ended prematurely when the Corporation asked him to recant some statements he had made about liberalizing currency, and he refused as a matter of principle, arguing that his right to free speech was more important than any discomfort he might have caused to prospective donors. As he put it, quite cogently, he could not recant "without surrendering that reasonable liberty of utterance . . . in the absence of which the most ample endowment for an educational institution would have but little worth." He submitted a letter of resignation, which the Corporation refused to accept, but a year later he accepted a new post as superintendent of Chicago schools. In retrospect, this leader of vision and talent was treated shabbily by the institution he had served so well. *Life* magazine ridiculed Brown on its cover, describing the vacant presidency, with a caption, "no gentlemen encumbered with a backbone need apply." [75]

Still, he accomplished much in his short time and set the University on a dynamic new course. In his annual report for 1892, Andrews had posed an existential question: "I cannot avoid the conviction that Brown University has reached a serious crisis in its history. It stands face to face with the question whether it will remain a College and nothing more or will rise and expand into a true University." [76] He had then answered his own question with a plan that crackled with electricity, calling for new professorships, a deeper library, more science, higher salaries, and, of course, fund-raising to pay for it all. By the time he left, enrollment was up, dramatically. After decades in which the size of the student body of the two colleges had hovered around 250, it was suddenly approaching a thousand. [77] In 1888, the faculty totaled twenty-six; eight years later, that figure had climbed to eighty-eight. [78] The professors came from around the country, and were more clearly recognized as experts in their fields. The curriculum was becoming more modern, with a larger emphasis on science and living languages. [79] Distinguished alumni were serving in the highest councils of the government. Inevitably, such a university, punching above its weight, was bound to attract students from a wider circle than Rhode Island and southeastern Massachusetts.

In the fall of 1892, as the country was enjoying the excitement of a spirited presidential campaign (Grover Cleveland defeated Benjamin Harrison), a young man in New York was wrestling with the agonizing question of where to go to college. John D. Rockefeller Jr. was heir to one of the greatest fortunes in history, assembled by his father, the founder of Standard Oil. But despite their incalculable wealth, the Rockefellers lived with relative austerity, and the younger Rockefeller was uncertain of his ability to socialize at a large New England college. Brown, with its smaller size, fit his sensibility better, and its denominational outlook was consonant with his own enthusiastic membership in the Baptist church. He exchanged letters with family advisors (one of whom, William H. P. Faunce, would soon be president of Brown), and they made many of the arguments later generations have made—that he would know his professors better at Brown, and that, as Faunce wrote knowingly, "Providence is more healthful than New Haven." [80]

Even before his arrival in September 1893, John D. Rockefeller Jr. won a major victory by persuading his solicitous mother that he needed to live with students his own age, and not with her. He narrowly avoided that fate, judging from one of her letters to him: "How much I wish I could be with you at Providence! It seems as tho' I ought to be, and it would give me much pleasure to be. You will get on all right, but I could help you decide matters." [81] One can almost sense his relief at his escape.

That was the beginning of a series of similar victories in which, over four years, the younger Rockefeller fought to become what he desperately wanted to be: a normal college student, liked by his friends for his own qualities. Instead of a richly appointed private residence, he moved into Slater Hall. He and Brown took to each other instantaneously, and he was soon known far and wide as "Johnny Rock."

It may have helped that he entered in an unusually large class of 175, and one that was economically and racially diverse (he wrote earnestly back home, "Grandmother will be interested to know that there are three colored men in the class"). He made friends with ease and enjoyed what by all accounts was a rich, variegated, and typical existence at Brown. One of his chief diversions was managing the football team, which put him at the center of the most important ritual on campus. An amusing story recounts a time his father came out to see a Brown football victory in New York, against the legendary Carlisle Indians, and became so excited that he jumped out of his seat and joined the team at field level. "I can still see him running up and down wearing a very prominent tall silk hat," his son recalled years later.[82]

But Johnny Rock did a great deal more than that. He taught a Bible class at a Baptist church in Providence, he joined the Glee Club and Mandolin Club, he played in the Providence Symphony Orchestra, and he attended the occasional sermon at a local African American church. He was elected president of his junior class, and was proud that on the occasion of the annual celebration (a huge party in which the junior class went to Newport, drank too much, and tried to get back to Providence), his tenure marked the first time that the entire class had returned under its own power. As he put it "When we landed at 2 a.m., again headed by the band, we marched up the hill every man on his own feet and without aid—a thing which has never been true of a Junior Celebration before." Even amid this kind of frivolity, Johnny Rock was discovering a serious side, and he was admired for his parsimony, his judgment, and his refusal to bend the rules, for himself as well as for others. His biographer noted another sea change:

> In one of his letters he speaks of a service conducted in a Negro church. . . . Perhaps even more important than his decisions regarding himself was the growing spirit of tolerance which he developed toward the other men who did not hold his views. . . . This change of view, this growing ability to distinguish between the letter and the spirit, the basic and the superficial, was probably the most important development during John's college life. It laid the groundwork for his future concern for interdenominationalism, and even more important it made him a wiser and more tolerant person.[83]

One other legacy of Johnny Rock's time at Brown had profound consequences for the rest of his life. Having acquired the beginnings of a sociable personality, he inevitably encountered women. His son David, at the dedication of the Rockefeller Library in 1964, remembered that he had discovered "the delights of dancing" while at Brown. It is difficult to imagine the straitlaced Rockefeller enjoying those delights, but in his case it produced handsome dividends, when he met a local beauty at a dance given near campus in the home of R. H. I. Goddard.[84] Her name was Abigail Aldrich, the daughter of Senator

Nelson Aldrich, who chaired the Senate Finance Committee and un-officially chaired the entire U.S. economy, through close consultation with Wall Street. It was bound to raise eyebrows when she met, and was wooed by, the shy young man from the oil dynasty.[85] Their marriage, in 1901, took place at the estate of Senator Aldrich in Warwick, Rhode Island—it was the great social event of its day.[86] The newspapers had a field day, with headlines such as "CROESUS CAPTURED," and "DANCES LED TO HIS MARRIAGE."[87] But it was a wise match, and with intelligence, vivacity, and grace, Abigail Aldrich Rockefeller would ease her husband into his responsibilities—another way in which Rhode Island shaped him.

Like John Hay, Johnny Rock had arrived on the campus shy and alone; four years later, he left Providence a much larger person. Well-adjusted, tolerant, and in love, he was poised for the great work that lay in his future. He had excelled in his studies, and to no one's surprise, he was elected to Phi Beta Kappa, a purely academic honor that had nothing to do with his wealth. His letters resembled Hay's, elegiac for the small city where he had grown to maturity. On the eve of graduation, he wrote, "We are a pretty mournful crowd up here at the thought of giving up so soon a life which has been so full of pleasure and happiness as well as profit." His mother wrote, "What an era his graduation day marks in a young man's history. It is like a mountain top on which he stands and looks both forward and backward."[88]

John D. Rockefeller Jr., circa 1915–1917.

That may have been a poetic way of referring to College Hill, but in Rockefeller's case it was true that he had climbed to a higher elevation. The tolerance that he learned at Brown manifested itself in the epic endeavors he supported throughout his life. When he arrived on campus in 1893, he found a letter from his grandmother, with a bit of advice, in the shape of a poem:

> Think truly, and thy thought
> Shall the world's famine feed.
> Speak truly, and each word of thine
> Shall be a fruitful seed.
> Give truly, thy life shall be
> A grand and noble creed.[89]

He was now ready to live out this creed. If his father had displayed a genius for acquiring wealth, the son displayed one for giving it away—but always with the seriousness of purpose that he learned at Brown. The list of Rockefeller donations over the course of the twentieth century is staggering, for its size (estimated at $537 million) as well as its diversity.[90] Even many years after his time at Brown (Rockefeller lived until 1960), it was possible to see the influence of his college on his philanthropy. The Baptist cause was never neglected, and he supported a huge range of churches and missionary activities in the tradition Adoniram Judson made famous a century earlier. But he also conspicuously supported the cause of religious tolerance, such as the interdenominational efforts of the Union Theological Seminary and the Riverside Church in Manhattan, designed to lessen religious tensions and bring adherents of different faiths to one communal location. Like the Judson Church in Washington Square, Riverside Church became known and respected for its moral leadership on the great questions facing Americans, and when Martin Luther King Jr. gave a brave speech there in 1967, turning against the Vietnam War, it was another form of tribute to the independent thinking Rockefeller encountered at Brown.[91]

Although Rockefeller never lost his Puritanical self-restraint, his donations were often daringly modern, and that too spoke to the undergraduate career of a shy young man whose mind had been opened by his classes and his colleagues. He supported birth control, African American colleges, the Museum of Modern Art, and, whenever he could, he fought against religious fundamentalism—a powerful political force in the 1920s. Throughout the Great Depression, his effort to build the huge midtown complex known as Rockefeller Center was a tremendous shot in the arm for the city where he lived, and the buildings stood for America's resilience. The spirit of tolerance seized him again in the aftermath of World War II, when the United Nations needed a place to meet, and its great champion, Franklin Roosevelt, was no more. Rockefeller had long supported other international causes such as the League of Nations, and he did not miss the opportunity to build the biggest interdenominational shrine of them all. The magnificent land that the UN complex now occupies in Manhattan, overlooking the East River, could only have been purchased by one man, and he duly bought it for $8.5 million in December 1946, donating it to the cause.[92] If John Hay's efforts had brought the United States into the world as a global power, then Rockefeller's efforts were bringing the rest of the world to the United States, as an arbiter for the disputes that would inevitably arise in the future.

To this day, a sharp observer can see his influence nearly everywhere—whether in satirical political sketches beamed out of Rockefeller Center on *Saturday Night Live*, or in debates over human rights at the United Nations, or simply in a splash of color on a museum canvas. A year after giving the gift of the land for the United Nations, Rockefeller returned to Brown for his fiftieth reunion. He spoke on that occasion about what college had meant to him: "Only here on the campus did I enjoy a completely independent personality. With you fellows I was hailed as 'Johnny Rock,' just one of a hundred others, but at least one who stood on his own feet. . . . There has been nothing in my life since then quite like this kind of comradeship."[93]

Rockefeller was born in 1874, only ten years after Brown's centennial, and lived until 1960, only four years before the bicentennial. His strikingly modern cast of mind was well captured by the building that bears his name, the John D. Rockefeller, Jr. Library. As his son David said, during the dedication ceremony in 1964:

> During Father's lifetime, he consistently refused to accept honors or have his name memorialized in any way. Nevertheless, I am convinced that he would have been greatly moved by this unsought and genuine expression of his Alma Mater's esteem. And I think he would have hoped, too, that this memorial at the College he attended would serve as a reminder to others of all that Brown meant to him. For here he formed friendships that endured throughout his life, and here were instilled in him many of those attitudes and beliefs which became the foundation of his philosophy of life and his creative philanthropy.[94]

Brown was still a small college on the day that it graduated Rockefeller in 1897. Its campus, though expanding, was diminutive in comparison with the major New England universities. There were conspicuous gaps in the College Green where one might have expected to see buildings. But they would come soon, brought in hastily by the onrushing century that would do so much to change the world, and the university along with it.

CHAPTER 4

DANCE OF
THE BROWNIES

Nippauochâumen. *We are dancing.*

—ROGER WILLIAMS,
A Key into the Language of America, 1643.

O N THE EVE OF A NEW CENTURY, Brown appeared to be
thriving, by almost any measure. Student enrollment
was up, complemented by new faculty appointments
and expansion of the curriculum. A new president,
William H. P. Faunce, was found in 1899, bringing with him most
admirable qualities. Like many of his predecessors, he was a Brown
alumnus (class of 1880) and a Baptist minister. Indeed, well before his
appointment, as the pastor of New York City's prestigious Fifth
Avenue Baptist Church, he had already performed the first of many
important services to his alma mater, by helping to convince John D.
Rockefeller Jr. to enroll. Only forty years old when hired, he would
serve for three decades, transforming the institution.[1]

In 1894, the *Brunonian* reported on a "Dance of the Brownies"
that united all of the members of this festive community, male and
female.[2] That phrase might apply more generally to a university
moving with increased freedom and confidence as it entered the
twentieth century.

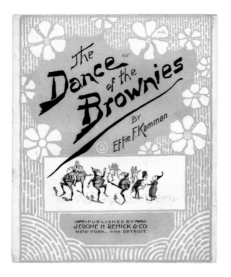

Over the course of the next half century, the Brownies continued to dance. Students came in much larger numbers, from a wider range of places and social strata. The undergraduate experience grew correspondingly more diverse, and more interesting. The faculty expanded at the same time, offering more courses, at more levels, in more disciplines. The campus grew, and with it, a world of extracurricular possibilities, including more engagement with the world beyond the Van Wickle Gates (installed in 1901). In short, a distinctive but still regional college evolved into a genuine university.

But before this growth could begin in earnest, Brown had to get past its 150th anniversary celebration and a war that challenged all of the assumptions of enlightened humanism on which the university was founded.[3]

1914

THE SUMMER OF 1914 marked the end of a long idyll, stretching back many decades, in which civilization was assumed to be advancing through inexorable laws of progress. The assassination of the Archduke Franz Ferdinand in Sarajevo on June 28 severely tested that theory, for humankind soon descended into a conflict so murderous, so uncivilized, and so comprehensive in its destruction that we are still recovering, a century after the fact.

History is always clearer in hindsight, and when the spark was ignited, almost no one could foresee the toll that the Great War would take. In Providence, the conflict seemed especially distant, competing awkwardly with Brown's 150th anniversary, an event designed to instill faith in a peaceful future. Throughout 1914, the happier work of remembrance went forward, as the university prepared to celebrate its sesquicentennial in style. It would indeed be a spectacular affair, far beyond any commemorative event the university had ever seen. Planning began in 1909, and it was clear that the event was going to be pitched to fundraising at a time when Brown needed, as ever, to shore up its endowment. In 1913, the *Providence Journal* reported on the celebration, to which "every important institution of learning will be invited to send delegates, and leading scholars will represent each of the great departments of knowledge."[4] By March 1914, invitations had been sent to 4,500 people, a who's who of prominent educators, leading citizens, and worthy dignitaries. A forlorn correspondence between the university and the White House tried to capture President Woodrow Wilson (who had been honored at Brown in 1903), but Wilson dithered for a long time and missed the celebration.[5]

Still, nearly everyone else came. Across four days in October, the alumni returned in throngs. Providence dressed itself up for the occasion. The First Baptist Church received a fresh coat of paint, and the

150th anniversary procession, 1914.

buildings and streets around the campus were festooned with laurel garlands and Japanese lanterns. Lectures were delivered by the great and near great. Collegiate songs were sung, and 900 local schoolchildren acted out episodes from Brown's history, covering everything from Native American rituals to more obscure topics ("the Warren Fire Department in 1802"). Torchlight processions led alumni through the campus, and the celebration continued over lavish dinners. A ten-mile-long iceberg off Alaska was christened "the Brown University glacier." It was a glorious time.[6]

COMING UP ROSES

AS IF INSPIRED BY THE CELEBRATION, Brown's 1915 football team had a remarkable season, culminating in its appearance in the Rose Bowl on New Year's Day, 1916. That the team lost to Washington State, 14–0, was a fact of minor consequence that did not in any way dim the luster of the achievement. To be sure, the Rose Bowl was not yet a marquee event (in the years before 1916, the Tournament of Roses had culminated in a different sort of athletic contest—an ostrich race).[7] But Brown's football team did appear, as the ancient footage on YouTube proves.

Rose Bowl Poster, 1916.

Even if the Brown team did not win, it was a memorable squad, led by a gifted African American athlete, Frederick Douglass "Fritz" Pollard, at a time when diversity was still rare in the Ivy League. Pollard's mother, a seamstress in Chicago, worked for a Brown alumnus, and she mounted a lobbying campaign, speaking to her adolescent son about the glories of the Brown football tradition, including the fact that an earlier African American, Edward Stewart, had played there in the 1890s.[8] When he finally made it to the campus, Pollard arrived with no application and no idea of how to enter the university. But he knew he was where he wanted to be:

> The cab driver took me up this steep hill, which I found out later was College Hill. And right straight ahead of me at the top of the hill were those big, beautiful iron gates leading to the campus. It was a cold, clear January day and the late afternoon sun was shining directly on the gates, making them sparkle. Oh boy, I got a lump in my throat.[9]

But it was not quite as effortless as that epiphany suggested. Pollard later confessed to some difficulty penetrating the nearly lily-white preserve of Ivy League football. He recalled:

> At Brown the day the team handed out the uniforms, the athletic department wouldn't give me one. Maybe they thought my color would stain the uniform. That hurt more than any of the other stuff, beatings and all. I went back to my segregated section of the locker room, down in the boiler room—even there they didn't want me—and I hid behind the lockers and cried my eyes out.[10]

The catcalls he endured from rival teams were even worse. But as he persevered, Pollard found acceptance, and he brought a double-distinction to Brown, for its powerful team and for the racial tolerance it emanated (while crushing its opposition). A New York newspaper wrote, "Mr. Pollard is doing a very great deal to help solve the race problem."[11]

Pollard's contributions as a player were impressive enough, as a star halfback and an All-American. But his leadership qualities were evident in nearly everything else he did as well. After Brown, he coached at Lincoln University, a historically black college in Pennsylvania, before joining a professional team, the Akron Pros, and leading them to the championship of the American Professional

The Providence Steam Roller, featuring four Brown alumni, including Fritz Pollard, on the occasion of an early NFL game against the Chicago Bears, December 9, 1925.

Fritz Pollard.

Football Association in 1920. The following year, Pollard was named the player-coach of the Pros, and thus became the first African American head coach in what would become the National Football League. Those teams were almost unrecognizable compared with what the NFL would become, but it is impressive that Pollard emerged as a leader from an environment that tolerated virulent racism (many of Akron's fans were transplanted Southerners), inconsistent playing conditions, and brutal, no-holds-barred competition. It would be another sixty-eight years before another African American was hired as a head coach in the NFL, in 1988. Indeed, the small number of African Americans in professional football indicates potential players were intimidated from participating in the late 1920s, and a color line was reinstated in 1933, preventing

them for a time from playing professionally altogether.[11] But they had dug in and set an impressive precedent.

Afterward Pollard coached barnstorming black teams, and he also played for the Providence Steam Roller, in the short period when Providence actually had an NFL team.[13] In a culture that tolerated some racial fluidity, he also briefly played for a team of Native Americans under the name "Charlie Lone Star."[14]

Pollard's travels in the twilight world of early professional football were noteworthy for a fellow traveler he brought with him. The great actor, singer, and activist Paul Robeson was working at a summer job at a hotel in Narragansett, Rhode Island, in the summer of 1915 when Pollard befriended him. They spent a summer socializing (often with the mixed-race descendants of Narragansett Indians), became lifelong friends, and shared many attributes—a desire to succeed in professions previously off-limits to African Americans, a fierce pride, and a ferocious competitive instinct on the gridiron. Indeed, that arena was satisfying for offering a chance to excel—and also to punish those who were not as evolved on racial matters ("The football field was really the only place where you could do anything that amounted to retaliation"). Pollard was faster, smaller, and slightly older than Robeson, and described himself as "a sort of big brother in a small package."[15] He mentored him in other ways, too, finding him part-time work and coaching him off the field. Robeson followed Pollard to Lincoln University, to the Akron Pros, and well into adulthood. In March 1918,

W. E. B. Du Bois featured Pollard and Robeson as "Men of the Month" in his magazine, *The Crisis*. Years later, when he became a film star, Robeson kept Pollard near to him throughout the shooting of *The Emperor Jones*.[16] In the 1930s, among his various ventures, Pollard started a Harlem newspaper (the *Independent News*), a musical talent agency (Suntan Studios), and a barnstorming, all-black football team (the Brown Bombers). There is no indication that this last organization was a tribute to his alma mater, but Brown had certainly helped his confidence, and over the course of his long life, this important pioneer often had cause to recall the undergraduate experience that accelerated and gave direction to his run.

THE BEARDED ICEBERG

ANOTHER BROWN ALUMNUS running effectively before the public was Charles Evans Hughes, class of 1881, who campaigned hard for the presidency against Woodrow Wilson in 1916, nearly unseating him. Hughes grew up in upstate New York, the only child of a Baptist minister whose father had emigrated (as many Baptists did) from Wales. He came to Brown as a transfer student from another Baptist institution, Madison (the future Colgate University), and instantly felt at home among the "jovial lot" of Brown students, situated on that "high and pleasant hill."[17] He competed hard at everything. There was a very rough annual football game between freshmen and sophomores (he recalled that it was "really a class fight, which could be called football only because a football was used").[18] Politics was another outlet, and during the 1880 presidential campaign, Hughes and his friends organized a "Garfield battalion" at Brown and marched in support of the Republican candidate, wearing caps and capes. Slowly, the young Baptist loosened up under the more permissive influence of Providence and thrilled to the theater, the opera, and the beer gardens of a growing city. Hughes also loved baseball, watching the city's major league team, the Providence Grays, along with the Brown nine—and he was the official scorer when Brown won the intercollegiate title of 1880.[19] As editor of the *Brunonian*, Hughes advocated a number of positions that were guaranteed to build up his popularity with students, including abolition of the grading system and support for their right to play cards, use profanity, go to plays, and enter taverns. But he remained a Baptist, attending local churches, and his grades were good enough that he graduated third in his class. To no one's surprise, he was named class speaker and "class prophet."[20]

Hughes then began a rapid ascent through New York society, law, and politics. A classmate and friend of President Faunce, he became a member of Brown's

Charles Evans Hughes with his wife, Antoinette.

board, and he joined John D. Rockefeller as a trustee of the Fifth Avenue Baptist Church. But he retained a certain independence of spirit, raising a "minor furor" when he invited Booker T. Washington to speak at the church. In defense of his unorthodoxy, he wrote, "I cherished the noble tradition of the Baptists as protagonist in the struggle for religious liberty."[21] He raised his own electoral prospects through a series of good works, including his service on a committee that investigated utilities for overcharging their customers. A moderate Republican, he ran for governor in 1906 and defeated the press baron William Randolph Hearst. During his tenure as governor, until 1910, he was allied with the progressive wing of the Republicans and under the particular influence of Theodore Roosevelt. He promoted sound business regulation, fought corruption, and tried to steer influence to commissions of experts rather than friends of politicians.

In 1910, Hughes was appointed by William Howard Taft to the Supreme Court, but despite his apparent removal from electoral activities, his political prospects brightened in 1916, as the Republicans sought to unite behind a single candidate. Hughes was nominated, and he did his best to bring together Taft's conservatives and Roosevelt's progressives, but that difficult task was challenging for a candidate who lacked Roosevelt's natural charisma. None questioned his integrity, but his formal reserve alienated some people, including Roosevelt himself (who called Hughes "the bearded iceberg").[22] Hughes's speeches were less fiery than Roosevelt's or, for that matter, Wilson's (Roosevelt complained, "A campaign speech is a poster, not an etching"). [23]

Nevertheless, it appeared on election night that Hughes had won—Wilson even went to bed planning to appoint his rival secretary of state and then resign, so that they could have an orderly transition.[24] But over the night, the South and Midwest went for Wilson, whom they believed would keep the United States out of war. If California had come through, Hughes could still have won, but a little-known blunder proved costly. While visiting a hotel in Long Beach, California, Hughes failed to meet with the state's governor, Hiram Johnson, who was also in the same hotel. Johnson was an important Progressive who had been TR's running mate in 1912, and he took offense at the slight, whether it was intentional or not (Hughes claimed it was not).[25] Without Johnson's enthusiastic support, Hughes lost that crucial swing state, and its thirteen electoral votes, by 3,800 votes. That small margin proved to make the difference, and Hughes lost the overall election by twenty-three electoral votes.[26] It was the closest (to date) that a Brown alumnus has come to the White House.

Despite that disappointment, Hughes continued to shape American history at the highest levels. He declined to run in 1920, but when Warren G. Harding was elected, he appointed Hughes as secretary of state, the fourth Brown alumnus to serve in that position, after William L. Marcy (class of 1808), Richard Olney (1856), and John Hay (1858). Just as Hay had steered the United States to unprecedented influence in the world, so Hughes took advantage of America's enhanced position after the Great War to enforce international disarmament, solidify the peace, and lower tensions that were still simmering.[27] From 1930 to 1941, he returned to the Supreme Court as chief justice at a time when nearly all ideas about the relationship between the federal government and the American people needed to be redefined. That inevitably brought him into a complex relationship with President Franklin D. Roosevelt, as we shall see.

To the end, Hughes remained true to his Brown education—as a leading Baptist (he was president of the Northern Baptist Convention), a proponent of religious freedom (he founded the National Conference on Christians and Jews), and a lifelong advocate for peace and international jurisprudence. He returned to the campus in 1937, delivering a thoughtful address to the alumni that reached back into Brown's history, but also validated the university's needs to expand and change. (Hughes devised a perfect sound bite for the occasion: "It is always Old Brown and it is always New Brown.")[28] A historical rhyme may be worth pointing out: throughout the nineteenth century, as we have seen, Brown had a special connection to Burma, where Adoniram Judson had made a significant impact. Today, the former home of Charles Evans Hughes is the residence of the Burmese ambassador to the United States.[29]

THE GREAT WAR

IF THE DEFEAT OF HUGHES IN 1916 owed something to the failure to lock in California, it also resulted from intense feelings over the war raging in Europe. Throughout the United States—and especially in the Midwest, where huge numbers of German Americans lived—the idea of joining the conflict on either side was anathema. Wilson campaigned that "he kept us out of war," a slogan that was persuasive, if a bit disingenuous. Every day that the war took its grim toll, it seemed prudent to continue that policy, and for many Americans, that meant a vote for Wilson.

But the war's impact was being felt with more urgency every day, even on a leafy campus far from Europe. On September 9, 1914, as preparations were nearing completion for the 150th, Brown suffered its first casualty. Students were shocked to learn that a well-liked professor of French, Henri Ferdinand Micoleau, had answered the call of his country and died at the first Battle of the Marne.[30] Over the next few years, even while the United States remained neutral, Brown students

Training on the Green.

chose service as ambulance drivers or as volunteers with Canadian troops (in a nod to early American history, they were described as coming from "the province of Rhode Island.")[31] The first Brown student to be killed in the war was Sergeant Florence J. Price of the class of 1906, killed in 1916 by a burst of shrapnel in the trenches, near Ypres.[32]

In the spring of 1917, American policy and public opinion began to change quickly, in the wake of serial German violations of American neutrality. Woodrow Wilson's war message of April 2 had an electrifying effect on young people around the country. In short order, 240 students withdrew to enlist in military, naval, or agricultural service to the cause, then another 116, and 52 others volunteered for the foreign ambulance corps. This hemorrhaging of students was only the first of a series of paroxysms that rocked the university during the Great War. The massive loss of students was a crisis in every sense—of empty classrooms, empty coffers, and parents imploring the administration not to let their sons do anything hasty. As President Faunce later recounted it:

> When war was actually declared, the minds of our students were thrown into a ferment and the campus was seething with eager and intense desire for action. As patriotic addresses were made on our campus or near it, wave after wave of emotion swept over the students and a novel and difficult situation was created. Parents were telegraphing from distant cities begging us to hold back their sons from rash and thoughtless decisions, while recruiting officers were attempting each to show that his branch of military or naval service was more attractive and more valuable than any other. Students were hurriedly enlisting without regard to natural fitness and with no knowledge of the work into which they were going. It was freely prophesied that the college would soon close and the students scatter till the end of the war. To steady our students and direct their fine loyalty into the channels where it would be most effective was a task of no small magnitude.[33]

But Brown adapted quickly to the new exigencies. In short order, a profoundly new regimen was developed that turned the university into something like a military academy. In cooperation with the federal government, Brown agreed to train young men for the officer corps, and to whatever other purpose the country needed. As Faunce wrote, "if any students were to remain in college, we must take immediate steps to provide military instruction by competent officers." This was an enormous change in the ethos of a university founded upon the inquisitive spirit of the Enlightenment. Faunce elaborated, "It may seem that the drill of the soldier is not easily reconciled with the ideals of liberal education. The soldier is not to reason why, while the whole object of a liberal education is to teach the student to search for reasons, to discover causes, and to base the real on the ideal."[34]

Accordingly, Brown set out to give intensive training in both "the theory and practice of the solder's life."[35] Theory was considerably easier—practice involved sudden new rules, such as reveille at 6:00 A.M., and taps at 10:00 at night, and strict military discipline throughout the day. Faunce reported, "At once our grounds became an armed camp."[36] The dining hall was now called a "mess," and the dormitories became a "barracks." It was not the first time that the campus had been connected to the theater of war; as Faunce remembered, "It was fitting that from our oldest building, whose rooms were occupied by French soldiers in the War of the Revolution, should go forth American students to reinforce the hard-pressed armies of France."[37] But it was a profound change all the same. After the war had ended, Faunce wrote:

> none of us could then see how complete was to be the overturn of our curriculum, how novel the experiment of federal control in liberal education, how perilous, yet inspiring, was to be the whole experience. The colleges and universities of America went to war as well as their graduates, and Brown University was for a time simply a training school of the Army and Navy. Every building, every dollar of our endowment, every teacher, and every male student over eighteen years of age and physically fit was devoted absolutely to the winning of the war.

There were other crises as well. As if the dangers of the trenches were not daunting enough, an influenza epidemic spread with virulence in 1918, turning the campus into something like a fortress. "When the influenza came," Faunce wrote, "it seemed necessary to establish quarantine, both to keep our students away from crowded halls and cars in the city and to keep infected persons from entering the campus. For four weeks sentries were posted at every gate by day and night, and no person was allowed to enter or leave the campus without a pass."[38] These changes greatly altered the mood on campus. Faunce noted how serious the students had become:

The feverish way in which they worked to attain that goal, the surrender of all fraternity life, all athletic sports, all dramatic and musical clubs, and the intense concentration of all students on a visible objective—all this has caused much searching of heart among the college teachers of the country.[39]

The way in which instruction was given changed as well. Most advanced classes were canceled, and every class reduced to basics. Such humanistic disciplines as philosophy, literature, music, and art almost vanished, to be replaced by "subjects of immediate utility, like Surveying, Navigation, Military Law." Romance languages were reduced to "military French." History became a course in "the Aims of the War."[40] Nautical science was taught in the top floor of University Hall, and a photograph from that time shows the officer candidates dutifully tying knots and making splices.[41] At the women's college, students organized themselves to aid the war effort, sending clothing and materials to the front.[42]

As the campus was enduring these transformations, Faunce tried to track the Brown men in the service. On March 21, 1918, he wrote an Easter message distributed to all Brown students, many of whom were already at the front. He described the university's military preparations, including the ROTC drills in the middle Green, and the fact that fifteen faculty members were also serving. He added this thought:

You see Brown is not asleep. It is meeting the crisis of the world with open eyes and eager spirit. Our campus has expanded till it covers the training camps at home and reaches into the trenches of France. The best part of my morning mail is now letters from our boys, scattered far and wide but united still. . . . It is glorious to be alive when the world desperately needs you. I am confident you will have patience, endurance, unfaltering loyalty to American ideals, and will show what college men can do to lead the world to freedom. [43]

They answered him in great numbers—their letters from the front remain gathered in a file in the Archives, one of the more

moving testaments to the spirit of the time. The toll was hard on
Brown. In 1918, only 81 students graduated, and in May of that year,
there were a mere 485 students.[44] Nearly two-thirds of normal classes
were canceled. But as it had done in previous wars, Brown made ends
meet. A War Emergency Fund was gathered to weather the crisis.[45]
And slowly, the end came. A false armistice announced the end of the
war on November 7. Then, four days later, it was truly over.

Brown students celebrated, of course, but they were also daunted by
a grim postwar landscape. Three stalwart European powers had disappeared (the German, Austro-Hungarian, and Russian empires), and a
fourth, the Ottoman Empire, was teetering on the brink of collapse.
The Russian Revolution, not quite finished with its violent birth pangs,
was threatening instability all around it. Around the world, approximately seventeen million people had died as a result of the conflict.
Forty-two of them came from Brown, out of 1,974 students and alumni
who had served.[46] They ranged from William W. Keen of the class of
1859 (who had given one of the principal historical addresses at the
150th) to members of the class of 1922. In his 1917 Baccalaureate
address, President Faunce asked a difficult question: "The old world—
the world of the Romanoffs and the Hapsburgs and the Hohenzollerns
is toppling into dust. What sort of world shall rise in its place?"[47]

Obviously, it was a very different one from the one the 150th
anniversary had begun to usher in only four years earlier. Political
instability followed hard upon the grim reckoning of the conflict, and
despite the relative well-being of the United States, Americans turned
on each other in the immediate aftermath of the war. During the "Red
Summer" of 1919, there were race riots in more than three dozen
cities, and between 1919 and 1920, Attorney General A. Mitchell
Palmer arrested thousands of Americans, often without proper war-
rants, for their political views.

In this turbulent atmosphere, Brown alumni played helpful roles.
Zechariah Chafee Jr. (class of 1908) emerged as a leading defender of
freedom of speech, through his writings and his teaching at Harvard
Law School. Well into the twentieth century, through the McCarthyism

of the early 1950s, Chafee was an indefatigable advocate for the old liberties, which he consciously linked to Rhode Island's proud heritage of dissent. Chafee's book *Freedom of Speech* came out at precisely the right moment to make a difference—1920—and helped to calm waters that had become dangerously roiled. "We cannot lead sterilized lives," he reminded Americans, for "Democracy is not a water-tight compartment. It is a great adventure, and in order to prepare for that adventure we have to teach [students] to think for themselves on the problems they will have to face when they grow up."[48] That philosophical statement, brave for its frightened time, came close to serving as a maxim for Brown University. And in 1920, another alumnus, Charles Evans Hughes, asked "whether constitutional government as heretofore maintained in this republic could survive another great war even victoriously waged."[49]

Celestial navigation being taught in Rogers Hall during World War I.

ROARING TWENTIES

A MONTH AFTER THE ARMISTICE, military control of the curriculum ceased, and the university went back to something like normal. But the United States had flexed its muscles on the world stage in a way that it had not previously, and it would never again be the relatively isolationist power it had been in the nineteenth century. Huge numbers of immigrants continued to pour into the United States from Europe and elsewhere, eager to enter an American mainstream that now spoke to them more than ever.

These restive conditions gave rise to two contradictory impulses. Many Americans desired nothing more than a return to normality, or "normalcy," as a successful presidential candidate in 1920 (Warren Harding) put it. Nostalgia for simpler times also animated the vexed desire to suppress the consumption of alcohol and the urban vice that was thought to accompany it. A temporary ban went into effect one week after the Armistice, on November 18, 1918, before the Volstead Act passed in October 1919 (it would endure until 1933). But if Prohibition was designed to bring back prewar norms of rustic virtue, it failed miserably, giving rise instead to organized crime syndicates that made a killing—literally—off the sale of alcohol.

At the same time, America was moving ahead with breakneck speed. Returning veterans were impatient to resume their lives, celebrate, marry, and start new enterprises. Rapid technological change was making life faster and easier, as automobiles continued their conquest of America, airplanes made distant journeys that might have seemed inconceivable only a few years earlier, and everyone flocked to the movie house. Women finally received the right to vote after the passage of the Nineteenth Amendment on August 26, 1919. In partial response to the war, a "lost generation" arose, skeptical of the pieties of an older generation that seemed to have lost its way, and easily captivated by the wit of comic writers such as H. L. Mencken or the darker portraits of F. Scott Fitzgerald and Sinclair Lewis. The fact that the consumption of alcohol was now illegal only enhanced its attractiveness, and most accounts of the twenties have to be filtered through the boozy lens of contemporary observers.

All of these contradictions were felt on the Brown campus. To be sure, life accelerated, as large numbers of young men returned to a campus now liberated, like them, from military regulation. Prohibition seems to have had little if any impact, and President Faunce complained, "There is much less drinking among students than formerly, but when liquor is introduced it is under conditions vastly more damaging than ever before. It now involves, as never previously, the elements of surreptitiousness and disrespect for law, the presence and participation of young women, and the lowering of morale in the "strategic centers of civilization." [50]

At the same time, the university was eager to restore its own version of normalcy. The return of so many students solved some of Brown's fiscal problems, but it created others, as Brown was forced to confront essential questions about its identity. How big should the student body be? What should the new criteria for admission be? To what extent was Brown capable of stretching to accommodate students of unlimited talents but of limited means?

These were important questions as the university entered the Roaring Twenties. They were not unique to Brown—many universities became ensnared in awkward questions about racial and religious quotas in the 1920s. Harvard, for example, began to substitute vague references to "character" for the academic qualities that had previously gained admission, and tried to reduce its Jewish population from about 21.5 percent, in 1922, to 15 percent. Columbia, regarded as quite open, still reduced its quota of Jewish students from 40 percent to 22 percent, between 1920 and 1922. Yale's numbers were substantially lower, and were cut back to about 10 percent in 1923; Princeton was not even near that level. [51]

These questions required serious attention as Brown sought to continue its rise in size and standing, while maintaining excellence, solvency, and character in the most inclusive sense. Clearly, more consistent policies were needed, and a strategy of growth. Colleges were becoming a more achievable aspiration for American families, thanks to a flourishing economy and a booming popular culture that liked to situate scenes within the once-sacrosanct halls of elite academic institutions (for example, Harold Lloyd's 1925 film comedy, *The Freshman*). As Brown became more popular, it, too, was forced to confront some of its internal inconsistencies. While it had always been less large and wealthy than its sister institutions in Cambridge, New Haven, and Princeton, Brown was still a place of conspicuous privilege, with a fraternity system that was not closely regulated, and palpable forms of elitism on campus. At the same time, Brown was an urban institution, not unlike Columbia, and attractive to the students from modest backgrounds who lived in the institution's backyard. Many of them commuted to Brown, earning the derisive epithet "carpetbaggers." Nevertheless, they were some of Brown's best students, and even if Brown retained forms of snobbery on campus, it was generally open to students who were willing to bear the cost and effort necessary to apply.

Rhode Island was an ongoing laboratory of democracy, and by extension, so was Brown. As the state saw its population swelling to new heights in the 1920s, with factory jobs attracting immigrants from eastern and southern Europe, those families inevitably turned their attention to the educational citadel guarding the approaches to Providence. To be true to its democratic mission, its sense of place, and its bottom line, Brown needed to ensure ongoing access to talented students from all backgrounds. In 1922, the lead editorial in the *Brown Alumni Monthly* called for open admission, regardless of background, and concluded, "It would be unfortunate if there were full and free admittance to our American Academe for Anglo-Saxons only."[52] But it would take time to ground those lofty sentiments in reality.

A satirical image of a carpetbagger, from the *Brown Jug*, February 1921.

Through his annual reports to the Corporation in the twenties, President Faunce tried to shed light on these important questions. As the head of an increasingly complex institution, in a time of rapid change, he understood that Brown had to adapt to new realities. But he also faced constraints, as he explained in 1924:

> The increase in the number of students in the University is beyond our desire or our capacity, and leads us to search for measures of restriction which can be imposed without injustice. . . . The selective process is forced upon us, and we must reject some if we are really to train others. To include all is to damage all. But how can such selection be wisely and fairly made? Shall we refuse admission to every student whose preparation is deficient by even half a "point"? That would mean the exclusion of some of the most vigorous and promising minds. Shall we admit annually a preferred class, consisting of the sons of alumni, or of those residing in a certain region, or those belonging to certain races or religions? Such discrimination would be out of harmony with all our tradition and ideals. Class distinctions are unknown in the true university planted in American soil.[53]

In spite of these noble aspirations, Brown did not always live up to their spirit. Fraternities continued to self-select among the wealthier students from established Anglo-Saxon families, and when Jewish students tried to organize a fraternity in 1928–29, President Faunce discouraged the idea. Brown applied highly inconsistent standards throughout the twenties, thirties, and forties, and the percentage of Jews dropped to 9 percent for the class of 1944, from 38 percent for the class of 1928. Following the example of other universities of prestige, Brown fell back upon unconvincing arguments of "character" to justify unofficial quotas.[54]

Upton Sinclair dismissed Brown as a school for spoiled rich kids in *The Goose Step* (1923):

> Here is an extremely wealthy institution, catering to the sons of the plutocracy, and almost as snobbish as Princeton. . . . Brown in

its day had such outstanding men as Lester F. Ward and Meiklejohn, now president of Amherst; but those days have passed, and
there has followed a regime of intellectual dry-rot. It is a League
of the Old Men, maintaining a caste system, based on seniority;
any young instructor who arises to suggest a new idea is quickly
taught his place. . . . Under such a regime what becomes of the
students? Exactly the same thing as we found happening to
students at Harvard, Wisconsin, and California; they get drunk.[55]

This harsh critique might have come as welcome news to earlier
Brown presidents, who could never find enough sons of the plutocracy
(at last, Brown was being denounced in the same breath as Harvard
and Princeton!). But Sinclair was a sensationalist, and despite some
lingering snobbery, the student body was growing larger, broader, and
better over the long haul. Extracurricular activities dramatized the
ways in which Brown was improving itself. As Faunce wrote, the
students had organized "their own college, within the college," a competitive world of musical groups, publications, and performances that
had replaced the old "quiet and still air of delightful studies" with "the
eager competition, the ceaseless enterprise, of the world around it."[56]

That effervescence bubbles forth in nearly every publication from
the era. An irrepressible spirit underlay the university, and if Faunce
was apprehensive at times, he still had the vision to see that the advantages of growth outnumbered the disadvantages. In other ways, too,
he was a modernist, fighting the rise of fundamentalism within the
Baptist church and urging that the Corporation dispense with the
ancient requirement that the president be a Baptist (which it did in
1928).[57] He also expanded the campus. Indeed, as he neared the end
of his thirty-year presidency—the longest in the university's history—
it was clear that Brown had been fortunate to find him when it did.
The way that Brown looks today is due, in no small measure, to
Faunce's vision. In addition to filling in the main Green, now
protected along the north side by Rockefeller Hall (later renamed
Faunce House), he oversaw new scientific facilities (Arnold and
Metcalf laboratories and an engineering laboratory), new dormitories,

Pembroke's Alumnae Hall, and a new football stadium and gymna-sium to satisfy Brown's hunger for sport. When the stadium was dedicated on October 24, 1925, all 27,000 spectators took a pledge to "the comradeship of American colleges" and to "the loyalties of the game and the loyalties of life."[58]

The endowment had risen from $1.7 million to $9.9 million, and the size of the student body and faculty had trebled over those three decades. It was noted in the presidential report of 1929 that nearly half of all the men who had ever graduated from Brown University (4,497 of 9,049) had done so under the Faunce administration. (Men still out-numbered women significantly; in the same report, the incoming class at Pembroke numbered 139.)[59] With that growth came a notable rise in quality—deeper treatment of the social as well as the natural sciences, a broader variety of languages, attention to modern literature, and the unstinting devotion to teaching for which Brown's faculty has always been known.[60]

Across the globe, the pace of change was quickening, but not always smoothly. Seven years after women achieved the vote, the Corporation declined a petition to name the distinguished educator and alumna Mary Woolley as trustee. The Women's College was renamed Pembroke College in 1928, and every year brought impres-sive gains in the number and quality of its students. In 1904, the *Sepiad*, a Pembroke literary magazine included a "Diary of a Brown Girl 2500 A.D.," that described a College Hill in which the men had become vestigial and not particularly useful relics ("There are only one hundred and fifty men left on the hill and they seem almost lost in the buildings").[61] That was not quite the case, but Pembroke raised the bar high for its academic achievement, and in some ways, its diversity. Four sisters from the African American Minkins family of Pawtucket distinguished themselves across a long period of atten-dance in the teens, twenties, and thirties, and Beatrice Coleman, class of 1925, received a Doctor of Humane Letters in 2014 for her distinguished teaching career (conferred posthumously because she died just before the commencement at which it was to have been bestowed).[62]

Rudolph Fisher, second from right, photographed in 1924 with other luminaries of the Harlem Renaissance, including, left to right, Langston Hughes, Charles S. Johnson, E. Franklin Frazier, and Hubert Delany.

And what of Brown's racial diversity? Although the university's numbers of African American students were not high, Brown attracted students of high distinction. Rudolph Fisher, of the class of 1919, a polymath with both medical and literary ambitions, exerted a strong influence on what became the Harlem Renaissance of the 1920s. After majoring in biology and English, he gave the commencement address, on "The Emancipation of Science," and subsequently received his master's from Brown as well.[63] But he was already feeling the pull of Harlem and spending time there in the early 1920s with his fellow Brown alumnus, Fritz Pollard, and their friend Paul Robeson, playing music in public, discussing ideas, and sharing in the excitement of a remarkable time and place.[64] Langston Hughes was particularly impressed by Fisher, calling him the "wittiest of these New Negroes of Harlem. [He] always frightened me a little, because he could think of the most incisively clever things to say, and I could never think of anything to answer."

Fisher became the superintendent of a Harlem hospital, but never stopped writing. His 1932 work, *The Conjure-Man Dies*, is considered the first novel to feature an African American detective, and, as such, was a precursor to such iconic 1970s figures as Shaft, Dolemite, and Foxy Brown (in no way related to Brown University). But after a promising literary debut, he died too young, of an intestinal ailment, at age thirty-seven.

Other groups were finding their place at Brown as well. In the early decades of the twentieth century, steamships were bringing large numbers of immigrants to Providence from Italy and Portugal, and nearly every demographic change in Providence was eventually reflected in the college on the hill. Jewish students were also coming in increasingly large numbers, and organizing student groups— a Menorah Society in 1915, and a fraternal organization known as "The Lambs."[65] Without doubt, their entry into the full range of extracurricular activity, particularly that rooted in the fraternity system, was blocked by lingering forms of anti-Semitism, and by admission restrictions that were often tacit rather than explicit. But it was never comfortable to sustain snobbery at an institution as dedicated to intellectual freedom (and as modestly endowed) as Brown University. Nor was it likely to last in an age that was trending toward more opportunities for all, albeit inconsistently. As Brown became more diverse, its environment happily encouraged satire.

JUGGLERS

It was inevitable that the collision of an older Brown, steeped in wealth and tradition, and a newer Brown, open to more recently arrived Americans, would produce occasional friction. Fortunately, it also produced art. In the 1920s, two extraordinary writers emerged at Brown, and though they were quite different from each other, they became best friends, brothers-in-law, and brothers in arms, creating a new kind of American culture—lightning-fast, cinematic, and caustic toward the older hierarchies. The humorist S. J. Perelman had a gentler voice, though plenty acerbic on occasion; the novelist Nathanael West wrote devastating critiques of American popular culture and its tendency to promise more than it could deliver.[66]

Perelman, the son of recent Russian immigrants, grew up in Providence in something quite close to poverty. If the Industrial Revolution had brought self-reliance and wealth to Rhode Island, it had also brought considerable squalor, as documentarians such as Lewis Hine made clear in their exposés of working conditions in Rhode Island's mills. The senior Perelman did not work in a factory, but in the edges around the industrial economy. As his son later remembered:

> My father had a speckled career. He had a drygoods store and was a machinist and an unsuccessful poultryman. It was the American dream that if you had a few acres and a chicken farm there was no limit to your possible wealth. I grew up with and have since retained the keenest hatred of chickens. My chief interest always was to be a cartoonist, and I began very early to draw cartoons in my father's store on the long cardboard strips around which the bolts of Amoskeag cotton and ginghams were stored.[67]

Perelman's school friends recalled that he drew some of his first cartoons on the very eggs that he had brought to eat, from his father's farm in Cranston.[68] Eventually, the captions grew longer, and he began to think of himself as a writer. His vocabulary steadily became prodigious, nurtured by a keen ear, voracious reading at the Providence Public Library, and an early love of James Joyce.[69]

After a writing contest judged favorably by a young Brown professor, Perelman followed his high school career by trudging up College Hill in 1921 to attend Brown as a freshman.[70] From the beginning, it was clear that his extracurricular education was more important to him than his classes. As he later recalled, "Simply stated, I became interested in the life creative because I was a comic artist in college. I was more interested in working for the college humor magazine, the *Brown Jug*, than I was in trigonometry and all those necessary adjuncts."[71]

The *Brown Jug* was a humor magazine, founded in February 1920, that gave students a much-needed vehicle to make fun of their elders. Its first issue, entitled "Coming Out," featured a cover with a girl in party dress, emerging from a bandbox and holding a small bear. The "Coming Out" number was followed by more than a decade of sophisticated issues that gave Brown humorists (who called themselves "Jugglers") a chance to write for a slick magazine that sold in train stations and newsstands, far from campus. It offered serious professional training for

A cover of the *Brown Jug* drawn by S. J. Perelman.

writers and editors and, in Perelman's case, a platform to help shape the raucous twentieth-century culture still coming into focus.[72]

Early numbers of the *Jug* contained cruel depictions of "carpet-bagger" students that Perelman might easily have found hurtful; yet he poured himself into the work of the magazine, ultimately becoming its editor in chief. He was absorbing a great deal of information, although apparently not much from his classes. He loved the theater, and in the 1920s, downtown Providence was significant theatrical destination, full of show palaces that theatrical stars visited on the circuit between New York City and Boston. Perelman had a part-time job managing a cigar store on Washington Street, just above Fay's Theater, and one night he saw a comedy troupe called the Marx Brothers performing "a rancid little act" that he found very funny.[73]

A spirited reminiscence of his undergraduate career makes it clear where Perelman's priorities lay:

> For six months after seeing Erich von Stroheim in *Foolish Wives*,
> I exhibited a maddening tendency to click my heels and murmur
> "Bitte?" along with a twitch as though a monocle were screwed

into my eye. The mannerism finally abated, but not until the
Dean of Brown University had taken me aside and confided that
if I wanted to transfer to Heidelberg, the faculty would not stand
in my way.[74]

Perelman's tone suggests a certain coolness toward the administration, which was reflected in his writings at the time. Perelman
admired a young professor of English, Percy Marks, who had written
a racy novel about Brown, *The Plastic Age* (1924), whose most famous
scene described the women of "Sanford College" checking their corsets
before attending a dance. It even committed the sacrilege of ridiculing
the college's obsession with football—a specific satire that Perelman
would remember and put to good use with the Marx Brothers. Percy
Marks was also Jewish, and when Brown dismissed him, not long after
his novel was issued, Perelman was livid.[75] Around that time, his writing took on a harder edge:

> Ah the college boys, the college boys! I daresay that if all the
> sub-freshmen who are intending to come to Brown could see it
> for what it is, a fraternity-ridden and lethargic academy of very
> middle-class "boosters," they would change their minds about
> starting for Providence next fall. From the dot of nine o'clock
> when we rush in to fear God for fifteen minutes every morning
> till Cap Cameron [the campus guard] puts the last blowsy drunk
> to bed, the spectacle is the same.[76]

That edge was still apparent years later, when he recalled the university's social universe: "There were nineteen fraternities. As a Jew,
I wasn't invited to join any of them. That is, until I started to write and
became editor of the humor magazine. Then two of them asked me to
belong. I refused them flat, and that gave me great pleasure."[77]

It was rapidly becoming clear that neither Brown nor Rhode
Island could hold Perelman, and he left before he could graduate with
the class of 1925, an oversight that was rectified forty years later, when
he received an honorary degree.[78] But even in his fits of pique,
Perelman had learned a great deal from Brown—including how to

divert his flashes of anger into effective satire. Anyone could make a sociological observation about fraternities, but Perelman was learning how to make people laugh. He honed that skill upon moving to New York City, where he first worked for a small magazine called *Judge*. He later reminisced, "What I didn't know was that I was hitching my star to a wagon that was gathering night soil." *Judge* was so insolvent that the staff painted its walls gray, so that no one would be able to see the treasurer, who always wore a gray suit.[79]

Eventually, Perelman brought his skills to the *New Yorker*, and to the group of brothers whose "rancid" act he had seen in downtown Providence. The Marx Brothers were approaching apogee and had turned to Hollywood at just the right moment, as sound came in, permitting them to comment on America through a variety of noises, spoken and unspoken. With his eye for detail, sharpened at Brown, Perelman helped them turn sociological observations about the wealthy into gold, first in *Monkey Business* (1931), then in *Horse Feathers* (1932).

That alone would be enough of a literary legacy. But one of Perelman's enduring friendships was with another Jewish student, named Nathan Weinstein.[80] Weinstein had grown up wealthier than Perelman, in New York City, but had overcome a few obstacles of his own. He was called "Pep," sarcastically, because he exhibited so little energy as a child (the name came at summer camp, when he slept for a day after a modest hike).[81] High school also had proven to be too much of a challenge for him, and he had dropped out, making it unlikely he could attend Brown. But he had secured admission to Tufts University, outside Boston, not yet as reputable as it later became (its mascot was Jumbo the circus elephant, in deference to P. T. Barnum, a major donor).[82]

However, Weinstein's grades there were not good—his performance in French was so execrable that he received a "double F." He was asked to leave and had few options until he happened upon the idea of transferring to Brown, sending the much better grades of a different student, also named Nathan Weinstein.[83] That implausible ruse worked, and given a second chance, Pep did not waste it. He entered Brown fully accepted, accredited, and ready to go.

But despite his wealth, he too fell short of full acceptance in the fraternity-dominated world, and spent most of his time at Brown with a small circle of friends who loved writing, including Perelman. They daydreamed about words and pranks (Perelman talked Weinstein out of a plan to turn a rare elephant folio in the John Hay Library into the top for a coffee table).[84] In a rare burst of activity, he secretly wrote the speech of a classmate, Quentin Reynolds, who had been elected to give the Spring Day speech. As Reynolds later remembered,

> He labored long and hard and brought forth an amazing satirical dissertation. I didn't understand a third of it, but dutifully I memorized it. Part was in Greek, part in Latin and part in what we call "double-talk" today. It had a continuity of sorts—its theme concerned what one would find if one could discover the actual wooden horse of Troy and penetrate the inside of the animal.

That inside contained a menagerie of fantastic creatures, all of whom turned out to be unsuccessful authors. Much of the speech made it into a later novel, *The Dream Life of Balso Snell*.[85]

Weinstein continued to reinvent himself, first as Nathanael von Wallenstein Weinstein, and, finally, as Nathanael West. Perelman wrote of his shape-shifting friend, "I love his sudden impish smile, the twinkle of those alert green eyes, and the print of his cloven foot in the shrubbery."[86] They grew closer after graduation, when they moved to New York City together to conquer the fortress of American literary culture. For a while they lived together as part of a group of Brown friends, all writers. Quentin Reynolds was among them, and he co-wrote Perelman's second book, *Parlor, Bedlam and Bath*. Another was a young woman who wrote advice columns in the *Brooklyn Daily Eagle* under the byline "Susan Chester." This source lit the fuse that led to West's great novel about the people who write in to newspapers.[87]

In other words, two of the greatest works of the 1930s were germinating in that house of sarcastic Brown alumni—*Horse Feathers* and *Miss Lonelyhearts* (1933). Indeed, the Huxley College of *Horse Feathers* may have been modeled on Brown (a wonderful song and dance routine by Groucho, "I'm Against It," looks at the world with a certain constructive irreverence). Perelman eventually married West's sister Laura, who also called herself Lorraine, and attended Pembroke College from 1928–29. *Miss Lonelyhearts*, in addition to its stature as a great American novel, bequeathed the name "Homer Simpson" to later generations.[88]

Groucho Marx as President Quincy Wagstaff of Huxley College, likely modeled on Brown University.

NEW DEAL

The long presidency of William Faunce concluded in 1929, just as the American economy was heading off the rails. The Great Depression hit Rhode Island hard, and by many measures, Providence never fully recovered. Many of the shuttered mills in the periphery simply stayed closed, their jobs migrating to the South, where wages were lower, and ultimately to foreign countries. The city population in 1930 reached a plateau (252,981) before beginning a long decline (in 2010 it was 178,075).

In its search for a new president, Brown once again looked within the ranks of its alumni and found Clarence Barbour of the class of 1888, who would serve eight years, until 1937. Although the charter stipulation that the President be a Baptist had been removed, Barbour fit that original requirement. A reminiscence by Thomas J. Watson Jr., class of 1937, reveals that religion was still very much a part of the social calculus that would lead a family to a particular university. Watson was not a very good student, but his path to Brown was eased by his father's standing in the business community (as the founder of IBM) and friendship with Barbour:

> I said, "Why don't we go to Brown?"
>
> We drove to Providence, checked into the Biltmore Hotel, Dad called the admissions office, and up we went the next morning. He said to the admissions officer, "I'm Thomas Watson, I run the IBM company, and my son would like to consider coming to Brown. By the way, who is the president of Brown?"
>
> The admissions guy said, "Clarence Barbour."
>
> "That's very interesting," said Dad. "He was my pastor when I lived in Rochester, New York." In those days, Brown's charter required that the university president be a minister.
>
> We went to Clarence Barbour's office, said hello, and Barbour got somebody to show us around the campus. When we returned, the admissions officer was looking at my record. He said, "He's not very good but we'll take him." [89]

The university's publications do not reveal much attention to the poverty and privation that many families were wrestling with, but obviously those hardships were felt on campus, especially by the so-called carpetbaggers. Despite his privileged upbringing, the younger Watson conveyed the dualistic quality of Brown in his autobiography, noting the poverty of some students and the wealth of his own set:

> If you'd visited Brown University in 1933, the effects of the Depression would have been obvious. The campus looked run-down and a good number of students seemed undernourished. Many of them commuted by bus from places like Pawtucket, because they couldn't afford to live at school.
>
> However, I fell in with the minority of students who had the money to behave as if the 1920s had never stopped roaring. I belonged to the Psi Upsilon fraternity, which was known for its fun-loving ways. Every night of the week our crowd would head downtown to drink and dance at the Biltmore Hotel. We had apartments, cars, and a pretty fast life. On weekends we drove off to ski resorts in Vermont or to Smith or Vassar for girls.[90]

Brown was increasingly an important local employer, and throughout the years of the Depression and New Deal, its alumni were deeply engaged in the effort to restore the vigor of the U.S. economy. Several were especially prominent. Tommy "the Cork" Corcoran, one of Franklin Roosevelt's most talented advisors, was a member of the class of 1922. Charles Evans Hughes continued to play an essential role in the government, as chief justice of the Supreme Court, although that became a vexed position indeed as the court rejected many of the pillars of the New Deal, earning the wrath of FDR and his millions of supporters. "The Bearded Iceberg" had few political tools with which to fight back. He had also moved to the right as he aged: *Time* magazine reported that "the pure white flame of Liberalism had burned out in him to a sultry ash of Conservatism."[91] FDR became so frustrated by the Supreme Court's rejections that he considered a scheme to pack the court with new members, before cooler heads prevailed.

At the same time, Hughes had the acumen to sense that the times demanded change. He was sensitive in many ways to the progressive winds that were blowing across the landscape, just as he had himself embodied the hope for a better politics as a young man. With his appointment as chief justice in 1930, he fortified the arguments on behalf of free speech that Oliver Wendell Holmes Jr. and Louis Brandeis had been making vainly for years. The Hughes Court struck down state suppressions of free speech and the hoisting of unpopular flags (such as the hammer and sickle), state taxes on newspapers, and city ordinances designed to restrict activities of such unpopular religious denominations as the Jehovah's Witnesses. Although opposed to many New Deal initiatives in the beginning of FDR's presidency, Hughes began to change course in 1936, supporting increased government regulation of the economy, in a spirit more closely aligned with his earlier Progressivism. He wrote the majority opinion that validated the Wagner Act, legitimizing unions and collective bargaining, and also supported the Social Security Act. He further advanced the work of democracy by protecting due process for African Americans in the South and by asking a Southern justice, Hugo Black, to write a vigorous opinion defending equal access to justice the case of *Chambers v. Florida* (1940).[92]

John D. Rockefeller Jr. was also critical to the recovery, in his own inimitable way. By committing his prestige and fortune to enormous building projects such as Rockefeller Center in midtown Manhattan, Rockefeller instilled confidence and created jobs. As noted earlier, Rockefeller also lent his might to the creation of the Museum of Modern Art (its first incarnation opened ten days after the stock market crash of 1929), to the scrutiny of the heavens (by building the Palomar Observatory), and to the study of the past (Colonial Williamsburg). Throughout the 1920s, and beyond, he was a quiet voice for tolerance in a country that was becoming ever more divided. As American Protestants (and Baptists in particular) split into evangelical and liberal camps, over the Scopes controversy and other irritants, he consistently supported interfaith dialogue, modernity, and reason. His old friend William Faunce was solidly behind him, which occasionally drew the ire of Southern Baptists onto Brown University.[93]

And we should not forget S. J. Perelman. By helping the Marx Brothers, he gave a precious form of relief—laughter—to Americans in dire need of diversion. But the Marx Brothers' transformation from traveling vaudevillians into Hollywood heroes did not come effortlessly. As Perelman later recalled, there were moments when he and Groucho did not see eye to eye. Indeed, Perelman's Brown education nearly made him unfit for Hollywood, by teaching him to love words too much:

> My own relationship with Groucho was, in a sense, a baffling one. I loved his lightning transitions of thought, his ability to detect pretentiousness and bombast, and his genius for disemboweling the spurious and hackneyed phrases that litter one's conversation. And I knew that he liked my work for the printed page, my preoccupation with clichés, baroque language, and the elegant variation. Nevertheless, I sense as time went on that this aspect of my work disturbed him; he felt that some of the dialogue I wrote for him was "too literary." He feared that many of my allusions would be incomprehensible to the ordinary moviegoer, whom he regarded as a wholly cretinous specimen.[94]

Despite all those words, the movies were made, and Rockefeller's buildings were built, and the New Deal was able to navigate its way past the Bearded Iceberg. By the late 1930s, it was clear that the United States had survived its greatest financial crisis, and that Brown alumni had played a significant role in that survival.

Closer to home, Brown not only survived the crisis, but it continued to grow. To be sure, there were limits imposed by economic and physical constraints, but the arrival of a new president in 1937 strengthened the mandate for change. Henry M. Wriston would become one of Brown's transformative leaders. He was the first non-Baptist to lead the university and, like Faunce, a young president as well. He came from Lawrence College in Wisconsin and, with no shortage of confidence, the young Wriston seemed like a logical choice to help lead Brown into a new era of growth. He would do that, but first, Brown had to brace itself for another unwelcome intrusion from the theater of world politics. Everyone was ready for change in 1937, but few saw a great global conflagration coming, the second in as many generations. There were premonitions—the *Brown Daily Herald* covered the rise of Hitler with dismay in the early 1930s.[95] But isolationism remained a potent force on campus. The *Pembroke Record* spoke for many in April 1938, with an article titled, "Neutrality Is Favored Here."[96] As late as October 1939, an overwhelming 96 percent of students opposed entering the war.[97]

Yet Wriston had been sounding the alarm. In the spring of 1937, he warned students in no uncertain terms, "If war comes and America becomes involved, your lives are at stake." He steadily advised Brown men to prepare to fight and disparaged isolationist sentiments, with a prescience that was not universal at the time.[98]

WORLD WAR II

ON THE DAY THAT THE JAPANESE ATTACKED PEARL HARBOR— December 7, 1941—they also attacked American installations throughout the Pacific. One of these was a military base in the Philippines called Camp John Hay. The attack was obviously an assault on American troops, but it was also a symbolic blow to many of the peaceful initiatives that John Hay had undertaken as secretary of state, including his work toward a resolution of the Russo-Japanese war in 1905, the last year of his life. Camp John Hay was later used by the Japanese as an internment camp for American and British soldiers.[99]

As in 1917, the onset of war greatly disrupted the life of Brown. But in short order the campus adapted itself to a war footing. Within five months of their graduation, 71 percent of the college's class of 1942 had enrolled in the armed services, and another 21 percent was doing work linked to the war effort.[100] In order to rush students through graduation and into service, Brown agreed to teach year-round so that students could complete eight semesters in three years.[101] Accordingly, the new year of 1942 brought a commencement in May and another in October— the first fall commencement since 1869. Uniformed personnel were seen

Members of Brown's Naval Unit pass through the War Memorial Gate, built to honor "the men of Brown who in the World War gave their lives that freedom may endure." A generation after World War I, these students faced another global conflagration.

everywhere on campus, and a military celerity began to dominate the rhythms of campus life. Change came in nearly every realm. Buildings were repurposed, and a palpable seriousness descended upon campus. For the first time, men and women were allowed to swim together in the Brown pool.[102] Commando drills were held on Lincoln Field, and

Brown's Naval Unit trains on a campus obstacle course.

lessons in how to survive a burning oil spill were held in the pool. As it had in the First World War, Brown offered its campus for training purposes to the national war effort. Brown became one of eleven centers for meteorological training—of crucial use to aviation—and again offered a training ground for Naval officers.[103]

As with previous wars, women's lives were transformed by the new regimen of life. New opportunities were suddenly available for the undergraduates of Pembroke in both curricular and extracurricular activities. Brown and Pembroke integrated all their classes in 1942, and the Brown and Pembroke newspapers briefly merged in 1943 (the result was called the *Brown Herald-Record*). The academic offerings saw a striking increase in science courses and the applications of knowledge that might contribute to the war effort (the Pratt-Whitney Aircraft Corporation paid for eleven Pembroke students to study engineering). It was a time of both sacrifice (coffee rations were cut by 35 percent, sugar rations by 40 percent) and liberation.[104]

Of course, Brown's men and women went overseas as well. By the summer of 1942, more than 900 alumni were serving their country, and 7 had already died by then.[105] When Pembroke created a Pembroke Defense Program, nearly 450 students signed up.[106] At least 35 faculty and staff members left the university in the months after Pearl Harbor to lend their services to the war effort.[107] Those figures would only rise over the next three years. The men and women of the Brown-Pembroke community participated in every theater of the war and in every service. They served as ace pilots, as commanding officers, and as rank-and-file members of a global fighting force. Major General Royal Lord, class of 1921, helped to plan the D-Day landings.[108] Lieutenant Colonel Charles Morhouse, class of 1925, was General Douglas MacArthur's personal physician.[109] One undergraduate was captured in Italy, served time in a German POW camp, and through resourceful use of conduits, was able to complete course credit toward his Brown degree.[110] Another graduate, a Chinese American named John Sen, class of 1943, worked among the Japanese Americans consigned to internment camps.[111] John Fujio Aiso, class of 1931, was the highest ranking Japanese American in the U.S. Army, rendered invaluable service in military intelligence, and received an honorary degree from his alma mater in 1950.[112]

In 1946, the *Brown Alumni Monthly* issued a list of all those who had died in the war. They ranged from the classes of 1907 to 1947, and died everywhere the war was fought.[113] They died in Patton's invasions of North Africa and Sicily, and in the skies over Germany. Two were killed on the beaches of Normandy on D-Day. They died in the island-hopping campaigns of the Pacific. They died above the water, through kamikaze attacks, and below, in submarines. Two died in the sinking of the USS *Indianapolis*. They died far from home, in Japanese and German POW camps. They died patrolling the home waters of the United States. All in all, 177 alumni gave their lives. When the war finally ended, the bell of University Hall rang out, as it had for all victories since the eighteenth century, and the students poured onto the Green.[114]

Now and then, Brown's service to the war effort touched upon an older history. A harbor defense installation in Narragansett Bay was named Fort Varnum, after one of Brown's first graduates, James Varnum (class of 1769).[115] In 1945, a Victory-class cargo combat ship was named *Brown Victory*, and at her commissioning an alumnus, Colonel Ashley Greene, class of 1921, spoke of the Brown idea:

> Brown stands for a faith based upon wisdom and understanding. Founded by Baptists, inspired with the liberalism of Rhode Island, the school retains that liberal spirit which reveres tradition but welcomes invention—a spirit with breeds sturdy loyalty, initiative, and respect for humanity, which is vital to democratic leadership.[116]

In Burma, one of the war's hot spots, the allied campaign was facilitated by the presence of yet another Brown-educated missionary, Brayton C. Case, class of 1910, who had been living there since 1913. He advised General Joseph Stilwell, and helped set up food-distribution networks for the Allied armies, drawing upon his missionary experience and agricultural expertise.[117] But another group of Brown-affiliated missionaries encountered a horrific end. On the island of Panay in the Philippines, a group of eleven Baptists were beheaded by the Japanese after refusing to heed warnings to leave. This episode was all the more tragic for the fact that the missionaries were devoted to the cause of peace, spoke Japanese, and some of them had brought up their children in Japan. Among them were James Covell, a member of the class of 1920, and Dorothy Dowell, of the Pembroke class of 1918. One newspaper account of the time claims that the missionaries named their last redoubt "Hopewell," the name of that place in New Jersey where the first inspiration struck to found a new Baptist college, nearly two centuries earlier.[118]

But if the war brought loss to Brown, it also expanded the scope of the university's mission and its reach. Around the world, Brown and Pembroke alumni saw the war up close, and they returned to the United States educated in new ways. Throughout the war, the *Brown Daily Herald* featured contributions from around the world, describing the activities of a network of students and alumni, suddenly globalized. The writings of President Wriston and others from the Brown community added to the rising clamor for a world based on more effective international law, just as President Faunce and Brown faculty and alumni had done in the aftermath of World War I. In his 1943 commencement address, Wriston argued, "It is essential that we do not postpone an association of nations until some distant Nirvana."[119]

Another old friend, Brown's former dean, Alexander Meiklejohn (class of 1893), was an eloquent voice for tolerance throughout the war and its aftermath. It may have helped that he himself was an immigrant to the United States, but he also had a rare gift of reaffirming what was uniquely valuable in the American approach to human rights while avoiding a descent into patriotic hyperbole or cant. His writings reached many Americans in their day, conveying a seriousness of purpose and a grasp of American history that had been profoundly shaped by his time in Providence. He served for many years with the leadership of the American Civil Liberties Union, advised the creation of UNESCO in 1945, and never lost his affinity for Brown. When he was awarded the Rosenberger Medal in 1959, he called it the highest honor of his life. Well into the twenty-first century, his ideas about the First Amendment continue to shape Supreme Court deliberations over campaign funding and over whether individual rights extend to corporations.[120]

Freedom of worship, in particular—that ancient Rhode Island idea—was anointed by President Roosevelt in 1941 as one of the goals for the world to come, and Brown alumni persevered in service to that ideal. The reliable defender of free speech, Zechariah Chafee, brought out a new edition of his book in 1941, just in time for another war, and in countless ways the men and women of Brown and Pembroke defended the Brunonian ideals that Wriston himself, in his many orations and writings before the Brown community, often linked to the war effort. In his remarks before the university convocation on September 24, 1941, he recalled the Civil War, still within living memory of a handful of alumni, and said, "Those students of Brown turned from books to guns with the same reluctance as you do today, and only when it seemed necessary to vindicate in action the fundamental values for which the University itself stood."[121]

Brown was also involved, indirectly, in the culminating event that ended the war, the development and detonation of the atomic bomb. Richard Chace Tolman, a grandson of Elizabeth Buffum Chace, was a key scientific adviser to the Manhattan Project. A Brown dean, Samuel T. Arnold, class of 1913, was instrumental in managing the Project.[122] And a future president of Brown, Donald Hornig, was at ground zero when the Trinity Project (the first detonation) was finally realized. Indeed, he was the last person to see the bomb and spent the night before its detonation guarding the device. When it went off, at 5:29:45 A.M. on July 16, 1945, he described it as "one of the most aesthetically beautiful things I have ever seen." But of course, that beauty was in the eye of the beholder.

THE WORK OF PEACE

IF BROWN WAS INVOLVED IN THE WORK OF WAR, it was also involved in the work of peace. President Wriston used his position as a kind of pulpit in the years that followed the war, speaking eloquently on the challenges facing Americans as they sought to build a new global architecture. Throughout the resurgent crises of the late 1940s and early 1950s, he offered a reassuring message of calm determination, urging Americans to stay focused on their immense new responsibilities and to avoid the distractions and internal divisions that had squandered the last peace.

From the moment the war began—indeed, even before that— Wriston was active, helping to define the postwar order. At the 1942 commencement, he spoke eloquently of the need to achieve solidarity between nations, after the fighting was done, and to remember the spiritual aspirations that linked human beings:

> As the nationhood of the United States could not endure half slave and half free, so the peace of the world cannot survive a division in the ideology between the state as master and the state as servant . . . between the individual as slave, and man as a son of God. . . . The central political problem of the world is continuously to expand the areas of self-government, as the central economic problem is to expand wealth. . . . But the world at war reveals that the standard of living is basically spiritual, not economic. War offers its stark and final proof that man does not live

by bread alone. The world at peace must show that these lessons have been learned. The structure of the post-war world cannot be founded upon power. It must be founded upon moral intangibles which control power.[123]

In his final years as president, Wriston spoke often of the ethical imperatives that must guide a great university. He particularly liked the language in the Brown charter that spoke to moral guidance. He used his considerable powers as a writer to remind Americans of their new authority as shapers of the postwar order. It was a world in which the nation's colleges and universities would play an ever more prominent role. The GI Bill gave millions of Americans a chance to achieve a college education and the economic opportunity to launch new careers after that. New government funding, particularly in the sciences, swelled research budgets. Brown's traditional role as an exponent of innovative educational strategies was relevant again, as Wriston pushed through yet another curricular revision, the second of three to be called

Henry M. Wriston using a new medium—television—to explain "Operating a University" to Rhode Island viewers, February 15, 1954.

the New Curriculum.[124] When universities became an unexpected battlefield in the contest of ideas that launched the Cold War—and Senator Joseph McCarthy, in particular, attacked them as disloyal—Wriston offered a spirited rebuttal.[125]

Other Brown thinkers contributed to that defense. Once again, Zechariah Chafee rose to remind Americans of a tolerant tradition that was all too easily forgotten in the fearful early days of the Cold War. He not only published extensively throughout the postwar period, he also advised the United Nations as it was going through its birth pangs.[126] That the UN was located where it was—in a vast multi-ethnic city that represented democratic inclusiveness—stemmed in no small degree from the idealism as well as the wealth of John D. Rockefeller Jr.

Inclusiveness was also on Wriston's mind as he turned his attention to matters closer to home. In the 1930s, Harvard and Yale had undertaken major new residential complexes, called Houses at Harvard and Colleges at Yale. In the early 1950s, Wriston pursued a similar vision of a new enclosed quadrangle, just south of campus, that would greatly expand the living space for students of the college and bring the added benefit of making fraternities (invited in) more accountable to the university. Although smaller than the Harvard and Yale systems, it was plenty ambitious, requiring the destruction or relocation of a huge number of old houses, which Wriston described, impoliticly, as "the greatest slum clearance since Sherman burned Atlanta." Alarmed local citizens responded by forming the Providence Preservation Society, arguing that the destruction of old homes was a curious way to advance the humanistic ideals of a university seeking to live by the example of its founding. But the result was an indisputable forward step for the college, unifying much of its student life in the friendly confines of what would ultimately be known as Wriston Quad. It is easy to disparage the Ratty on nearly every imaginable count, and indeed, that is one of the essential conversations of the Brown experience. In many ways, that was exactly Wriston's point. He understood that a central place to eat and talk, uniting the community, would be helpful to Brown's democracy. Of course, it would become even more so after men and women were allowed to eat together, several decades later.[127]

In 1954, the Ivy League officially came into existence as an athletic conference, giving formal recognition to what had been an accepted phrase for some time. At the same time, it was gratifying for Brown to be acknowledged as the peer of the elder institutions that had often stopped short of giving the university its full due. In the early years of intercollegiate athletics, Harvard and Yale had simply refused to travel to Providence for football games. The great victory over Harvard in 1916, made possible by Fritz

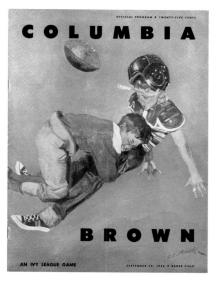

Brown prevailed over Columbia, 20–0, in the first official football game of the newly formed Ivy League in 1954; this program is from September 29, 1956.

Pollard's heroics, was all the sweeter for that reason. Brown would always benefit from the company of Harvard, Yale, and Princeton. But to be smaller, less wealthy, and right was familiar territory to Rhode Islanders. And to be on the playing field at all was gratifying.

Wriston stepped down in 1955. It was the same year that a new chapter of the NAACP opened on the Brown campus, a sign that, for all its progress to date, Brown still had some distance to go. The decade to come would offer ample opportunity. Speaking of the acceptance of women on campus and their continued absence from the Corporation, Wriston wrote in 1947, "our successors 50 years hence will be amazed at the hesitation and the doubts which have so far precluded their election." That amazement extended to other categories as well. But with an enhanced reputation, and full confidence in the future, Brown was ready for the many challenges still looming.

CHAPTER 5

THE BROWN DECADES

Núnnowwa. *Harvest time.*

—ROGER WILLIAMS,
A Key into the Language of America, 1643.

No period, of course, is uniform in its colour any more than in its
morals or manners; there are always gradations; there are likewise always leftovers and intrusions, reminders of a dead past that
is not yet dead or promises of a venture into a future still unborn.
But the Brown Decades mark a period, a period we have yet to
explore intimately and reckon with.[1]

—LEWIS MUMFORD
The Brown Decades

NOT MANY PEOPLE REMEMBER Lewis Mumford's 1931
study, *The Brown Decades*, which described the rise of
American architecture in the aftermath of the Civil
War.[2] It told the story of a nation growing in all directions, gaining confidence, and learning to express itself with eloquence
and force. Whether measured by influence, or wealth, or the sheer fact
of bricks and mortar, the United States grew so rapidly in the aftermath of the war that it seemed nearly unrecognizable to those who
remembered the simpler republic of the antebellum.

Opening Convocation, the ceremonial start of the academic year.

Something similar could be said about Brown in the seven decades that followed World War II. In the second half of the twentieth century, the university underwent a transformation so profound that it might be called an awakening. The number of departments, programs, and buildings grew exponentially; the endowment portfolio thickened to respectability; and a series of strong presidents left their mark. In terms of bricks and mortar, the change was particularly striking, as the campus expanded, with a dizzying range of eclectic buildings, and a new feeling that change was not only inevitable, but constant.

Perhaps most important of all, the students were different—they came from farther afield, they applied in larger numbers, and they began to reflect the wider world, in all of its magnificent diversity. The faculty more than kept up. As a result, the university, already distinguished, grew into something very special. Its reputation rose as measured by conventional means, such as incoming SAT scores and magazine rankings. But it evolved well past those overrated benchmarks into a university that was unlike the others—an Ivy League institution that gave students near-total freedom to design their academic experience, embraced teaching to an unusual degree, and celebrated its natural tendency toward heterodoxy. The result was a high level of student motivation and a half century and more of progress. Brown's historic virtues—its tight-knit academic village, its teaching excellence, and its freedom of conscience—remained firmly in place. As its historic liabilities (poverty and insularity) began to recede, the result was an institution achieving new levels of excellence, fulfilling the worldly hopes of its founders, and at times, daring to think beyond the world. A pamphlet created for the 1964 bicentennial brimmed with the jangly optimism of the mid-sixties, promising that "Brown's environment is getting better all the time." To a large extent, that cliché was true.

With growth, the pace of life quickened. Brown had always maintained a strong presence within its neighborhood, but now the circumference of the university's influence grew wider. A new curriculum eliminated most distribution requirements, attracting strong individuals to what had already been a place of some iconoclasm. But in fact, what made Brown thrive was not simply its freedom, but its focus, and the discipline with which first-rate minds attacked problems of relevance. To an impressive degree, Brown's scholars were achieving new kinds of usefulness and reputation, on the national stage as well as locally. Throughout the convulsions of the sixties and seventies, Brown grew in size and stature, but in the words of the old college song, it remained ever true to an older ideal.

In many ways, that ideal became the nation's in these years. Freedom of conscience impelled more and more Americans to speak out against internal injustices and inconsistencies in the 1950s and 1960s, and no movement was more convulsive than the seismic struggle for Civil Rights, led by a great Baptist preacher, albeit one with little connection to Rhode Island. Still, Martin Luther King Jr. came to Brown, along with many of the nation's other leaders, recognizing that Brown's traditions spoke to the nation at large. The ancient imperatives—to expand knowledge and fight orthodoxy—were very much in the air, although not always in ways that Brown's founders would have predicted.

In this respect, Brown was not unique—universities were on the front lines in the 1960s, demanding change and often getting more of it than they were prepared for. On campuses ranging from Ole Miss to Kent State, simmering tensions exploded into crises, with the government playing both helpful and harmful roles as the decade unfolded. To a surprising extent, students found themselves at the center of moral issues with profound consequences for the nation at large, from the Vietnam War, which touched their lives intimately, to wider questions relating to race, justice, and the definition of a good society. To their credit, they often had better answers—or at least better questions—than an older generation that had compromised some of its authority. It was inevitable that Brown undergraduates would seek to engage these urgent matters, and they did, with results that were less destructive than on other campuses, but no less profound. The university, in turn, reciprocated, and if the conversation became strained at times, it remained respectful for the most part.

NEW FRONTIERS

ONE REASON THAT CHANGE WAS COMING SO ABUNDANTLY was simply demographic. Between 1946 and 1964, the baby boom introduced 78.3 million new Americans, roughly the population of the entire United States in 1900 (76 million). Universities quickly swelled to greet these new prospects, fattened by a growing number of federal subsidies, especially in the so-called STEM disciplines, made urgent by the Cold War. In the wake of the Soviet Union's successful launch of Sputnik in 1957, enormous appropriations were set aside for universities to train scientists, particularly through the Defense Education Act of 1958.

Another reason for the exponential growth of universities was democratic. Following World War II (and the GI Bill, in particular), Americans from all backgrounds felt a rising sense that college was a realistic option and something close to a right. Brown University historian James T. Patterson titled his history of the period *Grand Expectations*, a phrase that well encapsulates the surge of optimism that followed victory in 1945 and the specific belief that those who had

Brown welcomes back veterans, 1947.

fought for their country deserved a chance to enter the economic mainstream. Predictably, the percentage of American youth matriculating went up strikingly. According to Patterson, 216,500 students received university degrees in 1940, and 497,000 received degrees in 1950, and "The total number of degree-seeking college and university students increased from 2.3 million in 1950 (14.2 percent of people aged 18 to 24) to 3.6 million (22.2 percent) in 1960," and to 7.9 million (32.1 percent) in 1970.[3] Nearly 500 veterans came to Brown, beginning in the fall of 1947, to attend an improvised Veterans College, and they performed with distinction, encouraged by President Wriston's strong support.[4]

The result of this growth, and the federal largesse that stimulated it, was a new intimacy between government and the academy, and a loose sense that what was good for the one was good for the other. Throughout Brown's history, the federal government in Washington had been a distant entity, brought vividly onto campus at moments of national emergency, but absent the rest of the time. Now, in the years after World War II, it became something larger and more immediate—

a lender of money, a shaper of new pathways, a measurer of standards, an enforcer of justice, and a recruiter into the vastness of government service. That would have many positive effects on Brown, always struggling to compete with the older Ivies for privilege and position; but as many young people began to question the purpose of national policy in the 1960s, Brown's nearness to the government would also bring some cause for self-reflection. Like Harvard and Yale, Brown had a cozy relationship with the Central Intelligence Agency in the 1950s and 1960s.[5] The full cost of this partnership was, like so many questions relating to the CIA, difficult to answer.

Amid all this growth, a young new president was appointed who embodied the ambitions of the postwar generation. Barnaby Keeney was only 41 when named president in 1955. A decorated war veteran, he had earned a doctorate in medieval history at Harvard, then came to Brown as an assistant professor, before ascending quickly through a series of deanships. He also continued to serve intermittently as a consultant for the CIA, including during his presidency, a form of dual loyalty that was common at the time.[6]

With pots of federal money available for expansion, and a surge of potential students, it was a flush time for all universities. Keeney surfed those waves with skill. Undergraduate enrollment rose from about 3,600 to 4,600, and the graduate school more than doubled, from about 400 to 1,100. The ranks of the faculty swelled from 496 to 911. Keeney raised more than $82 million, including large grants from the Ford Foundation. New programs were begun not only in science, but also in area studies of relevance to the Cold War, such as East Asia. Upon Keeney's retirement ten years later, a Providence reporter assessed what had been the "explosion" of growth that had taken place: "In a dozen different ways the University hurled itself upwards and outwards: more students and better students, more faculty and better faculty, more buildings and better buildings, new programs, new ideas, new money, and more money."[7]

That change was soon visible on campus. Despite the fact that Brown was landlocked within a tightly knit, well-defined zone of historic houses, the university expanded radially in nearly every direction.

To accommodate rising demand, it needed more of everything, beginning with beds. So in 1957, what is now called Keeney Quad opened, bringing six new dormitories. Manifest destiny continued as Keeney oversaw two significant acquisitions of real estate in 1955 and 1957. Seventeen miles away, in Bristol, the university acquired a lovely waterfront property on Mount Hope, the traditional encampment of the Wampanoag Indians, which gave Brown a new museum of native artifacts and a program in anthropology. Closer to home, Brown purchased a spectacular thirty-nine-acre green space in the middle of the East Side, the former poor farm known as the Dexter Asylum. The land was transformed into a handsome set of playing fields, long known as Aldrich-Dexter.[8] A hockey rink, which doubled as an enormous theater, Meehan Auditorium, opened in 1961. The Pembroke campus saw Morriss and Champlin residence halls added in 1960, and Emery and Woolley halls, with new dining facilities, in 1963. In a short span of years, a campus that had remained largely static atop College Hill had greatly enlarged its footprint.

Befitting the government's keen interest in funding the sciences, new science buildings began to spread like bacterial spores: the Hunter Laboratory of Psychology (1958), the Prince Engineering Laboratory (1962), the J. Walter Wilson Biology Laboratory (1962), Barus and Holley (1965), and the striking Center for Computation and Visualization, which was designed by Philip Johnson in 1961 at the height of IBM-inflected optimism about the technocratic future. Donated by Thomas J. Watson Jr., class of 1937, and his mother, the building was a monument of sorts to Thomas J. Watson Sr., whose number-crunching wizardry had done so much to accelerate the processing of information. Its austere Greek lines suggest some kinship with the past, but the main purpose of the building in 1961 was to house the IBM 7070 computer, then allegedly the largest on the East Coast. In other words, at the zenith of the Cold War, Brown had a larger computer than the Pentagon.[9]

For all of his eagerness to build temples to science, Keeney remained concerned about the parts of the university that were growing less quickly—the old-fashioned humanistic elements, traceable back to the Greeks, that had not been altered by Sputnik's overflight. Accordingly, he spoke out volubly on the special character of the humanities, and eventually he was drafted into service on their behalf. In 1963, he chaired a National Commission on the Humanities, which called for a renewed emphasis on humanistic instruction to offset a growing imbalance with science and recommended the creation of a "National Humanities Foundation."[10]

Keeney also tried to put his thumb on the scale in another way. He was concerned that schools were educating increasingly homogeneous students; as he put it, bluntly, "At college age, you can tell who is best at taking tests and going to school, but you can't tell who the best people are. That worries the hell out of me." Accordingly, he exercised a president's prerogative to make sure that places were reserved for applicants with "outstanding characteristics," not always measurable by scholastic aptitude tests and IBM punch cards. As much as 10 percent of an incoming male class might be populated by these unclassifiable students, who ordinarily would not have had high enough grades to enter an Ivy League school; they referred to themselves as "Tom Sawyers."[11]

They gave Brown character. But just as the original Tom Sawyer had lacked racial sensitivity (Huckleberry Finn would have been a better model), so Brown was sluggish when it came to extending these broad principles to minority groups. Accounts from the era portray a campus in which African Americans came in very small numbers and suffered from ostracism and even intimidation. In 1949, J. Saunders Redding, class of 1928, became a visiting professor, and in so doing, the first African American professor at an Ivy League institution.[12] When Augustus White III, class of 1957, arrived at Brown in 1953, he was one of only five African Americans in his class. Overcoming considerable adversity, he would enjoy a stellar career at Brown, breaking the color line in the fraternities and going on to serve as a trustee and fellow; he had a long and distinguished career as an orthopedic surgeon.[13] But despite his success, racial progress was glacial in the 1950s.[14]

As Keeney was making his mark on Brown, another young man of the World War II generation was rising quickly and speaking for

Senator John F. Kennedy in Providence, November 1960.

his cohort on the national stage. John F. Kennedy spoke in Providence on the day before his election in November 1960, and by a special providence, Martin Luther King Jr. was on campus that week, giving separate speeches on integration at home and globalization abroad.[15] It was an electric time, and King noted that the world was poised at that moment between "the dying old and the emerging new." When it became clear that Kennedy had won a razor-thin election, King gave a press conference in Faunce House, expressing his hopes for the new administration and noting Kennedy's religion as an encouraging sign. King called it "a great victory for tolerance in the nation," a sound bite that seemed tailor-made for Brown and the Baptist inheritance.[16]

Sometimes together, sometimes in opposition, Kennedy and King would go far to define the new frontiers of the 1960s, including many that were inconceivable to Kennedy when he coined the phrase "New Frontier." Similarly, Keeney's many innovations at Brown would continue to bear fruit, long after his departure in 1966, including in ways that he likely would have found bewildering. If these were thrilling years for undergraduates, thrust into the forefront of a widening platform of debate, they were that much more difficult for the nation's college presidents. As the baby boom generation matriculated in ever-larger numbers, they brought a questioning spirit that undermined many of the assumptions that universities, like so many American institutions, rested a bit too comfortably upon.

Keeney was adroit in recognizing this spirit, and to a degree, encouraging it. He himself gave speeches on the history of human rights, in keeping with his interest in humanistic discourse. In 1962, he reported to the Corporation that students were increasingly questioning authority—following an older Brown tradition, but surprising in a society that revered hierarchy more than it cared to admit. A year later, he pointed out some of the dangers of Brown's growing codependency with the federal government, including the administrative burden of asking for and then receiving grants on a permanent basis, and the difficulty of protecting Brown's interests when those of the government were also involved.[17]

This included a specific encumbrance, the obligation to swear loyalty to the government in order to receive its pots of money. An ongoing debate, carried out in *Brown Daily Herald* editorials as well as President Keeney's reports, probed the difficulty of this obligation and the financial cost of rejecting it.[18] President Eisenhower himself had opened up the "military-industrial complex" to criticism, in his farewell address, delivered five days after Brown's Center for Computation was inaugurated.

But as the years flew by, Keeney, too, was vulnerable to the rising skepticism of the young, and his long affiliation with the CIA would certainly have created problems for him if he had overstayed his time in office. He did not: the creation of a new National Endowment for the Humanities in 1965, after a bill proposed by Senator Claiborne Pell of Rhode Island, created an opportunity for Keeney to bring his talents to Washington, and he was spared the difficulty of presiding over Brown during the late 1960s.[19]

Of course, much of the change that appears rapid in retrospect was incremental at the time. If an anthropologist had wandered onto the Brown campus at any moment in the late 1950s or early 1960s, he or she would have encountered a habitat much like the other elite universities of the time, with a social system that revolved around fraternities, anemic racial diversity, considerable sexism, and a high degree of conformity among both men and women. To be sure, this calm could be shattered by the occasional iconoclast—Robert Edward Turner III, for example, who blazed an incandescent path through Brown for several years in the late fifties, acting the part of an unreconstructed Southerner with flair. According to a classmate, he showed up at Brown as "a strange mixture of states-rights revisionist, rebel, war lover, Dixiecrat and humanitarian." He shot his .22 rifle toward the Green from his window in Maxcy Hall, denounced most of the faculty, and adopted a few theatrically far-right positions. Perhaps inevitably, he was drawn to the classics professor John Rowe Workman, a specialist in the history of disaster, but also a gifted teacher who believed that "the real humanist will always go out of his way to be different." Workman recalled, with understatement, that Turner "was superb in bringing out argumentative tendencies in other students."[20]

After testing the authorities in a number of ways (including his father, who was "horrified" at his decision to major in classics), Turner was thrown out for a minor parietal violation. Decades later, Ted Turner would emerge as a gifted sailor, a visionary of the cable television industry, and a surprisingly left-of-center philanthropist, dedicated to environmental stewardship.[21]

In fact, an anthropologist *did* come to Brown—the most famous of them all, Margaret Mead, in 1959. Deeply conversant in the sexual practices of premodern peoples, she might have found much to study at

Ted Turner in the Coast Guard, following his colorful career at Brown.

Brown and Pembroke, particularly as the old walls separating the sexes were beginning to crumble. But instead, she spoke of social justice, in a language that would soon become common on the Brown campus: "What we need is some sort of ethical rationing of our time and our resources for an uneasy peacetime—where the rich countries, the Haves, and the Have-Nots, work closer together, for the same goals—a world which will be free from want and free from fear, and ruled by law."[22]

Those questions were asked with a growing frequency in the 1960s, and to an impressive degree, they were being asked by the students themselves, impatient for change. As Martin Luther King Jr. had said, during his visit to Brown in November 1960, "there is no greater tragedy than to live in a monologue rather than a dialogue."[23] The deeply American problem of racial inequality was being examined with a new insistency, and in the early 1960s Brown students distinguished themselves with their courage, agitating for racial progress long before the Civil Rights Act of 1964 and the Voting Rights Act of 1965. It was clearly a subject of interest to the *Brown Daily Herald* and *Pembroke Record*. In May 1964, a Pembroke student and a graduate student were arrested in Florida for participating in an interracial sit-in.[24] In October, the *Brown Daily Herald* sent reporters to Mississippi for a full month to report from the front lines of the Civil Rights movement.[25] Brown's fraternities were caught uneasily in their own struggle to deepen civil rights—protesting against national boards that refused to approve their desire to integrate more quickly, while appearing slow to change on a campus that was growing impatient with the old mores. On this issue, as on so many, it was becoming impossible to stand on the sidelines. Not all enjoyed the new inquisitive spirit—to some, it felt like the Inquisition. Dwight D. Eisenhower decried the young in the same language a Congregational elder might have used in 1764 to describe the Baptists, as lacking respect for tradition, and for general "laxness in dress, appearance and thinking."[26] But at Brown, to be inquisitive *was* to respect tradition.

HOLBROOKE

FROM AN UNLIKELY SOURCE OF DISSENT—Scarsdale, New York—came an undergraduate who embodied the questioning spirit animating Brown undergraduates at the dawn of the new decade. Later in life, Richard Holbrooke, class of 1962, might have become Brown's fifth secretary of state, if fate had dealt him a slightly different hand. As an undergraduate, he joined the staff of the *Brown Daily Herald* at a time when it was beginning to report stories and express opinions more assertively. His restless ambition led him naturally to the editor's chair, and from that perspective, every question was worth asking.

Brown was the smallest college in the country to have a daily, yet Holbrooke was not one to be disturbed by the modesty of the opportunity. Instead, he filled the chair with gusto. "I spent a lot more time here than I did in my classes," he remembered, touring the *Brown Daily Herald* office in a return visit in 2007. He often proclaimed his favorite poem to be Matthew Arnold's "The Buried Life," including its line about "the longing to inquire"—although his memorial volume cites several different favorite poems, perhaps proving the point.[27] Holbrooke would spend much of his career living out the mantra of the 1960s to "question authority." At the *Herald*, he chose an unlikely interview to make his first splash. In June 1959, he went across country to Palo Alto in order to interview Alexander Kerensky, the seventy-eight-year-old former revolutionary who led Russia for 110 days in 1917, at the beginning of the Russian Revolution. There was still plenty of life in Kerensky, and they spent much of their time singing boisterous songs.[28]

Holbrooke being Holbrooke.

In December 1960, Holbrooke became editor in chief, just in time to follow JFK's New Frontier. Holbrooke brought some of its restless feeling into the newsroom, questioning decisions made in University Hall, and publishing the work of Pembroke writers in what had largely been a male forum. Those were heady days, with crises coming in quick succession, both domestically and abroad. Holbrooke paid close attention to the civil rights movement, and in February 1961, he secured a scoop when he published a detailed look at the Black Muslims (or Nation of Islam), written by a reporter, Katherine Pierce.[29] The Black Muslims had recently invaded the United Nations Security Council to protest the murder of Patrice Lumumba, and Holbrooke (a future ambassador to the United Nations) gave considerable space to the story. One thing led to another, and a rising star of the Black Muslims, Malcolm X, expressed his desire to come and speak to an audience at Brown University. Holbrooke extended an invitation, and the controversial minister appeared on campus on May 11, 1961. He spoke to a rapt crowd of 750 in Sayles, and near the end of his remarks, offered to debate Martin Luther King Jr., if he would come to Brown.[30] "The university went crazy," Holbrooke recalled with a smile, remembering the event as he began an Ogden lecture in 1997.[31] A recording of Malcom X speaking recently surfaced, and it still crackles with electricity. In defending an oft-maligned religion whose freedom of worship was guaranteed by the Constitution, Malcolm X sounded much like a member of Brown's original Baptist cohort.[32]

Holbrooke used the *Herald* to advance his own ambitions as well. In the spring of 1960, after securing employment as a stringer with the *New York Times*, he blustered his way into a Paris summit meeting between President Eisenhower and Nikita Khrushchev. That summit meeting went disastrously, but Holbrooke had acquired a taste for statecraft. He made his first visit to the U.S. Department of State while on spring break from Brown, in 1961, and after graduation, failing to find work with the *Times*, he joined the foreign service. A year later, he was sent to a distant outpost called Vietnam, a place so far away that even he did not know where it was, except that he knew it was "someplace in Southeast Asia."[33]

Just as S. J. Perelman had taken a worldview from his Brown experience and applied it to the world at large, so too Holbrooke carried the traits he had sharpened at Brown to his remote posting. Vietnam proved an excellent classroom, particularly for learning skepticism of official pronouncements, a subject in which he soon had an advanced degree. But he loved the foreign service, earning quick recognition for his drive and his command of language.[34] One of his early essays advocated an enormous overhaul of the Department of State, calling for a secretary of state who "is willing to upset a few established applecarts along the way," and one suspects Holbrooke would have been quite willing to serve if asked.[35]

1964

Brown's bicentennial came at a time of considerable distraction. Once again, the United States was at war—in August, the Tonkin Gulf Resolution escalated American military involvement in Vietnam, and increasingly it began to feel like the United States was at war with itself. Domestic unrest was disturbing the peace in Harlem, Philadelphia, and Rochester, where riots broke out calling attention to the racial divides that undermined American claims of equal opportunity. That had an immediate effect on college campuses, just beginning to become flash points for expressions of discontent in their own way. The two causes often overlapped—at the University of California, students who had worked on the "Freedom Summer" in Mississippi led a "Free Speech Movement" that roiled the campus throughout the fall of 1964.[36]

At exactly the moment Berkeley was witnessing the first sparks of its own revolution, Brown was immersed in its bicentennial proceedings.[37] There were paeans to the past—the university's redoubtable senior fellow, John Nicholas Brown, delivered a learned discourse on the progress of the institution—but new winds were blowing on College Hill. Brown's campus was not as restive as Berkeley's in 1964, but it was changing quickly all the same. The campus welcomed a remarkable new building that still breathes the fresh air of modernity, when the John D. Rockefeller, Jr. Library was dedicated (that air has

The John D. Rockefeller, Jr. Library, under construction.

become even fresher since the library's many smoking rooms have been converted to new uses). David Rockefeller gave the principal speech that day, recalling what Brown had meant to his father, who had died only four years earlier. He also reflected on the strikingly different university that was coming into existence, with a global reach and a connectivity that his father could only dream about as an abstemious young Baptist:

> I am informed that the day is not far off when a student in Nigeria wanting to read a chapter in Brown's unusual collection of Chinese literature, or a Professor in Buenos Aires wanting to review the Lincolniana which my father presented to Brown, will be able to have the material flashed to him by novel television techniques or other data-processing equipment. There will be a time when the a great network of cooperation and technology will make the entire university library system of this country the common property of a transcontinental student body.[38]

A variety of other speakers were induced to appear at the campus as well, including, for the first time since George Washington,

Barnaby Keeney, center, escorts President Lyndon Johnson and Lady Bird Johnson.

a president of the United States. On September 28, Lyndon Johnson flew to Rhode Island to give the culminating address of Brown's celebratory observance, to a large crowd of 4,700 people gathered in Meehan Auditorium. To their frustration, President Johnson was a hundred minutes late for his speech—in high election season, he could not resist the temptation to pause and press the flesh, and it was estimated that he saw 150,000 Rhode Islanders during the eight-mile drive from the airport to Providence. Indeed, nearly everyone in Rhode Island who did *not* attend Brown University heard him en route. He gave fifteen impromptu speeches along the way and shook hands with all he could see, in full view of the surging crowds (this despite the fact the Warren Commission had just issued its report on the Kennedy assassination the day before). That was excessive— Rhode Island was in no danger of voting for Barry Goldwater, and the state had only four electoral votes to offer to the Great Society. But Johnson, whose derisive nickname was "Landslide," after barely winning an election early in his career, was taking no chances.

When Johnson finally arrived, he thanked every local pol he could think of and then launched into a long stem-winding oration, interrupted ten times by applause. He had some familiarity with the university (he had received an honorary degree in 1959), and he artfully turned Brown's story into a homily on why Americans should support "full freedom of conscience, the freedom to believe, and the spirit of free inquiry on which our American system stands." There were dutiful references to Roger Williams and Brown's charter, perfect for the occasion, and an expression of gratitude to "the little state of Rhode Island for the quality of the manhood it has produced," showing that even at the high tide of liberalism, the Great Society had some evolving to do on gender sensitivity. Near the end, Johnson made a little news when he called for the creation of what would become the National Endowment for the Humanities, soon to be headed by Brown's president, Barnaby Keeney. It was not Brown's brainchild, but still, the NEH was an impressive after-effect of the bicentennial.[39]

Brown was mostly rapturous after this visit from a president at the height of his powers. He had declared war on poverty in March, signed the great Civil Rights Act on July 2, and received the Democratic nomination by acclaim on August 26. On September 3, Congress passed the Wilderness Act, which set aside 9.14 million acres of forests.[40] Johnson was heading for one of the great landslides of American history. But ever true to its creed, the *Brown Daily Herald* chided LBJ for his lateness and general corniness. An editorial published two days later pulled no punches, calling the speech "a venture in triviality" that insulted the intelligence of the audience.[41] The last gibe may have been the harshest: "Maybe we should have had Dean Rusk after all" (a reference to the none-too-scintillating secretary of state). Several months later, the president lived up to his reputation for sensitivity to press criticism when he met a Pembroke student in a White House receiving line and asked her why the *Brown Daily Herald* was being so hard on him.[42]

That was a small foretaste of what the rest of the 1960s had in store. Within five years, LBJ would no longer be president, and the biggest crowds at Meehan Auditorium would be for Janis Joplin, who headlined Brown Spring Weekend on April 26, 1969.[43] At commencement a few weeks later in the same auditorium, a mass of undergraduates would turn their backs in protest over an honorary degree given to Henry Kissinger—because of the war that Lyndon Johnson was accelerating at almost the exact moment he came to Providence. His press criticism would expand quite a bit beyond the *Herald*, into a nonstop torrent of disapproval for a president whose extravagant promises of a Great Society and a victory in Vietnam were undeliverable. But for a brief and glorious moment in 1964, a president brought his traveling road show to Brown University and conflated its story with the nation's.

PAINT IT BROWN: THE SIXTIES, CONTINUED

In retrospect, that sun-dappled day marked a high-water mark of sorts, for a kind of unquestioning faith in the federal government that would prove difficult to sustain across the 1960s. One of the many paradoxes of that tumultuous decade is that universities had never done better—they were swollen with funding and students and new buildings—but as they tied their destiny to that of the federal government, they unwittingly invited an argument about America's future that grew bitter at times, and even violent.[44] That argument took place on campuses across America. In 1962, the Port Huron Statement, a manifesto for much of the tumult to follow, called upon universities to embrace their role as agents of change and to resist the temptation to divert knowledge toward militaristic ends. Throughout the long decade to come, campuses became inadvertent battlegrounds for one national crisis after another.[45]

A half century later, that furor has not entirely subsided. A form of anti-intellectual conservatism began around the same time— Ronald Reagan's rise coincided with his strong response to the "intellectual elite" protesting at Berkeley, and Newt Gingrich would later cite 1965 as the precise moment that a "culture of irresponsibility" seeped into American culture. The memory of the 1960s continues to drive a partisan wedge into politics to this day.[46]

Many would dispute Gingrich's choice of words, but they would agree that Brown, like so many universities, was changing rapidly and

grappling with thorny issues in the 1960s. As Brown entered its third
century, it was clear that the old hierarchies were less dominant, and
that a great deal of change was coming from the bottom up. Brown
professor James Patterson has called 1965 a "hinge" of history—a year
that attitudes began to change and young Americans began to question the assumptions of an older generation they increasingly regarded
as out of touch. At Brown, it was easy to detect signs of both rising
prosperity and a new spirit of critical inquiry, inside and outside the
classroom, rising just as quickly. It seemed like a new building went
up every year, and admissions statistics were rising as well: the *Brown
Alumni Monthly* reported in May 1965 that applications had gone up
30 percent in two years. Graduate students were coming in much
larger numbers—there would be 1,450 in 1968, up from 350 in 1945.[47]
To accommodate them, a futuristic Graduate Center was built and
dedicated in October 1968.[48]

But inevitably some deconstruction accompanied all that construction, and a rising tide of skepticism, a refusal to accept the platitudes of
America's leaders as the nation sank ever deeper into the quagmire of
Vietnam. It was not entirely surprising that dissent would emerge at a
university that had valued freedom of conscience so highly since its
founding. In the early sixties, controversies had erupted over matters
relating to personal freedoms on campus, such as the prescription of
birth control pills, and curfews, and parietal rules.[49] But slowly and
surely, dissent grew, fanned by student outrage over a wide range of
deeper problems that were not exactly new, but felt newly urgent, including the enduring legacy of racism and poverty in the United States,
and the obvious dissembling of the executive branch on other matters.

Without too much difficulty, that unblinking gaze was soon
transferred to the university itself, which was deriving financial support from the government and investing in a variety of corporations
that were doing business with the military. It did not take acute detective work to see that the Brown campus was not nearly as diverse
as its bicentennial rhetoric claimed. To be fair, that charge could
be leveled at all of the Ivy League colleges, still languishing in
Eisenhower-era pallor. But as Brown continued to grow at an

impressive clip, it was all the more important that its growth be inclusive. The times demanded it; Brown's democratic ethos demanded it; and more than ever before, the students demanded it. They understood that they too were stakeholders, and their arguments for equal opportunity were also about demanding more power for themselves, in a world rapidly flattening before the demographic assault of the young. In a 1967 editorial, the *Brown Daily Herald* complained that students felt left out and wanted nothing more than "intellectual honesty, emotional sincerity and mutual concern"—not far from what the Baptists were hoping to find in 1764.[50]

Universities, for all of their appeal to youth, were in many ways resistant to change and clung to something much older than American democracy, a cult of learning that was as redolent of the Middle Ages as it was of the Enlightenment and its aftermath. To this day, there are flickers of the medieval history that undergirds even the most progressive university—the caps and gowns, the snatches of Latin at commencement, the Masters of Arts and Doctors of Philosophy taking pride of place before the younger initiates in the commencement procession. But in the 1960s, as students demanded a role in shaping their rules and education, it was all the more important to respect transparency, and to align university priorities with those of a new generation, impatient for change. Feeling the power of their generational might, the students began to act with an irrepressible energy never seen before. To their surprise, they discovered that they wielded real power. In early 1968, college students—including Brown students—swarmed into New Hampshire to work for a presidential candidate of their own, Senator Eugene McCarthy of Minnesota, and a deflated Lyndon Johnson decided soon after to walk away from his office, a shadow of the eminence who had entered Providence like Marcus Aurelius only four years earlier.

The cause of protest grew quickly, over issues that seemed small at first, but soon grew into a general refusal to toe the line, particularly regarding the war in Indochina. Campuses that had been proud to host military training in the two world wars now saw a different kind of combat in which students fought back against the authorities. There were flare-ups at Columbia University in 1968 and Harvard in 1969, when administrative buildings were occupied—and in the worst incident of them all, the National Guard killed four student protesters at Kent State University in Ohio, in 1970.

Brown was spared those extremes, but the times were volatile all the same. Any casual reader of the *Brown Daily Herald* and *Pembroke Record* issues of the middle and late sixties will instantly feel the energy crackling from the old pages, impassioned on every subject from coeducation to poverty to civil rights to music. Some conservative critics would later blame the pediatrician and writer Dr. Spock, saying that his gospel of tenderness had bred a generation of spoiled monsters. To be sure, some of it was rebellion for the sake of rebellion. Protest was in the air, and Brown, like so many universities, breathed it in. But much of it was rebellion for the very specific reason that older practices were unfair and undemocratic. A short walk around Providence could quickly confirm that many of the promises of the Great Society were far from being realized.

Many of the decade's most celebrated bards of nonconformity came to campus during those years, particularly for Brown Spring Weekend, an annual rite that began to attract well-known performers in the early 1960s. Bob Dylan played in 1964—barely: he was stopped trying to enter Wriston Quad without a pass. But he eventually found his way to the stage of Meehan Auditorium and thrilled the concertgoers. In keeping with the spirit of the time, he conducted a nonsensical interview with the *Herald* in which he mock-denounced folk singers as Communists and gave a number of enigmatic recommendations to would-be musicians, including eating frogs' legs.[51]

As the Vietnam War took its toll, the protests grew more serious. Brown students were quick to pick apart the sophistry of arguments made to placate them and asked hard questions about American foreign policy, racism, poverty, and the role of universities in addressing these problems. Many began to question admissions policies, which had permitted small numbers of African Americans to attend for decades, but had stopped far short of an aggressive commitment to inclusion. Others found it unconscionable that women were excluded from so many levers of power, both within and without the university. Their cause followed hard on the heels of civil rights, and sometimes dovetailed with it, as in 1964, when a small addition to the Civil Rights bill (intended to destroy its chances of passing) produced the unexpected result that women's rights were strengthened as well. Enlightenment came slowly—the official mascot for the 1964 Spring Weekend was a Brown Bear, equipped with a club, menacing a nearby female.[52] But once it came, it came inexorably.

Progress was also fitful on race, but one of the bicentennial year's more meaningful achievements was the creation of a new partnership with Tougaloo College, a historically black institution in Mississippi. As the Civil Rights Act of 1964 went into effect, Tougaloo's traditional sources of funding were drying up (the state of Mississippi tried to revoke its charter). But two Rhode Islanders served on the Tougaloo board and drew the matter to the attention of President Keeney.[53] The faculty voted unanimously to establish a formal cooperative agreement with Tougaloo in November 1964. Brown and Tougaloo began to seek grants together, to exchange students and faculty, and to arrange for Tougaloo seniors to spend a fifth year at Brown, and vice versa. Brown's chaplain, Charles Baldwin, gave particular attention to the cause of Tougaloo and even served as its interim president.[54] Fifty years later, the partnership is going strong.

Brown also began to pay more attention to its own underperformance, especially after the arrival of a young new president, Ray L. Heffner, in 1966. Heffner tried to lead in promising new directions (his inaugural address attacked homogeneity), but in most ways he was simply playing defense. Throughout his tenure, students pressured Brown to do more to address its anemic diversity and to step up its relationship with the depressed city encircling the campus. Black pride was noticeably on the rise, offering a way forward for a university that had never opened its doors quite as wide as it wanted the world to think. In April 1967, an Afro-American Society was founded on campus, and a year later, in April 1968, the first Black Arts Festival was held. In the same month, James Brown headlined Brown Spring Weekend, to ecstatic reviews, and a few days later, a new kind of

On December 5, 1968, 65 of Brown's 85 African American students walked off campus to protest the University's inadequate commitment to diversity.

course was announced, History 166, "Problems in American Negro History in the 19th and 20th Centuries." But these halting steps did not address the real issue at hand, and, in December 1968, most black students walked off campus and demanded that the university recruit more students of color. In response, Brown guaranteed 11 percent representation in each incoming class and $1.2 million in support.[55] Respect for African American culture deepened in other ways, as well. A program in Afro-American Studies was created, and new faculty members were hired to staff it.[56] These beginnings were modest, but they began to address an old injustice. Within four years the number of black students at Brown would rise from 85 to 417.[57]

As the national debate on race continued throughout the sixties, Brown entered it in another way as well. In 1967, after yet another series of race riots had roiled America's cities, President Johnson turned to a Brown alumnus, Governor Otto Kerner of Illinois (class of 1930), to head a commission investigating the causes of the riots. The so-called Kerner Report was issued on February 29, 1968, and was blunt in its criticism of systemic racism. "Our nation is moving toward two societies, one black, one white—separate and unequal." In the last weeks of his own life, Martin Luther King praised it as a "physician's warning of approaching death, with a prescription for life."[58]

After his 1960 visit, King returned to deliver a sermon in April 1967. He issued a blistering critique of the Vietnam War, along with an attack on poverty, and asked, "What does it profit a nation to gain the whole world and lose its soul?"[59] Only three weeks earlier, on April 4, he had turned against the war for the first time, at Riverside Church in New York City, the Gothic shrine to religious tolerance that John D. Rockefeller Jr. had built. Just after King's second visit to campus, the *Brown Daily Herald* published an editorial supporting his stance on Vietnam.[60]

That conflict, quickly metastasizing in Southeast Asia, was another issue driving a wedge between the students and their elders. If earlier generations of Brown students had joined eagerly in the fighting of wars, this one was different. It did not seem vital to American interests, it was doing precious little to advance democracy abroad, and it seemed to be weakening it at home as well, asking poor Americans to do most of the fighting. Many faculty members joined Brown's students in protesting the war; teach-ins and sit-ins and lectures argued against the unwinnable struggle, and the *Herald* freely offered advice on ways to avoid the draft. In the early stages of the war, any male student making "satisfactory progress" toward a degree could get a deferment. But students in lower grade ranges were more vulnerable, and those from poorer backgrounds even more so. A lottery system was instituted on December 1, 1969, but the feeling of injustice persisted.[61] Brown and Pembroke students organized a moratorium in protest. There is no such thing as a typical letter home from that time, but one student, trying to explain to her parents how personal and international politics were colliding, gave vent to a rage that was not always easy to articulate:

Dear Mother and Dad,

I'm sorry you people are not aware of the despair which seems to pervade this and many other college campuses. This despair goes beyond the lack of a Saturday night date or the scorn of a particular boy. It is a complete feeling of being helpless— seeing so much wrong and not knowing where to go. What good were all the hours of the Moratorium? The ghettoes in Providence are still there, the war is still there, air pollution is still there. The Lottery? Remember the Shirley Jackson Story? [62]

On campus, that disenchantment turned into a campaign to eliminate the ROTC program and ongoing criticism of the university's relationships with such war contractors as the Dow Chemical Company, responsible for the production of napalm and Agent Orange. There were many symbolic moments of disapproval, including student strikes and the public rejection of Henry Kissinger in 1969. The students met to discuss the issues, and marched, and held rallies everywhere they could—on the Green, in downtown Providence, on the State House lawn. They joined the great rallies in New York City and Washington in a determined effort to change the course of history. At the same time other Brown students answered the call in the traditional way and went to Vietnam in uniform. They served with valor as they had in so many earlier wars. [63]

Turmoil over Vietnam was only one of a set of external pressures adding to the overall sense of disequilibrium in the latter years of the decade. The cause of women's liberation was also gathering steam, in ways that touched on every question from housing to professional development (more Pembroke students were preparing for careers in law, medicine, and government) to the sexual revolution. The rise in women's empowerment led to serious questions about the viability of two coordinate colleges, male and female, when all might be united under one administration. Individually, any one of these pressures would have been difficult for Brown. Collectively, they marked the most serious set of challenges of the twentieth century—and perhaps the greatest since the British troops landed in Rhode Island in 1776. The challenges were not made easier by the fact that Brown was experiencing some disruption at the upper levels of its leadership. When he became president in 1966, Ray L. Heffner had promised that Brown would pursue "the spirit of free and disciplined inquiry."

There was plenty of inquiry, and considerable freedom, but increasingly less discipline. To be fair, these were perhaps the hardest years in which to preside in the history of American education.

Brown faced a particular conundrum. For generations, the existential problem that Brown presidents faced was how to raise enough funding to be competitive with Harvard and Yale. To attract the best students, Brown had to stay current in new disciplines, and top-of-the-line research facilities, libraries, dormitories, and athletic fields all cost money. Now, just as Brown was getting the federal grants and large gifts that had so often gone to the larger universities, it was being asked to answer accusations of institutional privilege. With financial aid, in particular, Brown did not have the same deep pockets that the larger Ivies did—but at the same time, its egalitarian traditions demanded that this problem be addressed with seriousness.

Heffner resigned after three years, but there was no student takeover of University Hall in the 1960s and no serious police action on campus.[64] Brown pursued genuine change in those years, responding to many of the students' demands and adapting the institution to the exigencies of the age. Throughout the decade, the university continued to teach and inspire as it always had, even in tumultuous times. That offered a measure of comfort, even as so many externalities looked different. To read the old ads in the *Brown Daily Herald*, it is remarkable to see how quickly fashion evolved from the early sixties, with its crew cuts and cardigans, to 1969, when a Thayer Street establishment was offering "big fat funky ties," "colorful bell

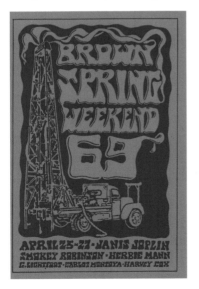

Brown Spring Weekend poster, 1969.

bottoms in all kinds of freaky fabrics," and "out of sight dresses for the chicks."[65]

Brown students never stopped expressing themselves, and that meant a lot of different selves. Self-expression was not hard to find within a youth culture that delighted in its extravagant nonconformity. On occasion, that self-expression could get quite loud. A plethora of stereo shops and a steady diet of FM radio ensured that most of the major rock and folk acts came through town (in 1966, WBRU received an FCC license to broadcast on FM and became an important outlet for independent music).[66] Remarkably, Jimi Hendrix played at the old Marvel Gymnasium, on March 8, 1968.[67]

But a quieter form of self-expression could also be found among the same kind of diligent students who had been attending Brown for two centuries. The most out-of-sight event of the decade was surely the lunar landing of July 20, 1969—and the head of NASA at the time was a Brown alumnus, Thomas O. Paine, class of 1942. In an interview, Paine gave his opinion that the Apollo mission represented a "triumph of the squares—meaning the guys with crew-cuts and slide rules who read the Bible and get things done."[68] That too was a part of the Brown story—and the university's eighteenth-century founders would have understood most of that statement, except for the strange part about short hair.

NEW CURRICULUM

ALL OF THOSE REVOLUTIONS were important and transformational. But the change that left the most enduring impact on student life at Brown was an effort to rethink the way that undergraduates approached their education. The "New Curriculum" was not entirely new—it drew on many older ideas, including several "new curricula" from years past. From its founding, Brown hoped to teach young people differently than the institutions that preceded it—that was the whole point. If Harvard and Yale were too regimented in the eighteenth century, then the Baptists would try a more creative approach.[69]

The result was a long tradition of educational innovation. Brown attracted gifted teachers from the beginning—one early graduate, William Williams of the class of 1769, opened a school at Wrentham and sent scores of his students back to Rhode Island College.[70] Throughout the nineteenth century, great educators came through Brown, as faculty members, as undergraduates who would go on to their own teaching careers, and as administrators. Horace Mann, of course, was nearly a household name, but the list of innovators included Francis Wayland, who became a nationally recognized expert on pedagogy. His "New Education" dismantled many of the older ideas of classical learning and tried, with incomplete results, to effect a newer approach. Alexander Meiklejohn founded the Experimental College at Wisconsin, which pioneered "classless" classes and highly individual attention well before the 1960s (his motto was "think or get out").[71]

In the boom years following World War II, Brown continued to press this advantage and tinkered with curricular reform. In the academic year 1953–54, a new set of classes known as "the IC Program" (for Identification and Criticism of Ideas) was created, designed to stimulate participation and free exchange. IC Classes were capped at twenty and taught around hexagonal tables, with a focus on great books in a range of disciplines.[72]

As the students began to question more and more assumptions in the middle of the 1960s, at Brown, more than any other college, they also wanted to rethink the way in which they were educated. Fittingly, a movement seeking greater independence began with students seizing the reins. In 1966, a group of seventy students, constituting itself as a GISP (Group Independent Study Program) began to agitate for a new approach to learning at Brown. The group was winnowed to twenty-five, and in 1968 it issued a "Draft of a Working Paper for Education at Brown." Its two principal authors were Ira Magaziner, class of 1969, and Elliot Maxwell, class of 1968.

Unlike so many revolutionary ideas of the 1960s, this one took root and endured. Perhaps that was because this revolution was uncharacteristically deliberate and engaged all members of the community in its process. Magaziner, Maxwell, and their fellow students, including Beverly Hodgson, first woman editor of the *Brown Daily Herald*, looked deeply at Brown's own history of curriculum reform. Magaziner later estimated that a million student-hours of preparation went into the reform effort.[73] A university committee was created to consider the report, and it offered an "Apologia" that tried to break down the searing problems of the times into the most elemental building blocks:

> The members of the Committee are keenly aware that we have been dealing with critical and complex issues in a time of change and stress. At several points in the discussions . . . we have had to reconcile differences of opinion with respect to our understanding of certain of the terms we have used. Words, we know, are often treacherous things, vehicles of confusion and contention, agents of subterfuge; and we are imprisoned by them, held in solitary confinement, for nothing is more intensely and stubbornly personal than language.[74]

Over several marathon faculty meetings in the first week of May 1969, a new philosophy of education was debated and ultimately endorsed by the faculty, affirming the importance of every student's active participation in shaping his or her education. All distribution requirements were eliminated, a Satisfactory/No Credit grading option was introduced to encourage student experimentation in new fields, special "modes of thought" classes for freshmen were created, and the number of classes required for graduation dropped to twenty-eight (later increased to thirty-two).[75]

It was quite a week; by the time it ended, President Heffner had resigned. But with these sweeping changes, Brown became a genuine leader in education reform, far more flexible than its peer institutions.[76] This dynamism would soon be reflected in a rising tide of popularity that essentially has never waned.[77] Jimi and Janis may have come and gone, along with the bell bottoms, the freaky fabrics, and the big, fat, funky ties—but the curricular reform movement of the late 1960s turned out to be anything but ephemeral and has become a deeply rooted component of Brown's identity.

The spirit of change lingered on in other ways. In the spring of 1970, student anger came to a boil over a number of politically charged issues. In one difficult week in May, campuses around the country exploded in anger when it was revealed that the Nixon administration—despite its vague promise to wind down the war—had invaded the neutral nation of Cambodia. They then erupted a second time when the four protesting students were killed by National Guardsmen at Kent State, on May 4. At Brown, the feeling was intense, and the students voted to strike in protest, 1,895 in favor, 884 against. The faculty endorsed the strike, 247–47, and supported it some more by voting to make final exams optional. Over the next two weeks, a self-proclaimed "free university" came into existence, surprisingly close to the Socratic ideal, with students and professors engaged in a running conversation about war, ethics, and justice. Seeing these groups of students, arguing with their bearded teachers while seated in the groves of academe, a casual passerby might have wondered if he or she was in ancient Greece. There was levity in the air—a list of student nominees for honorary degrees included Mickey

The student strike, May 1970.

Mantle, the Gabor sisters, and Ho Chi Minh. But there was also a dead seriousness, as undergraduates vented their rage at Nixon's heavy-handed tactics and a society whose values they did not recognize as their own. The chasm would only deepen over the next few years.[78]

TROUBLE AND RENEWAL

THANKS TO NEW ADMISSIONS POLICIES IN THE LATE 1960s, incoming classes began to reflect America's racial demographics somewhat more accurately, and Brown looked and felt different. That meant a student population that included more African Americans—one of the goals of student protests in the 1960s. Brown also began to attract Asian Americans in larger numbers, thanks to the changes in immigration law in the mid-sixties that had greatly expanded Asian immigration— one of the better legacies of the Great Society.[79] The university community was greatly enriched by this growing diversity, which dovetailed nicely with the implied openness of the New Curriculum. Brown also turned greener, as students began to express concern over pollution and the environment, especially after the first Earth Day on April 22, 1970.[80] In the wake of the 1969 Stonewall Riot in New York City, early stirrings of gay activism were felt on campus as well. In 1970, an organization called "Brown Gay Lib" began to host social events and defend the concerns of a minority that had surely been present nearly as long as the university itself. On December 9, 1970, Brown's gay liberation movement was officially sanctioned by the Cammarian Club; the first "Gay Liberation" dance was held May 22, 1971.[81]

In academic affairs, as well, things continued to move quickly in the wake of the New Curriculum. In the first year of its implementation, 1969–70, 97 percent of undergraduates opted to take their classes on a pass/fail option.[82] More important, they formed independent study groups and took chances in exploring new disciplines. The campus looked different, too—the Sciences Library was completed in the spring of 1969, and the List Art Building added a radically new look to College Hill when it was completed in 1971.[83]

But as a geologist might have observed, the substrata of the old Brown remained firmly in place. And some traditions gave way more easily than others. The novelist Thomas Mallon wrote perceptively, "Everywhere on campus one found solderings of the aborning and the obsolete, like the modern glass doors stuck into the Romanesque arch of Wilson Hall."[84] To be sure, the core elements of the campus experience remained the same, often subtly reminding students of the deeper history that enveloped them (noticing the candles burning in University Hall's windows on the night of the Kent State murders, Mallon thought they were for the students, and learned that they had first been lit in honor of another revolutionary figure, George Washington). In more than a few ways, history repeated itself: as they did in the 1770s, the revolutionaries on College Hill ran off pamphlets by the thousands (a "People's Print Shop" worked overtime in Sayles Hall), wore their hair long, and dreamed of ways to resist intrusive authority.[85]

Brown's beleaguered administration handled the crises, one after another, as best it could. In the particularly vexed year 1969–70, the university was led by an acting president, Merton Stoltz, a provost and economics professor. Then, a new president was found in Donald Hornig, a former Brown professor who had been at Princeton as well. Hornig's experience working in the development of atomic weaponry was not exactly reassuring to a student population whose nerves were on edge over militarism.

Hornig's first challenge was to balance the books. Having survived the party of the 1960s, Brown now had to survive the hangover—the austerity measures that Hornig deemed necessary to restore a sound fiscal footing. Brown's finances were not strong as it went through the convulsions of the sixties, which added to the difficulty of acceding to demands such as those for deeper financial aid. Hornig inherited a budget shortfall of $4.1 million, yet further budget cuts were highly unpopular on a campus straining to move forward.

Brown, which had never stopped growing through all the tumult, committed to another significant parcel of land in 1969, when it picked up eleven nearby acres from Bryant College.[86] Three years later, Brown grew some more when it launched a new version of a medical school, after a hiatus of nearly a century and a half. A Master of Medical Science program was begun in the 1960s, and it graduated its first class in 1969. A full medical degree program was launched in 1972 and graduated its first MDs in 1975. It would be difficult to think of a way in which the university has left a more positive impact on its city and state, bringing talented doctors to train and teach in Rhode Island, spinning off jobs in hospitals and research facilities, developing new technologies of healing, and generally helping the community to lead longer, healthier lives.[87]

In January 1970, the *Brown Daily Herald* ran a front page editorial, titled "Pembroke Dead at 78." Once again, students were leading the charge for reform, and a Pembroke Study Committee issued a draft report, calling for a merger of the two administrations. They wanted a new, unified college to be administered by two deans, a man and a woman, with gender parity throughout.

The official change took a year, and the two college administrations became one in the summer of 1971. For decades, undergraduates from Pembroke and the men's college had taken classes together and shared many of the same undergraduate experiences, while maintaining separate administrations, admissions, placement services, and dormitories. Now all of that would be united under one roof—including, for the first time, several coed dorms.[88] Older alumnae may have felt ambivalence, after having done so much, through considerable adversity, to build a distinguished institution and a campus. But that was offset by a recognition that women would, in principle, be entitled to the same services, rules, and opportunities as men, although real change took years to accomplish. Women's studies courses were initiated in the early 1970s, the Sarah Doyle Center was founded in 1975, and a series of internal reports and working groups would lead to the Pembroke Center for Teaching and Research on Women in 1981.[89] With the passage of Title IX in 1972, women athletes at Brown began to receive equal treatment, a process that would be complete only after Brown and the women athletes settled a Title IX lawsuit. That proved to be extraordinarily effective in stimulating decades of growth in women's sports.

Louise Lamphere and the Department of Anthropology, 1970–71.

Still, progress came fitfully, as became clear when Brown decided not to grant tenure to a female professor of anthropology, Louise Lamphere, who had been one of those leading the way forward in the development of classes in women's studies. Lamphere then did something that would have been unthinkable a decade earlier—she sued, on the grounds of sex discrimination. The consent decree that settled the case mandated specific timetables and goals for the hiring of women faculty members. By requiring written standards for tenure decisions, teaching evaluations, and nationwide searches (rather than relying on old boy networks), that decree contributed significantly to Brown's improvement in faculty quality. The results would soon be apparent: in 1976, 2.5 percent of tenured faculty members were women; by 1991 that figure had climbed to 16 percent, and junior faculty had risen to 43 percent female, from 8.5 percent in the same span. In 2008, Lamphere made a significant gift to Brown to endow a professorship in her name, within the Department of Anthropology and the Pembroke Center.[90]

Money issues also continued to plague Brown. In those years of lean budgets, compounded by a sagging national economy, unpopular decisions were almost inevitable. As the United States recovered from the shocks of an oil embargo and the "long national nightmare" of

Watergate, Brown wrestled with its own difficulties. Hornig announced a plan to reduce expenditures by $6 million, which included raised tuition, the removal of seventy-five faculty members, and a 4.5 percent reduction in financial aid. This was a lightning rod, especially since minority rates of admission and matriculation were in decline from their higher numbers a few years earlier.

Like some of his predecessors, Hornig did not always communicate effectively with a campus grown restive. Students and faculty were deeply conscious of the rights and causes they had fought for and secured a few years earlier, and they were in no mood to see them rolled back. The Watergate bombshells did not increase the reverence students felt toward authority figures, and student activism continued to flare up. Having avoided an occupation of University Hall in the late 1960s, when Columbia and Harvard were beset with troubles, Brown finally experienced its own version of a student takeover. On April 12, 1975, students voted 3,880–774 to strike and then boycotted classes for four days. On the morning of April 24, about 40 of them occupied University Hall, where they remained for thirty-eight hours.[91] They called themselves the "Third World Coalition," and they were supported by approximately 400 students outside the building. They issued twenty-one demands, most of which were accepted by the administration.[92]

These events took their toll, and Hornig resigned in 1976. The university turned again to Merton Stoltz, as acting president. Throughout that year, the United States celebrated its bicentennial, with help from Brown's gifted cadre of American historians and the deep holdings of the John Carter Brown Library.[93] That sense of the past, and of Brown's own institutional grandeur, offered much-needed ballast in a time of drift. But it was unclear how much longer the university could survive its own contradictions—venerable yet poor; inclusive but conflicted; dedicated to freedom of conscience, but capable of bureaucratic shortsightedness. To begin the world over again, as Thomas Paine hoped to do in 1776, may have struck some of Brown's leaders as an attractive proposition when they began to cast their net for a new president.

SWEARER

In 1977, Howard Swearer took the helm. He had no previous connection to Brown, but like Henry Wriston, he had presided over a small Midwestern college (Carleton) with distinction. As with Wriston, he brought a great deal of Midwestern common sense and something more than that—an unflappable confidence that Brown was going to solve its problems and fulfill a larger destiny. In retrospect, that is exactly what happened. The Swearer presidency was a tipping point, as Brown recovered from its perennial fiscal problems and the insecurities that attended them. With financial health came something Brown had not enjoyed in a long time—peace of mind. That in turn permitted a healthy ambition to unfold, and the university emerged as a great international institution of higher learning, no longer confined to a stony corner of New England. All of these encouraging trends built on earlier developments in the long history of the university. But they coalesced meaningfully between 1977 and 1988, guided by a steady hand.

Howard and Jan Swearer, escorted by the Brown Band.

Swearer's success emanated from some old-fashioned reasons. Under his leadership, budget decisions were made crisply and communicated effectively, and it helped immensely that he was an effective fund-raiser. Brown had ten balanced budgets between 1978 and 1987, and Swearer led a capital campaign that raised $180 million over five years. The endowment, which had been in decline, quadrupled. Gifts rose sevenfold. Research grants tripled.[94]

That made everything easier and created a wide field for Swearer's vision. He championed a large agenda of growth, particularly in new centers. A center for public service (later named the Swearer Center) offered undergraduates a meaningful opportunity to volunteer and work off-campus. The Pembroke Center officially opened in 1981, directing new research on gender through fellowships, research grants, and expanded offerings in the curriculum. Other new programs and centers studied alcohol addictions, environmental studies, hunger, and population problems. What is now the Watson Institute for International Studies gave Brown a significantly enhanced platform to convene and shape debates on public policy, particularly in the international realm (like Thomas J. Watson Jr., who served as ambassador to the Soviet Union from 1979–1981, Swearer was a Soviet specialist). The Watson Institute grew incrementally, from first steps in 1979, to the dedication of an Institute for International Studies in 1986 (former President Jimmy Carter spoke, along with his secretary of state, Cyrus Vance). In 1991, the Institute was renamed after its principal benefactor.

It helped, too, that Swearer was temperamentally well suited to preside over Brown. He enjoyed the challenges that students and faculty brought to him on a daily basis. As a young man, he had served in both the Army and the Peace Corps, and had little patience with those who sought disruption for the sake of disruption. But he was committed to protecting the reforms of the 1960s, and under his watch Brown continued to grow more diverse.[95] Women were faring better in the new Brown, especially after Swearer settled the Lamphere case in 1977, and were attending in ever-greater numbers. In 1970, women constituted 41 percent of American college students; by 1979, they were a majority.[96] At Brown, that important change began a year earlier;

Students occupy the John Carter Brown Library, 1985.

in 1978, 740 women and 660 men were admitted into the class of 1982 (though it was not until 1993 that the total number of women exceeded that of men, 3,090 to 2,902.[97]

A student takeover of the John Carter Brown Library in 1985 by the Third World Coalition was successfully resolved, and it led to a relocation of the Third World Center to Partridge Hall and a recommitment to the gains of 1968 and 1975. There were still inevitable points of disagreement; students demonstrated against apartheid and Reagan-era nuclear policies for much of the 1980s. But these demonstrations caused less disruption than they had in the 1960s, and students, faculty, and administrators generally enjoyed a mutually beneficial tolerance, confident that open-mindedness had become one of the defining characteristics of a very successful university.[98]

As these new programs were being launched, Brown continued to grow and, indeed, to flourish. A new wave of building took place in the 1980s, including a geology and chemistry building, an information technology center, and two new athletic buildings. Perhaps because of Swearer's confidence, or the New Curriculum, or perhaps simply because the time was right, the university also grew significantly more popular. In other words, Brown got hot. For as long as anyone could remember, it had occupied a lower rank in the Ivy League pecking order—excellent in its way, but unlikely to threaten Harvard or Yale in its admissions yield. In his memoir, Brown history professor Abbott Gleason put it succinctly when he remembered his childhood, and the traffic jams he and his family used to endure as they went through Providence on the way to somewhere more pleasant: "Providence was not a place where you went voluntarily, but, sometimes, passing through couldn't be avoided."[99]

But in the late 1970s and early 1980s, the university was generating a buzz, and stealing students away from the older Ivies. John F. Kennedy Jr. rejected Harvard to come to Brown, a fact much noticed at the time. When he later founded *George* magazine, it was to a large extent a Brown enterprise, its editorial ranks populated with talented alumni. That pattern repeated itself across the rapidly changing media landscape, as Brown alums popped up everywhere. They certainly populated the world of arts and letters, as writers (Marilynne Robinson, Edwidge Danticat, Rick Moody, Lois Lowry), actors (Laura Linney), musicians (Mary Chapin Carpenter), sportscasters (Chris Berman), cartoon characters (Otto, the bus driver on *The Simpsons*), people who never existed (Carrie Bradshaw and even Siri), and in one case, as a significant reshaper of the media universe. Ted Turner, after several different careers, launched CNN in 1980, ending what had been a network monopoly on news dating back to the dawn of television.

Otto.

Why did Brown catch on? For reasons, perhaps, that had always been there, but which were now more evident than ever, as if a curtain had been pulled back. The new students were attracted by Brown's size, its teaching excellence, and to no small extent, the New Curriculum, which continued to evolve even as it settled into comfortable middle age. Brown began to excel in all of the ways that were

The Griffins of *Family Guy* visit an imaginary Brown campus with ample parking.

quantifiable (the *U.S. News* annual report), and in quite a few that were not, including the quality of student life and the happiness of undergraduates. In retrospect, the seismic changes of the 1960s had settled well, as the campus offered a rich combination of new and old. Brown had expanded its campus in a way that greatly enlarged its ability to house and feed students, but had retained the intimacy of an academic village, its distances walkable, its teachers accessible, and its charm evident on nearly every corner.

It helped that Providence, too, was changing, beginning a self-proclaimed "Renaissance," a term that fit its Medici-like politics as well as its genuine rebirth. Stirred in no small part by the presence of the Rhode Island School of Design, a thriving cultural scene developed, including high-quality theater and a first-rate local music scene. A thousand flowers bloomed, in the form of small bands that sprang up in the factories and lofts that were as much a legacy of the Industrial Revolution as the School of Design itself. Some bands actually made it out. Talking Heads originated in Providence before taking their preppy funk to New York City. Brown Spring Weekend continued to attract high-end talent, including U2 in 1983 and Bob Dylan, in a return engagement, in 1997.[100]

Some of the feeling of this time and place is captured by Pulitzer Prizewinner Jeffrey Eugenides, class of 1982, in the opening pages of *The Marriage Plot*. The novel begins with a languorous look at College Hill on the morning of graduation, with the sun rising over "the smokestacks of the Narragansett Electric factory, rising like the sun on the Brown University seal emblazoned on all the pennants and banners draped up over campus, a sun with a sagacious face."[101] The central character has a classic Brown dilemma—how to be in love, while deconstructing love (she has been taking Semiotics).

As with the original Renaissance, the partnership between university and city-state was important to each. Brown's doctors worked in and taught through local hospitals. Brown's resurgence included an ever-accelerating medical program, expanding offerings in the sciences and attracting serious research funding. Brown also reached out to Providence and Rhode Island through new teaching programs. A national figure in education, Ted Sizer, came to Brown in 1983, and by advocating school reform from the bottom up, he fit congenially within a long Brown tradition. Brown's Continuing Education programs, built upon a tradition going back to Francis Wayland, opened up the campus to the wider community. A summer academy was launched in 1982 and, from modest beginnings, soon began to attract significant numbers of high school students, adult learners, people learning English as a second language, and others eager to join what became known as the Brown Learning Community. This community deepened Brown's scope and mission, including during emergencies (in the aftermath of Hurricane Katrina, sixty-three refugees from New Orleans institutions were invited to spend the semester).[102]

Brown also changed in subtle ways on campus, expanding the personal freedoms defined in the 1960s and the sense of the community's obligation to protect them. In February 1988, sexual orientation was added as a protected category for the university's non-discrimination policy, and Brown's LGBT population expressed itself more freely.

Brown also eagerly embraced the communications revolution that began with the advent of personal computing, and adapted adroitly to the teaching as well as the practice of computer science. In more and more ways, Brown felt connected.

In short, it felt as if Brown University had finally fulfilled its destiny. Applications continued to rise steeply. Talented new faculty members were easily recruited, complementing an established faculty that was growing more venerable with every cycle of national and international awards.[103] Historic liabilities—poverty and provinciality—receded in significance, and Rhode Island even began to attract people who were not required to live there. It is not possible to credit all of the responsible parties for Brown's surge in the late twentieth century, but any list ought to include Swearer's senior leadership team, including Sheila Blumstein; the indomitable trustee and later chancellor, Arte Joukowsky; beloved veteran faculty members, including Barrett Hazeltine; and a community of alumni and friends that had never relinquished its belief in Brown's mission. The idea of Brown had reached its fullest expression yet.

GOLDEN AGE:
GREGORIAN, SIMMONS, AND PAXSON

In 1988, Swearer stepped down after eleven transformative years that bestowed a sense that a Golden Age had begun, worthy of Marcus Aurelius. The university, energized, turned to the task of finding his successor and found one in an unexpected location. Vartan Gregorian was the president of the New York Public Library, not a university at all (although he had been provost and faculty member at the University of Pennsylvania). But while at the library, he had raised $327 million and had galvanized New York City's intellectual community around that institution. Gregorian's followers showed up in force to celebrate his arrival at Brown—Arthur Schlesinger Jr. gave a talk and Calvin Trillin wrote a poem—and it was clear that a new kind of luminary had arrived, nearly as exotic for his Manhattan friendships as his Armenian-Iranian heritage.[104]

Gregorian's inaugural address, in April 1989, came at a moment when some of the reforms of the 1960s were coming under fire. Arthur Schlesinger Jr., a liberal for most of his life, was then writing his book *The Disuniting of America*, which criticized the fragmentation of American learning from a conservative point of view. Grandiloquent theories about "the end of history" were becoming fashionable.[105] At the same time, a new generational energy was palpable around the world, from Berlin to Beijing, and everywhere there were computers (the World Wide Web was invented in the same year). Gregorian marveled at how far the information revolution had already extended—the world had 2,000 databases!

In his address, the new president spoke thoughtfully about how Brown would adapt to these trends. Presciently, he recognized the historic value of Brown's size and emphasized that he did not want the university to disappear into a "multiversity" of large graduate schools (although Brown grew significantly on his watch).[106]

Gregorian also built on the legacy of earlier presidents by encouraging student involvement in the wider community. In his inaugural, he promised to deepen Brown's efforts to fight poverty and the larger fragmentation of society. He strengthened a program of Howard

Vartan Gregorian, left, with Chancellor Artemis Joukowsky.

Swearer's, the Campus Compact, that organized service projects, and made Brown its headquarters. He launched a Leadership Alliance, joining the Ivy League universities and America's historically black colleges. He worked extensively with the local education community—a local school in Fox Point bears his name.[107]

Gregorian reached out to Rhode Island in another way, consonant with Brown's long-term vision. As the medical school grew, it deepened the range and quality of the university's interactions with the community. A welter of programs were combined to form HELP (Health and Education Leadership for Providence), joining together four private colleges and four hospitals to offer better treatment, education, and opportunity.[108] As with other recent presidents, Gregorian oversaw growth on campus as well.[109]

All of this building took money, of course, and here Gregorian's success was prodigious. The Campaign for the Rising Generation ultimately netted more than $500 million. By the end of his presidency, Brown's endowment had passed the $1 billion mark, a remarkable achievement for a university that had come close to the brink of bankruptcy in the early 1970s. There were eleven new departments, 275 new faculty members, and financial aid had doubled. That allowed Brown to continue, as it had under Swearer, implementing the promises of the 1960s. Applications soared, and Brown was now perennially listed highly in the guides compiled by *U.S. News* and other sources (all the more impressive for the fact that their rankings are weighted toward the research capacities of much larger universities).[110]

Gregorian also strengthened Brown in an intangible but important way. It says nowhere in Brown's charter that the purpose of the college is to increase a student's sense of contentment—and surely such a purpose is alien to many larger schools—but for several generations, pollsters have noticed that Brown students are unusually happy with their situation. In his memoir, Gregorian wrote, "I spent much effort building Brown as a community rather than treating it as a corporation."[111] With his accent and avuncular ways, Gregorian endeared himself to students, and if he was not exactly ursine, still, he resembled a bear enough to embody the university to thousands of undergraduates.

When he announced his resignation in 1997, to head the Carnegie Corporation of New York City, the *Brown Daily Herald* ran a headline, "Students Lament Life After Greg." A student commented, "he embodies Brown—right down to the goatee."[112]

The university had broken with tradition now so many times, in its new presidents, that there were few ways left to innovate. Non-Baptists and non-New Englanders were now the rule more than the exception, yet once again, the Corporation deviated from tradition. In fact, they did it twice in a row. The first time, it found E. Gordon Gee, the president of Ohio State University and a newcomer to private institutions. Two years later, he departed for Vanderbilt University, and after Sheila Blumstein served as interim president for a year, the Corporation offered the job to Ruth Simmons, the first African American and the first woman to lead the university. Indeed, she was the first African American woman to lead any Ivy League institution, and soon renewed the momentum that Swearer and Gregorian had begun.

Like previous Brown presidents, Simmons had served as the president of another college (Smith). But she was utterly unlike her predecessors in many other respects. She was raised in Houston's Fifth Ward, the youngest of twelve children born to sharecroppers Isaac and Fannie Stubblefield, and the great-great-granddaughter of slaves. She grew up with a reverence for the transformative power of education, having been helped by a kindergarten teacher named Ida Mae Henderson and by mentors at every level of her own steady rise, which included a scholarship to Dillard University and culminated in a PhD in Romance Languages from Harvard. She became a scholar of French literature and of Caribbean literature in particular—especially the work of Aimé Césaire. And she acquired deep administrative experience, having earned plaudits not only at Smith, but also at Princeton. In her first appearance on campus, she made her priorities clear— "It is the duty of education at every level to care about the opportunity for children of limited resources to establish an intimate relationship with ideas and high ideals." More sharply, she insisted that universities remain "the province of excellent minds and not just fat purses."[113]

Students celebrating Ruth Simmons, 2012.

Simmons quickly became immensely popular on campus, even iconic (her silkscreened image was a T-shirt favorite). She also turned out to be an impressive fundraiser. The "Boldly Brown" campaign netted $1.61 billion for the university, an amount that exceeded the entire American economy in Brown's early years. That funding allowed Brown not tain its intellectual ambitions, but to expand them, recruiting new faculty, keeping established faculty, and always deepening the university's commitment to financial aid and diversity. Brown also made its own statements about wealth, as it was accumulating it—such as the 2003 decision to divest from tobacco companies. As President Simmons said, "Universities—whether implicitly or otherwise—always teach values."[114]

Growth was particularly rapid in the sciences and, once again, Brown's footprint began to expand. Since 1770, the elevated location atop College Hill had worked well within the context of Providence, offering a lofty aerie for the intellectuals, while downtown bustled just below. But in the early years of the twenty-first century, that unofficial boundary dissolved. The Rhode Island School of Design began to expand its campus westward with dazzling effect (one could almost hear Talking Heads singing "Take Me to the River"). As Brown grew,

new land parcels near downtown beckoned, especially after the relocation of Interstate 195 freed up 19 acres of attractive real estate within
walking distance of Brown and Rhode Island Hospital. Some Brown
facilities—a laboratory for molecular medicine and offices for fundraising and tech support—had begun to move into what was then called the
Jewelry District. Accordingly, plans went into effect to create a 360-acre
Knowledge District, in a partnership with the city and state, local
hospitals, and the private sector. It promises to be as important to the
Brown of the future as any development of the last century.[115]

The timing was good for many reasons, including the rapid
growth of the medical school. Since its restart in 1972, the school had
grown quickly, becoming important to Rhode Island's economic as well
as physical health. In typical Brown fashion, it had developed in its own
way, permitting students to harmonize their medical education with
their other intellectual interests and to learn about alternative healing
alongside high technology. In 1984, the Program in Liberal Medical
Education introduced an eight-year plan that has become a much-
admired feature of Brown education. In October 2004, the Sidney Frank
Hall for Life Sciences opened, greatly expanding Brown's research
capacity. Three years later, the entire medical school was renamed after
a generous donor, Warren Alpert. In August 2011, the downtown
campus of the Warren Alpert Medical School was dedicated.

That was progress into the future; but Brown was also making
progress understanding the past. In 2003, Simmons convened a
Steering Committee on Slavery and Justice and asked for a full report
on the links between slavery and the university's founding. As it
turned out, they were extensive, surprising many who thought that
slavery was confined to the South or that its influence could never
reach an institution designed for the virtuous ends described in the
Brown charter. It took some courage to stare at these problems
unblinkingly. In the long run, the process proved cathartic, and the
candid way in which the university examined its own history won far
more admirers than detractors. In October 2006, the committee issued
the *Slavery and Justice Report*, a long and lucid look at the manifold
ways in which Brown's early history dovetailed with slavery. That

opened up an important new conversation on campus, led to informative exhibitions, and ultimately a new Center for the Study of Slavery and Justice. It also started a national conversation, as the *New Yorker* issued a long portrait of Simmons. Certainly, it helped that Brown's president was African American; but she was also an intellectual historian, a scholar who had worked on precisely the problem of how we reconcile ourselves to the past (Aimé Cesaire's poetry never stopped wrestling with the colonial legacy in the Caribbean). In an address at Touro Synagogue in Newport, in 2007, Simmons asserted "the importance of remembering" and continued:

> In wrestling with how to tell a difficult story from colonial times in a truthful yet uplifting way, we have learned that, even in the most difficult circumstances, the uncovering of older histories can recreate community, re-inspire fidelity to founding principles and embolden important new actions consistent with those ideals.[116]

The *Slavery and Justice Report* said to the world that Brown knew exactly where it had come from and where it was going, and it was lauded for its willingness to confront its past. Meanwhile Simmons had won nearly every possible honor: in 2001 she was selected as America's best college president by *Time* and in 2007 she was named one of the top leaders in the United States by *U.S. News and World Report*. In 2011, after accomplishing so much, Simmons announced that she would step down. The university turned to an old tradition and found its next president at Princeton University, where James Manning, Howard Swearer, and Ruth Simmons had all been trained.

A distinguished economist, Christina Paxson had served as the dean of the Woodrow Wilson School of Public and International Affairs. She had undertaken extensive research, with a particular focus on focus on international economic problems and on the relationship of economic factors to the health and welfare of children. Specifically, she had done deep work on the health impact of Hurricane Katrina in New Orleans, on the impact of AIDS on orphanhood in Africa, on the seasonal impact of weather on economic health in Thailand, and on the economics and demography of aging.

This concern for the vulnerable fit in seamlessly at a university with a highly refined social conscience. She demonstrated in her earliest remarks that she understood Brown—particularly noting the "constructive irreverence that makes every day interesting"— and urged students to reflect on the best ideals in the university's past. That included the DNA inherited from Roger Williams, the Baptists, and Brown's many defenders of human rights over the centuries. But she also praised the more recent legacy of the New Curriculum (now the Open Curriculum), emphasizing both its freedom and the responsibility it demands. And she reasserted that "diversity is far more than a legal concept, or a mathematical equation—but a profoundly ethical belief that our differences enlighten and enhance us."

Paxson elaborated in her inaugural address, proclaiming that "the major purpose of a university is to invest in the service of the common good: in scholarship that enlightens us; in discovery that helps us become healthier and more productive; and, perhaps most important, in the cultivation of creative and talented young people who will lead us." Unlike most economists, she eschewed what was immediately measurable, to probe Brown's particular strengths as an incubator of young imaginations. She defended the rights of students to take time to figure themselves out ("We are not in the business of producing widgets"), to expect the unexpected. Her speech offered a defense of the right to be different, a right that the university had certainly claimed throughout its history. She reasserted that Brown's purpose was "to invest in the long-term intellectual, creative and social capacity of human beings"— human beings who would not only survive in the world, but change it for the better. And she insisted that "the *status quo* can be, and must be, improved upon—including the *status quo* of the institution itself."

In short order, she was defining the Brown of the next generation. She emerged in 2013 as a defender of universities in general and the humanities in particular. She celebrated the opportunities of a world-class education—the research breakthroughs that happen because of research originally undertaken for a different purpose, or the interdisciplinary cross-fertilization that occurs naturally on a campus as interconnected as Brown's, leading to "engineers who love

Christina Paxson.

literature; historians who go on to medical school; and economics concentrators who study theater."[117] She praised the faculty who are there on the front lines, and cited her predecessor, Francis Wayland, on the miracle of good teaching.

Needless to say, while Paxson was sharpening the definition of Brown, the alumni were out in force, saying in their own way what their education had meant to them. There is likely no better argument for the success of Brown's approach to education than to point to the very long list of happy and successful graduates who emerged enlightened and inspired by it. This book was nearly finished when it was announced, in January 2014, that Janet Yellen, class of 1967, was confirmed as the chair of the Board of Governors of the Federal Reserve System. It was a historic announcement, obviously, for the simple fact that no woman had headed the national bank before. But it also brought her full circle to a discovery she made as an undergraduate. Although originally a philosophy concentrator, she was deeply affected by the teaching of two professors, George Borts and Herschel Grossman, who taught her that economics was "a systematic way of thinking," and that it had "real social impact." Under their tutelage, she had an epiphany of sorts, as she later explained to the *Brown Alumni Magazine*: "I remember sitting in Herschel Grossman's class and thinking, 'Gee, I didn't realize how much influence the Federal

Reserve has on the health of the economy. If I ever have a chance at public service, [a Fed post] would be a worthwhile thing to do.'"[118] Her ambition was realized, to put it mildly. And in her long prior career as an academic, and as a specialist on unemployment, she never lost her memory of what the classroom offered as a place to sharpen ideas. Remembering Professor Borts, she said, "George was both an inspired and an inspirational teacher, and what he taught me some forty years ago has stayed with me, deeply, for life."[119]

Two other alumni joined her in the inner councils of national and international policy making in 2014. Jim Yong Kim, class of 1982, as president of the World Bank, also wields one of the determinative voices on global economic policy. Like Janet Yellen, he came to that position from an unusually variegated background. A Korean immigrant (he came to the United States at the age of five), he transferred to Brown from the University of Iowa, majoring in biology before going on to earn an MD and a PhD in Anthropology from Harvard. He applied this interdisciplinary training, and the required political acumen, to the challenge of delivering health care more efficiently and less expen-

sively in the developing world, a challenge he worked on in a variety of positions in the academic world, government, and a non-governmental organization, Partners in Health. When Dartmouth College announced his selection as president in 2009, he became the first Asian American to lead an Ivy League university, and he was appointed to lead the World Bank in 2012.

Thomas Perez, class of 1983, also benefited from a wide range of experiences while at Brown. The child of Dominican immigrants, President Obama's

Janet Yellen, after being nominated by President Obama to become the Chair of the Federal Reserve, October 2013.

secretary of labor has credited Brown with his early training. He met a huge range of students from different backgrounds, majored in political science and international relations, and worked as a teaching assistant for Professor Edward Beiser's class on the politics of the legal system. As he later summarized it, "Tom Perez, Catholic boy from Buffalo. His mentor is Ed Beiser, Orthodox Jew from New York City . . . that's a microcosm of why Brown was so remarkable for me." Like so many Brown students, he also learned outside the classroom, including stints working in a warehouse and as a garbage collector. As the head of the Civil Rights Division of the Department of Justice, he fought voter-identification laws in South Carolina and Texas and challenges to immigrants in Alabama and Arizona, while defending Americans with disabilities, Muslims, and others in the margins.

Of course, no list of Brown and Pembroke alumni who found their way to usefulness and reputation can ever be completed. In 2014, the 250th year, four Brown alumni were running states, including Maggie Hassan, class of 1980, who won election as governor of New Hampshire after vowing to reverse cuts in education funding. Rhode Island's then governor, Lincoln D. Chafee, class of 1975, openly supported President Nixon as an undergraduate, only to emerge, while serving as a Republican in the U.S. Senate, as one of the most thoughtful critics of President George W. Bush. These alumni, so different from each other, all found a vital propulsion during their time at Brown, usually because of a mentor or a class that changed their way of thinking—or a decision they made to get into that class, because it fit into a course of study they had designed. In all of these ways, they are only a tiny microcosm of the whole.

The undergraduates, of course, were also defining Brown in their own way. In a university that places such a premium on their presence, and the full inclusion of every conceivable constituency, it would be churlish not to mention this perpetual source of renewable energy on campus. They become more astonishing every year and have already overcome one huge obstacle—the increasingly high hurdle of admission. The 1,537 members of the class of 2017 emerged from a pool of 28,919 applicants. They include 782 women and 755 men. Sixty

Brown at dawn.

percent came from public schools, and 46 percent receive need-based aid. A growing percentage—15 percent—come from abroad, and only 18 percent now come from New England, which would have shocked the founders.[120] On campus, they do their best to concentrate on what are now seventy-nine concentrations. That list is likely to grow.

With the future defined, the university community turned to the past in 2014, and to another anniversary moment. For nearly as long as Brown has existed, an acquaintance with its origins has offered a source of renewal and a chance to return to the original spring. It was a quest for intellectual honesty that led the first settler to the headwaters of Narragansett Bay, and a similar yearning, more than a century later, that caused the first teachers and students to trudge up this hill. A quarter of a millennium after the founding, it has become no easier to climb. But the reward keeps getting better, as the university continues to improve upon the founding principles and pursue usefulness and reputation in as many different ways as there are students. Today, what once was a small Baptist seminary has graduated students from 181 countries.[121] It is large enough to dazzle, and its tens of thousands of alumni seem to be everywhere, talking, acting, engaging. But it is also small enough to cohere and to give constant new life to the founding idea. What started in Rhode Island in 1764 has clearly never ended and never will.

AT THE TOP OF THE HILL, the weary traveler pauses again before the grandeur of the Van Wickle Gates to take it all in. The Brown seal is still there, of course, at the top of a bit of flamboyant ironwork. Its four open books may become anachronistic in the digital age, when the printed page is a relic of a slower era. Yet the fact that four books are open at the same time speaks to the attention-challenged of the twenty-first century.

The students are everywhere, darting from class to class, chattering happily. But there is continuity as well as chaos. Something about that sun still inspires hope, the word emblazoned in the college seal in Latin. On July 3, 1776, a significant day, John Adams wrote to his wife, Abigail, "Through all the Gloom I can see the Rays of ravishing Light and Glory, I can see that the End is more than worth all the Means."[122] A legend from the Constitutional Convention of 1787 records that Benjamin Franklin saw a similar sun, painted onto the back of George Washington's chair, and determined that "it is a rising, and not a setting sun."

Artist's conception of NASA's Curiosity rover on the surface of Mars.

The same might be said of Brown in 2014. It was an audacious attempt to stare into the sun, using the latest astronomical instrument, that helped to bring the university to this elevation. As noted earlier, the instrument can be found, not far away, in an alcove of the John Hay Library, where its brass continues to reflect the glint of the celestial orb it measured in 1769. A few buildings away, scientists still scan the skies, monitoring the progress of the rover Curiosity as it scuttles like a crab on the Martian surface. Elsewhere on campus, they turn their gaze earthward, at the fragile planet we cling to, for all our heavenly aspirations. They ponder old truths, handed down over the millennia, and they search for new ones, drawing upon deep wellsprings of creativity. In nearly every category of intellection, scholars test the boundaries of what is known, from the vastness of the cosmos to the tiny, irreducible building blocks of life itself. Brown's DNA is woven from these living strands, and the excited chatter of students suggests the ongoing relevance of the experiment begun a quarter of a millennium ago. For every answer found, there are more questions created and more answers yet to come. So it will always be. As Roger Williams wrote, at the dawn of Rhode Island, "a little *Key* may open a *Box*, where lies a

A key, centuries old, found in 2013 below the surface of the Quiet Green by students in an archaeology class.

bunch of *Keyes*."[123] Undoubtedly the search for knowledge will live on, which means that no history will ever be complete. Here's to 2064.

NOTES

EPIGRAPH: Marcus Aurelius, *Meditations*, Book 1.16. *Marcus Aurelius and His Times: The Transition from Paganism to Christianity* (Roslyn, NY: W. J. Black, 1945), 15–16; translation by George Long, revised by Classics Club editors. The father is his adoptive father, the emperor Antoninus Pius.

CHAPTER I. BROWN BEGINS

1. Roger Williams, in *A Key into the Language of America* (London: Gregory Dexter, 1643). Reprint, edited by Howard M. Chapin (Providence: Rhode Island and Providence Plantations Tercentenary Committee, 1936), 62, 94, 98, 178, 100.

2. It is worth noting that the heliocentric seal is not entirely consistent—in some places on campus, the sun's face includes a mouth, in other places just a nose and two eyes.

3. Stephen Hopkins, *The Rights of Colonies Examined* (1765; Providence: Rhode Island Bicentennial Foundation, 1974), 11, 28. Reprinted in London in 1766, the book was titled *The Grievances of the American Colonies Candidly Examined*.

4. *Slavery and Justice: Report of the Brown University Steering Committee on Slavery and Justice* (Providence, Brown University, 2006), 9, 10, 16. Stephen Hopkins was also a slave owner, though he later opposed slavery; ibid., 18; Craig Steven Wilder, *Ebony and Ivy: Race, Slavery and the Troubled History of America's Universities* (New York: Bloomsbury, 2013), 122. For more details on Rhode Island and the slave trade, see Jay Coughtry, *The Notorious Triangle: Rhode Island and the African Slave Trade, 1700–1807* (Philadelphia: Templeton University Press, 1981).

5. Bernard Bailyn, *Voyagers to the West: A Passage in the Peopling of America on the Eve of the Revolution* (New York: Knopf, 1986), 8.

6. James Hedges, *The Browns of Providence Plantations: Colonial Years* (Cambridge: Harvard University Press, 1952), 43.

7. Bailyn, *Voyagers to the West*, 10.

8. Gertrude Selwyn Kimball, *Providence in Colonial Times* (Boston: Houghton Mifflin, 1912), 21.

9. Ibid., 37.

10. See Ted Widmer, "1643: A Nearer Neighbor to the Indians," in eds. Greil Marcus and Werner Sollors, *A New Literary History of America* (Cambridge: Harvard University Press, 2009); Williams, *A Key into the Language of America*; John M. Barry, *Roger Williams and the Creation of the American Soul: Church, State and the Birth of Liberty* (New York: Viking, 2012).

11. William G. McLoughlin, *Rhode Island: A History* (1978; New York: W. W. Norton, 1986), 5. Although the Massachusetts Puritans often dismissed Rhode Island as culturally barren, Roger Williams was one of the best educated of the early English arrivals, with a Cambridge degree from Pembroke College and competence in seven languages—English, French, Latin, Greek, Dutch, Hebrew, and Narragansett.

12. Gordon Wood, *The Radicalism of the American Revolution* (New York: Knopf, 1992), 122.

13. Hopkins, *The Rights of Colonies Examined*, 5–6.

14. William G. McLoughlin, *Soul Liberty: The Baptists' Struggle in New England, 1630–1833* (Hanover, NH: University Press of New England, 1991), 20; Carl Bridenbaugh, *Fat Mutton and Liberty of Conscience: Society in Rhode Island, 1636–1690* (Providence: Brown University Press, 1974), 3. William Greene Roelker lists several entertaining insults to Rhode Island in "The Browns and Brown University," in *Essays Honoring Lawrence C. Wroth*, ed. Frederick R. Goff (Portland, ME: Anthoensen Press, 1951), 237.

15. Hedges, *The Browns of Providence Plantations: Colonial Years*, 49. See also McLoughlin, *Rhode Island: A History*, 68.

16. Wood, *Radicalism of the American Revolution*, 140.

17. *Slavery and Justice*, 16. See also Coughtry, *The Notorious Triangle*.

18. Wood, *Radicalism of the American Revolution*, 51; William Piersen, *Black Yankees: The Development of an Afro-American Subculture in Eighteenth-century New England* (Amherst: University of Massachusetts Press, 1988), 15, 22, 117–122; Lorenzo J. Greene, "Some Observations on the Black Regiment of Rhode Island in the American Revolution," *Journal of Negro History* 37 (April 1952). Christopher L. Pastore gives slightly different figures in *Between Land and Sea: The Atlantic Coast and the Transformation of New England* (Cambridge: Harvard University Press, 2014), 104.

19. Hedges, *The Browns of Providence Plantations: Colonial Years*, 39.

20. Records of Land and Property Held by Harvard University, 1643–1835 (Series 12, Narragansett Farm, Harvard University Archives).

21. Thomas Williams Bicknell, *The History of the State of Rhode Island and Providence Plantations*, 5 vols. (New York: American Historical Society, 1920), vol. 2, 657; Edwin S. Gaustad, *George Berkeley in America* (New Haven: Yale University Press, 1979), 32, 51; Garry Wills, *Mr. Jefferson's University* (Washington, DC: National Geographic, 2002), 46–47.

22. Antoinette F. Downing, *The Architectural Heritage of Newport, Rhode Island, 1640–1915* (Cambridge: Harvard University Press, 1952), 80–82.

23. The classic study remains Downing, *The Architectural Heritage of Newport*; on Harrison, see Carl Bridenbaugh, *Peter Harrison: First American Architect* (Chapel Hill: University of North Carolina Press, 1949). See also Pastore, *Between Land and Sea*, 175.

24. Wilder, *Ebony and Ivy*, 94; Stephen Hopkins, the future chancellor, met with Berkeley as well (95).

25. Kimball, *Providence in Colonial Times*, 26–27.

26. Lawrence C. Wroth, *The Colonial Printer* (1938; Charlottesville, VA: Dominion Books, 1964), 22–23. Mary Katherine Goddard, who became Maryland's official printer after moving to Baltimore, printed an important early copy of the Declaration of Independence.

27. Bridenbaugh, *Fat Mutton and Liberty of Conscience*, 65.

28. Reuben Aldridge Guild, *Life, Times, and Correspondence of James Manning, and the Early History of Brown University* (Boston: Gould and Lincoln, 1864), 143–150; Charles Rappleye, *Sons of Providence: The Brown Brothers, the Slave Trade, and the American Revolution* (New York: Simon and Schuster, 2006), 9. The full transcription of the 1792 marker is: "He was one of the original Proprietors of the Providence Purchase, having been exiled from Massachusetts for conscience sake." The Browns owned several vessels named *Rising Sun*; see Hedges, *The Browns of Providence Plantations: Colonial Years*, 299.

29. Hedges, *The Browns of Providence Plantations: Colonial Years*, 1.

30. Kimball, *Providence in Colonial Times*, 38–39; William B. Weeden, *Early Rhode Island: A Social History of the People* (New York: Grafton Press, 1910), 30–31.

31. Edwin A. Burlingame, *Plat of the Rhode Island College Property of 1770, and Plats of the Succeeding Brown University Properties in 1870, 1904 and 1938: Together with an Abridged History of These Properties* (Providence: The University, 1938).

32. Rappleye, *Sons of Providence*, 6.

33. Ibid., passim. Also helpful is William Greene Roelker, "The Browns of Brown University," *Brown Alumni Monthly*, December 1948, 3–8.

34. Ezra Stiles, who drafted the first version of the college charter, purchased a slave in 1756 and freed him in 1775; James Manning, the first college president, had two slaves early in his life, though he later helped Rhode Island pass a law for graduated emancipation in 1784. See James McLachlan, ed., *Princetonians, 1748–1768: A Biographical Dictionary* (Princeton: Princeton University Press, 1976), 393; Wilder, *Ebony and Ivy*, 121–22, and *Slavery and Justice*. Wilder praises Brown University (288) for its work in acknowledging its past.

35. Hedges, *The Browns of Providence Plantations: Colonial Years*, 9.

36. W. W. Keen, "The Early Years of Brown University (1764–1770) While Located in Warren, Rhode Island" (typescript, 1914, 150th Anniversary Files, Brown University Archives).

37. Edmund S. Morgan, *The Gentle Puritan: A Life of Ezra Stiles, 1727–1795* (New Haven: Yale University Press, 1962), 134.

38. Ibid., 151.

39. Ibid., 309–10, 451–52; Wilder, *Ebony and Ivy*, 121. After moving to Connecticut, Stiles would take a firmer stand on abolition.

40. Morgan gives the date as 1761 (*The Gentle Puritan*, 204). Carl Bridenbaugh gives it as 1759; Carl Bridenbaugh, "Newport's Graceful Gestures," *Brown University Monthly*, October 1964, 11–13.

41. Andrew Delbanco, *College: What It Was, and Should Be* (Princeton: Princeton University Press, 2012), 67.

42. Keen, "The Early Years of Brown University," 2; Reuben Guild, "Brown University," *New England Magazine*, January 1886, 4. Morgan Edwards was a fervent admirer of Roger Williams and a talented polemicist for Baptist causes. His *Materials for a History of the Baptists in Rhode Island* offers important background (manuscript, 1771, Rhode Island Historical Society). He includes some autobiographical information in *Materials for a History of the Baptists in Pennsylvania* (Philadelphia: Printed by Joseph Crukshank and Isaac Collins, 1770).

43. All historians of the Baptists owe a debt of gratitude to the late William G. McLoughlin, long a professor of history at Brown. Works of particular relevance include *Isaac Backus and the American Pietistic Tradition* (Boston: Little Brown, 1967); *New England Dissent, 1630–1833: The Baptists and the Separation of Church and State* (Cambridge: Harvard University Press, 1971; and *Soul Liberty*.

44. Kimball gives 1638, *Providence in Colonial Times*, 25–26; McLoughlin gives 1639, *Soul Liberty*, 16, 22.

45. Rappleye, *Sons of Providence*, 9; McLoughlin, *Soul Liberty*, 32.

46. McLoughlin, *New England Dissent*, 128–48.

47. William Warren Sweet, *The Baptists, 1783–1830; A Collection of Source Material* (New York: H. Holt and Company, 1931), 4; Norman H. Maring, *Baptists in New Jersey: A Study in Transition* (Valley Forge, PA: Judson Press, 1964), 14. In 1740, eleven of twenty-one Baptist Churches in New England were in Rhode Island.

48. See McLoughlin, *Isaac Backus and the American Pietistic Tradition*, x–xi.

49. McLoughlin, *Soul Liberty*, 6–7; McLoughlin, *New England Dissent*, 329–40.

50. Sweet, *The Baptists*, 10.

51. McLoughlin, *Isaac Backus and the American Pietistic Tradition*, 1.

52. Alan Heimert, *Religion and the American Mind: From the Great Awakening to the Revolution* (Cambridge: Harvard University Press, 1966), 165–166.

53. Wood, *Radicalism of the American Revolution*, 20–21.

54. Delbanco, *College: What It Was, Is, and Should Be*, 41.

55. Keen, "The Early Years of Brown University," 8.

56. Isaac Backus, undated letter after 1764, William G. McLoughlin, ed., *The Diary of Isaac Backus*, 3 vols. (Providence: Brown University Press, 1979), 2: 607.

57. Reuben Aldridge Guild, *Historical Sketch of Brown University* (Providence: Snow and Greene, 1858), 1.

58. Some Baptists were upset when Hopewell Academy was allowed to expire after the successful launch of Rhode Island College, calling it "the crime of 1767"; Maring, *Baptists in New Jersey*, 67.

59. McLoughlin, *New England Dissent*, 492; Keen, "The Early Years of Brown University," 2. On "Nothingarians," see Jurgen Herbst, *From Crisis to Crisis: American College Government, 1636–1819* (Cambridge: Harvard University Press, 1982), 123.

60. Maring, *Baptists in New Jersey*, 22.

61. Walter C. Bronson, *The History of Brown University, 1764–1914* (Providence: The University, 1914), 15.

62. For more on Newport's important contributions to the idea of Rhode Island College, see Bridenbaugh, "Newport's Graceful Gestures," 11–13, and Bicknell, *The History of the State of Rhode Island*, 2:663.

63. Bicknell, *The History of the State of Rhode Island*, 2:666.

64. The controversy stemming from the charter and its rewriting is covered extensively in the early sources, including a long appendix in Reuben Aldridge Guild, *History of Brown University, with Illustrative Documents* (Providence: Providence Press Company, 1867), 119–45. See in addition Reuben Aldridge Guild, *The Early History of Brown University, Including the Life, Times and Correspondence of President Manning, 1756–1791* (Providence:

Snow and Farnham, 1897), 510–51; Bronson, *The History of Brown University*, 493-507; Keen, "The Early Years of Brown University," 14–16; John Nicholas Brown, "The Story of Brown's Amazing Charter," *Brown Alumni Monthly*, April 1964, 7–9; and Bicknell, *The History of the State of Rhode Island*, 2:664.

65. McLoughlin says March 3, 1764, signed into law October 24, 1765 (*New England Dissent*, 494); Hedges confirms (*The Browns of Providence Plantations: Colonial Years*, 194).

66. The policy on Jewish admission was developed after a gift from a Jewish donor, Moses Linds of Charleston, South Carolina; see Bronson, *The History of Brown University*, 98; Guild, *The Early History of Brown University*, 150; Wilder, *Ebony and Ivy*, 158–59. One scholar speculated that Benjamin Benneau Simons of the class of 1796 may have been Jewish; Leon Hühner, "Jews in Connection with the Colleges of the Thirteen Original States Prior to 1800," *Publications of the American Jewish Historical Society* (1910), 114.

67. McLoughlin, *New England Dissent*, 500.

68. Backus describes the September 1765 meeting (Backus, *The Diary of Isaac Backus*, 2:606–7).

69. Edwards, *Materials for a History of the Baptists in Rhode Island*, 329.

70. Jeannette D. Black and William Greene Roelker, eds., *A Rhode Island Chaplain in the American Revolution: Letters of Ebenezer David to Nicholas Brown, 1775–1778* (Providence: Rhode Island Society of the Cincinnati, 1949), xvii; Keen, "The Early Years of Brown University," 41. Edwards described the church in its early days: "Its dimensions are 52 feet by 44, with pews, galleries, and a little turret, wherein is a bell, but the galleries are not finished." Gertrude Selwyn Kimball, *Pictures of Rhode Island in the Past, 1642–1833* (Providence: Preston and Rounds Company, 1900), 70.

71. "Library" in Mitchell, *Encyclopedia Brunoniana*.

72. Wilder, *Ebony and Ivy*, 158–59; *Slavery and Justice*, 19–20; Guild, *History of Brown University with Illustrative Documents*, 211-26.

73. Guild, *The Early History of Brown University*, 89.

74. Backus, *The Diary of Isaac Backus*, 2:727.

75. Ibid., 2:728.

76. Keen, "The Early Years of Brown University," 11; Jay Barry and Martha Mitchell, *A Tale of Two Centuries: A Warm and Richly Pictorial History of Brown University, 1764–1985* (Providence: Brown Alumni Monthly, 1985), 21.

77. Guild, *History of Brown University with Illustrative Documents*, 177–78. According to Guild, a conversation between a local official named Darius Sessions and Moses Brown was crucial in galvanizing the action of the Browns. For more background, see 175–210. The young Benjamin

Franklin called Harvard students "blockheads" in his fourth Silence Dogood letter; see Benjamin Franklin, *Writings* (New York: Library of America, 1987), 13.

78. Kimball, *Pictures of Rhode Island in the Past*, 56, 72.

79. Hedges, *The Browns of Providence Plantations: Colonial Years*, 6, 10.

80. Ibid., 15, 123. This iron would be useful during the American Revolution, when it was used for cannons.

81. Ibid., 197. A helpful source on Brown's history of land ownership is Burlingame, *Plat of the Rhode Island College Property*.

82. Hedges, *The Browns of Providence Plantation: Colonial Years*, 199.

83. Ibid., 195.

84. Donald Fleming, *Science and Technology in Providence, 1760–1914: An Essay in the History of Brown University in the Metropolitan Community* (Providence: Brown University, 1952), 13.

85. Ibid., 14–15.

86. Ibid., 19.

87. Guild, citing Manning, in his *Historical Sketch of Brown University*, calculated the amounts as £4,280 raised by Providence, £4,000 raised by Newport (125).

88. Backus, *The Diary of Isaac Backus*, 2:770.

89. Ibid., 2:761

90. For helpful maps and background, see Burlingame, *Plat of the Rhode Island College Property*. An interesting letter from Moses Brown to Francis Wayland, May 25, 1833, recounts in detail how the four Brown brothers took charge of the land and buildings; Guild, *The Early History of Brown University*, 137.

91. Roelker, "The Browns of Brown University," *Brown Alumni Monthly,* December 1948, 3–8; *Brown Alumni Monthly,* October 1971, 26–31; Edwards, *Materials for a History of the Baptists in Rhode Island*, 322. In 1797, one exuberant undergraduate referred to College Hill as an "adoreable Parnassian Seat." J. Tallmadge to William E. Green, January 31, 1797, in Robert Perkins Brown et al., *Memories of Brown: Traditions and Recollections Gathered from Many Sources* (Providence: Brown Alumni Magazine, 1909), 24.

92. Henry M. Wriston, *Wriston Speaking: A Selection of Addresses* (Providence: Brown University Press, 1957), 65. John Brown dispensed punch "with a liberal hand"; William MacDonald, "Address," in *Exercises Commemorating the Restoration of University Hall* (Providence: Standard Printing Company, 1905), 39. MacDonald says that the bricks came from Rehoboth and the stones from Pawtuxet and Cumberland.

93. Robert P. Emlen, "Slave Labor at the College Edifice: Building Brown University's University Hall in 1770," *Rhode Island History* 66, no. 2 (Summer 2008), 35–46; Lawrence C. Wroth, "The Construction of the College Edifice, 1770–1772" (typescript, Brown University Archives).

94. Guild, *The Early History of Brown University*, 143; Black and Roelker, *A Rhode Island Chaplain in the American Revolution*, xvii; Bronson, *The History of Brown University*, 54–55; Barry and Mitchell, *A Tale of Two Centuries*, 14. The old schoolhouse also was the site of early classes in anatomy for Brown's medical school in the early nineteenth century, and classes for tubercular children; see Robert A. Kesack, "The Old Brick School House (1769)" (Providence: Providence Preservation Society, 2013).

95. Kimball, *Providence in Colonial Times*, 353.

96. Ibid., 353–54.

97. Solomon Drowne, journal, in ed. Marion E. Brown, "Solomon Drowne, Student: His Papers and Journals, 1753–1774" (Brown University master's thesis, 1954), 38, 44.

98. Bronson, *The History of Brown University, 1764–1914*, 63.

99. J. Stanley Lemons, *The First Baptist Church in America* (Providence: Charitable Baptist Society, 1988), 34.

100. Nathanael Greene was awarded an honorary degree in 1776; Barry and Mitchell, *A Tale of Two Centuries*, 18.

101. Wriston, *Wriston Speaking*, 66–67.

102. Greene, "Some Observations on the Black Regiment of Rhode Island in the American Revolution," 149. Greene estimated that 225–250 served (165), but concluded that they were "forgotten by the ungrateful nation for which they had sacrificed so much to establish" (172).

103. David's moving letters to Nicholas Brown the elder are collected in Black and Roelker, *A Rhode Island Chaplain in the American Revolution*.

104. *Historical Catalogue of Brown University, 1764–1904* (Providence: The University, 1905); Kenny, *Town and Gown in Wartime*, 11–14; Barry and Mitchell, *A Tale of Two Centuries*, 32.

105. Guild, *The Early History of Brown University*, 14.

106. Burlingame, *Plat of the Rhode Island College Property*.

107. McLoughlin, *New England Dissent*, 501; Bronson, *History of Brown University*, 78–80.

108. See McLoughlin, *Isaac Backus and the American Pietistic Tradition*, 136–66.

109. Backus, *The Diary of Isaac Backus*, 3:1294. In addition to George Washington, early honorary degrees were given to Thomas Jefferson (1787), Alexander Hamilton (1792), and John Adams (1797); Keen, "The Early

Years of Brown University," 49. More detail relating to the Washington visit can be found in Guild, *The Early History of Brown University*, 479–82.

110. Bronson, *The History of Brown University*, 138.

111. Moses Miller Jr., letter to William E. Green, July 7, 1799, in Brown et al., *Memories of Brown*, 31.

112. Fleming, *Science and Technology in Providence*, 21.

113. Bronson, *The History of Brown University*, 89–92; Guild, *The Early History of Brown University*, 462, 496.

114. Charles Evans Hughes, "The Historical Address," in ed. William T. Hastings, *A Century of Scholars: Rhode Island Alpha of Phi Beta Kappa, 1830–1930* (1932; Providence: D. B. Updike, The Merrymount Press, 1943), 13–16.

CHAPTER 2 . BROWN BAPTIZED

1. Heimert, *Religion and the American Mind*, 526–27.

2. Joshua Wolf Shenk, *Lincoln's Melancholy: How Depression Challenged a President and Fueled his Greatness* (New York: Houghton Mifflin Harcourt, 2005), 83.

3. MacDonald, "Address," 41.

4. Bronson, *The History of Brown University*, 75, 155, and 156.

5. The Browns were also book collectors—a fact of relevance, since many of their books would find their way into the John Carter Brown Library; Lawrence C. Wroth, *The First Century of the John Carter Brown Library* (Providence: Associates of the John Carter Brown Library, 1946).

6. Bronson, *The History of Brown University*, 225. His total gifts to the University came to $159,000; ibid., 227.

7. Nicholas Brown III, letter to T. P. Ives, February 9, 1833, quoted in Bronson, *The History of Brown University*, 222. I thank Sylvia Brown for bringing this to my attention.

8. Bronson, *The History of Brown University*, 157.

9. Steve Dunwell, *The Run of the Mill: A Pictorial Narrative of the Expansion, Dominion, Decline and Enduring Impact of the New England Textile Industry* (Boston: David R. Godine, 1978), 14. See also Caroline F. Ware, *The Early New England Cotton Manufacture: A Study in Industrial Beginnings* (New York: Russell and Russell, 1966); Barbara M. Tucker, *Samuel Slater and the Origins of the American Textile Industry, 1790–1960* (Ithaca: Cornell University Press, 1984).

10. The Browns and their later economic interests are capably handled in James Hedges's posthumously published work, *The Browns of Providence Plantations: The Nineteenth Century* (Providence: Brown University Press, 1968).

11. Pastore, *Between Land and Sea*, 199.

12. Dunwell, *The Run of the Mill*, 21; George R. Taylor, *The Transportation Revolution, 1815–1860* (New York: Rinehart, 1951), 222. Taylor identified the vernier caliper, developed by J. R. Brown of Providence, as a major step forward in precision technology.

13. Pastore, *Between Land and Sea*, 218.

14. The Corliss House was the home of Brown's admissions office from 1973 to 2013.

15. Karl Marx, a careful observer, watched the rise of the machine-tool industry with "a kind of horrified fascination" and saw it as "the badge of the nineteenth century." Fleming, *Science and Technology in Providence*, 36.

16. For more detail on how Rhode Island industries fit into the vastly expanding American economy, see J. Leander Bishop, *A History of American Manufactures from 1608 to 1860* (Philadelphia: E. Young and Company, 1866). David J. Jeremy cites several Providence inventors of important industrial applications, including a differential gearbox that would become important in automobiles, invented by Asa Arnold in 1822; see "Innovation in American Textile Technology During the Early Nineteenth Century," *Technology and Culture* 14 (January 1973), 58.

17. To cite only one example, Ebenezer David of the class of 1772 studied medicine before becoming a chaplain; Black and Roelker, *A Rhode Island Chaplain in the Revolution*, xxv. See also Frederick C. Waite, "The Third Medical College in New England, That of Brown University (1811–1828)," *New England Journal of Medicine* 207 (1932), 30–33, and Charles W. Parsons, *The Medical School Formerly Existing at Brown University, Its Professors and Graduates* (Providence: S. S. Rider, 1881).

18. Fleming, *Science and Technology in Providence*, 28–29; Barry and Mitchell, *A Tale of Two Centuries*, 31. Throughout his long life of service to the university, Drowne kept gardens with medicinal plants on campus and at his home, Mount Hygeia, in Foster, Rhode Island (Waite, "The Third Medical College in New England," 33).

19. For example, there was Elisha Bartlett, whom Donald Fleming called "one of the best American physicians of the nineteenth century" and by himself "a sufficient justification of medical education at Brown"; Fleming, *Science and Technology in Providence*, 30.

20. Parsons, *The Medical School Formerly Existing in Brown University*, 11, 13.

21. Fleming, *Science and Technology in Providence*, 30.

22. *Slavery and Justice*, 32.

23. See Christy Clark-Pujara, "The Business of Slavery and Anti-Slavery Sentiment: The Case of Rowland Gibson Hazard—An Antislavery 'Negro

Cloth' Dealer," *Rhode Island History* 71, no. 2 (Summer/Fall 2013); *Slavery and Justice*, 34. In its portrait collection, Brown has a likeness of Rowland Gibson Hazard and more than 300 other individuals connected with the university's history. The collection may be searched online at http://library.brown.edu/cds/portraits/.

24. Thomas Jefferson, *Notes on the State of Virginia*, ed. William Peden (1955; Chapel Hill: University of North Carolina Press, 1982), 165.

25. These tensions are explored in Pastore, *Between Land and Sea*; Theodore Steinberg, *Nature Incorporated: Industrialization and the Waters of New England* (New York: Cambridge University Press, 1991); Mitchell Brewster Folsom and Steven D. Lubar, *The Philosophy of Manufactures: Early Debates over Industrialization in the United States* (Cambridge: MIT Press, 1982).

26. Gary Kulik, Roger Parks, Theodore Z. Penn, eds., *The New England Mill Village, 1790–1860* (Cambridge: MIT Press, 1982), 253–88.

27. Peter J. Coleman, *The Transformation of Rhode Island, 1790–1860* (Providence: Brown University Press, 1963), 74–75.

28. Dunwell, *The Run of the Mill*.

29. On African Americans in Providence, see Rhode Island Black Heritage Society, *Creative Survival: The Providence Black Community in the 19th Century* (Providence: Rhode Island Black Heritage Society, 1985). The riots are also described in Joanne Pope Melish's introduction to William J. Brown, *The Life of William J. Brown of Providence, R.I., with Personal Recollections of Incidents in Rhode Island* (Durham, NH: University of New Hampshire Press, 2006), xxv–xxvi, a reissue of an important 1883 memoir. Brown mentions (87) that the African American community sometimes heard sermons from student ministers at Brown, but it would be difficult to claim that Brown was engaged in any meaningful form of outreach.

30. However, at least one graduate was on the side of Dorr and the reformers, Joseph Josten of the class of 1814, who presided over the "people's constitutional convention"; for background, see Marvin E. Gettleman, *The Dorr Rebellion: A Study in American Radicalism, 1833–1849* (New York: Random House, 1973); Erik Chaput, *The People's Martyr: Thomas Wilson Dorr and His 1842 Rhode Island Rebellion* (Lawrence, KS: University Press of Kansas, 2013). Usher Parsons, formerly of the medical school, was sympathetic to Dorr in principle, but opposed his military tactics; see Charles W. Parsons, *Memoir of Usher Parsons, M.D., of Providence, Rhode Island* (Providence: Hammond, Angell and Company, 1870), 38–39.

31. Bronson, *The History of Brown University*, 254.

32. Joseph L. Blau, *American Philosophic Addresses, 1700–1900* (New York: Columbia University Press, 1946), 410.

33. Amos Perry, *Memorial of Zachariah Allen* (Cambridge: J. Wilson and Son, 1882), 12.

34. Dunwell, *The Run of the Mill*, 71–73; the quotations that follow are from Amos Perry, cited by Dunwell, 71.

35. Allen served on the board for fifty-six years; Perry, *Memorial of Zachariah Allen*, 50. Allen was also a leading figure at Rhode Island Historical Society, where he gave addresses on Roger Williams and early relations between the settlers and the Native Americans.

36. Patrick Conley, "The War of 1812 and Rhode Island: A Bicentennial Bust," *Rhode Island History* (Winter/Spring 2014), 28, 33. Usher Parsons was the father of Charles Parsons, who would serve Brown and Rhode Island as a health expert in the late nineteenth century. See Parsons, *Memoir of Usher Parsons, M.D.* On his recollections of the War of 1812, see Usher Parsons, *Battle of Lake Erie: Discourse before the Rhode Island Historical Society* (Providence: B. T. Albro, 1854). He also wrote a charming book on local nomenclature, *Indian Names of Places in Rhode-Island* (Providence: Knowles, Anthony and Co., 1861). On DeWolf, see Parsons, *The Medical School Formerly Existing in Brown University*, 20.

37. Solomon Drowne, early alumnus and member of the medical faculty, was another advocate of Greek independence, giving an oration in 1824 that claimed, "There is a sort of magic in the name of Greece." Usher Parsons, *Sketches of Rhode Island Physicians, Deceased Prior to 1850* (Providence: Knowles, Anthony and Co., 1859), 32.

38. Bronson, *The History of Brown University*, 167.

39. Talbot Hamlin, *Greek Revival Architecture in America* (New York: Oxford University Press, 1944), 179.

40. Bronson, *The History of Brown University*, 171–73.

41. Ibid., 224.

42. The cult of Roger Williams was nourished throughout the nineteenth century by Brown alumni, who spoke about him in historical discourses and composed long epic poems about how and why Rhode Island had been created; two alumni of the class of 1813, Job Durfee and Zachariah Allen, were active on this front. Brown's librarian for much of the nineteenth century, Reuben Aldridge Guild, was also a prolific researcher into the life of Williams; see his *A Biographical Introduction to Roger Williams* (Providence: Publications of the Narragansett Club, 1866) and *Footprints of Roger Williams* (Providence: Tibbits and Preston, 1886).

43. Bronson, *The History of Brown University*, 137.

44. Ibid., 169.
45. Ibid., 138, 179.
46. Ibid., 180–82.
47. Ibid., 213, 241.
48. Ibid., 183.
49. Ibid., 185.
50. Ibid., 188.
51. Ibid., 184.
52. Martha Mitchell, *Encyclopedia Brunoniana* (Providence: Brown University Library, 1993); Fleming, *Science and Technology in Providence*, 12; Bronson, *The History of Brown University*, 187.
53. Francis Wayland Jr. and H. L. Wayland, *A Memoir of the Life and Labors of Francis Wayland,* 2 vols. (New York: Sheldon & Co., 1868), 1:19, 1:24.
54. Bronson, *The History of Brown University*, 207. A later memoir records that Wayland was a chewer of tobacco; Walter Lee Munro, *The Old Back Campus at Brown* (Providence: Haley and Sykes, 1929), 46.
55. Fleming, *Science and Technology in Providence*, 31.
56. Bronson, *The History of Brown University*, 224.
57. Jeremy Chase, "Francis Wayland: A Uniting Force in an Era of Disunion" (Brown University bachelor's thesis, 2006), 36.
58. Bronson, *The History of Brown University*, 315.
59. James B. Angell, *The Reminiscences of James Burrill Angell* (New York: Longmans, Green, 1912), 37.
60. *A Memoir of the Life and Labors of Francis Wayland,* 357. Chase, "Francis Wayland: A Uniting Force in an Era of Disunion," 45.
61. Fleming, *Science and Technology in Providence*, 40.
62. Bronson, *The History of Brown University*, 258–67.
63. Ibid., 275.
64. Ibid., 279.
65. Ibid., 284.
66. Ibid., 302.
67. Ibid., 233.
68. Ibid., 239.
69. Ibid., 244.
70. Ibid., 242.
71. Susan B. Ely, "Essay Burning in 1831," in Brown et al., *Memories of Brown*, 53–54.
72. Bronson, *The History of Brown University*, 245. Latham also records an outing "to roll nine pins." James B. Angell recorded early memories of "ball playing" in his *Reminiscences*, 14.

73. Bronson, *History of Brown University*, 246.

74. Ibid.

75. Sylvia Brown, personal communication.

76. Coleman, *The Transformation of Rhode Island*, 108, 220.

77. Kathleen Curran, ed., *Thomas Alexander Tefft: American Architecture in Transition, 1845–1960* (Providence: Department of Art, Brown University, 1988), 18.

78. Angell, *Reminiscences*, 28.

79. George Wilson Pierson, *Tocqueville in America* (1938; Baltimore: Johns Hopkins University Press, 1996), 441. A generation later, when the revolutions of 1848 were roiling Europe, democracy and its possibilities were the subject of animated discussion on campus; see Angell, *Reminiscences*, 24.

80. Fleming, *Science and Technology*, 33.

81. For example, for his views on the dependence of science upon religion, see Francis Wayland, *A Discourse, Delivered at the Dedication of Manning Hall, the Chapel and Library of Brown University, February 4, 1835* (Providence: Marshall, Brown and Co., 1835).

82. More recently, it was led by another Brown graduate, Peter Laarman, from 1994 to 2004.

83. Louis Filler, ed., *Horace Mann on the Crisis in Education* (Yellow Springs, OH: Antioch Press, 1965), 124. On Mann's rejection of his childhood Puritanism, see Howard Mumford Jones, "Horace Mann's Crusade," in ed. Daniel Aaron, *America in Crisis* (New York: Knopf, 1952).

84. Lawrence A. Cremin, *The Republic and the School: Horace Mann on the Education of Free Men* (New York: Teachers College of Columbia University, 1965), 110.

85. James W. Trent Jr., *The Manliest Man: Samuel G. Howe and the Contours of Nineteenth-century American Reform* (Amherst, MA: University of Massachusetts, 2012), 4.

86. Bronson, *The History of Brown University*, 184; Trent, *The Manliest Man*, 16; Barry and Mitchell, *A Tale of Two Centuries*, 33.

87. Brown et al., *Memories of Brown* 44.

88. Ibid.

89. Edward J. Renehan Jr., *The Secret Six: The True Tale of the Men Who Conspired with John Brown* (New York: Crown, 1995), 29–36. I am grateful to Tony Horwitz for his advice concerning Howe and his liabilities. See also Tony Horwitz's *Midnight Rising: John Brown and the Raid That Sparked the Civil War* (New York: Henry Holt, 2011), 209.

90. F. B. Sanborn, *Dr. S. G. Howe, the Philanthropist* (New York: Funk & Wagnalls, 1891), 351.

91. Bronson, *The History of Brown University*, 303.

CHAPTER 3 . BOOKENDS

1. William Roscoe Thayer, ed., *The Life and Letters of John Hay,* 2 vols. (Boston: Houghton Mifflin, 1929), 1:35; Joshua Zeitz, *Lincoln's Boys: John Hay, John Nicolay and the War for Lincoln's Image* (New York: Viking, 2014), 11–12; John Taliaferro, *All the Great Prizes: The Life of John Hay, from Lincoln to Roosevelt* (New York: Simon and Schuster, 2013), 24. Hay's nickname at Brown was "Thaddeus of Warsaw" (Taliaferro, *All the Great Prizes*, 25).

2. Taliaferro, *All the Great Prizes*, 15.

3. Her father, Nicholas Power, was a business associate and relative of the Browns.

4. Thayer, *The Life and Letters of John Hay*, 1:44.

5. Ibid., 1:41–42.

6. Ibid., 1:50–51.

7. "Centennial" runs to eighteen stanzas. *Celebration of the One Hundredth Anniversary of the Founding of Brown University, September 6th, 1864* (Providence: S. S. Rider, 1865), 256–59.

8. Taliaferro, *All the Great Prizes*, 117, 463–64.

9. Robert H. George, *Brown University on the Eve of the Civil War: Brunonians in Confederate Ranks, 1861–1865* (Providence: Brown University, 1965), 2.

10. Ibid., 14.

11. Henry S. Burrage, "The College During the Civil War," in Brown et al., *Memories of Brown*, 177. Another Brown alumnus in Confederate ranks was Henry Clay Hart of the class of 1852; in letters to his wife, he boasted that the South would soon invade "Uncle Abe's headquarters." Barry and Mitchell, *A Tale of Two Centuries*, 54.

12. George, *Brown University on the Eve of the Civil War*, 16.

13. Robin Young, *For Love & Liberty: The Untold Civil War Story of Major Sullivan Ballou & His Famous Love Letter* (New York: Thunder's Mouth Press, 2006), xxiv–xxvii.

14. Joseph E. Garland, *To Meet These Wants: The Story of Rhode Island Hospital, 1863–1988* (Providence: Rhode Island Hospital, 1988), 11, 21–24.

15. George, *Brown University on the Eve of the Civil War*, 2.

16. Ibid.

17. Ibid., 30.

18. Henry S. Burrage, ed., *Brown University in the Civil War: A Memorial* (Providence: Providence Press Company, 1868).

19. Henry S. Burrage, ed., *Civil War Record of Brown University* (Providence: [n.p.], 1920).

20. Brown won the intercollegiate championship in 1879 by beating Yale. Bronson, *The History of Brown University*, 416.

21. J. Walter Wilson and Diana Fane, *Brown University as the Land Grant College of Rhode Island, 1863–1894* (Providence: Brown University, 1966), 64.

22. Henry Fountain, "A Lost World Is Resurrected at Brown," *New York Times,* July 28, 2014; *Brown Daily Herald,* March 4, 2014; "'The Lost Museum' Finds a Bit of Brown History" (Brown University news release, May 14, 2014). Jenks was an alumnus of the class of 1838; for more biographical information, see *Historical Catalogue of Brown University, 1764–1904*, 177.

23. "John Whipple Potter Jenks," in Mitchell, *Encyclopedia Brunoniana*.

24. Burrage, *Civil War Record of Brown University*.

25. Maureen D. Lee, "Rhode Island's Star Soprano: Sissieretta Jones," *Rhode Island History* 72, no. 2 (Summer/Fall 2014), 43–44. A modest plaque commemorates her at the corner of South Court and Pratt Streets.

26. Ibid.

27. "African Americans," from Mitchell, *Encyclopedia Brunoniana*.

28. See April Kaminer, "New Contenders Emerge in Quest to Identify Yale's First African-American Graduate," *New York Times,* March 16, 2014.

29. "Those We Mourn: Inman Edward Page," *Brown Alumni Monthly,* February 1936, 185–86.

30. Today, African American alumni can join the Inman Page Black Alumni Council.

31. Ralph Ellison, "Portrait of Inman Page," in *Going to the Territory* (1981; New York: Modern Library, 1995), 144.

32. The oration was titled simply "Brown University"; see Leroy David, "John Hope at Brown University: The Black Man Who Refused to Pass for White," *The Journal of Blacks in Higher Education*, 22 (Winter 1998–1999), 125. Hope's wife, Lugenia Burns, was also an important activist on behalf of African American women. Her work in community organizing within Atlanta helped lay the foundation for the later civil rights movement.

33. Munro, *The Old Back Campus at Brown*, 5, 27, 40–44. See also *Brown Alumni Monthly*, October 1918, 49–52.

34. Jay Barry claimed that Richmond pitched the first perfect game in the history of professional baseball, on June 12, 1880. Jay Barry, "He Pitched Baseball's First 'Perfect Game,'" *Brown Alumni Monthly*, October 1964, 27. Remarkably, Richmond was the roommate of a future Brown president, William H. P. Faunce, also of the class of 1880 (Barry and Mitchell, *A Tale of Two Centuries*, 68). An interesting remembrance of old baseball at Brown may be found in *Brown Alumni Monthly*, October 1918, 49–52. A short passage on baseball at Brown is found in Charles Evans Hughes*, The*

Autobiographical Notes of Charles Evans Hughes, ed. David J. Danelski and Joseph S. Tulchin (Cambridge: Harvard University Press, 1973), 41–42.

35. The student, John Heisman (class of 1891) ultimately transferred to the University of Pennsylvania. Jay Barry, *Brown Alumni Monthly*, October 1968, 31–32.

36. Barry and Mitchell, *A Tale of Two Centuries*, 58.

37. Ibid., 51, 63.

38. Ibid., 97. The team included a future Brown dean, Alexander Meiklejohn. In the first intercollegiate hockey game, Brown defeated Harvard 6–0 in 1898. For a remembrance of early hockey, see Norman L. Sammis, "Hockey Was Our Game, Too," *Brown Alumni Monthly,* May 1965, 64. The earliest games were played on local ponds.

39. Aldrich received an honorary degree from Brown in 1892; *Historical Catalogue on Brown University, 1764–1904*, 586. A modern reflection on Aldrich's legacy may be found in Nelson W. Aldrich Jr., *Old Money: The Mythology of America's Upper Class* (New York: Alfred A. Knopf, 1988).

40. Fountain, "A Lost World Is Resurrected at Brown"; *Brown Daily Herald,* March 4, 2014.

41. Fleming, *Science and Technology in Providence*, 43–46.

42. Ibid., 47; Bronson, *The History of Brown University*, 448.

43. Lester Ward, "Our Better Halves" (1888), in eds. Michael S. Kimmel and Thomas Mosmiller, *Against the Tide* (Boston: Beacon Press, 1992), 313.

44. Lucille Salitan and Eve Lewis Perera, eds., *Virtuous Lives: Four Quaker Sisters Remember Family Life, Abolitionism, and Women's Suffrage* (New York: Continuum, 1994), 162. Elizabeth's son, Arnold Buffum Chace (1845–1932), was the eleventh chancellor of Brown.

45. Grace E. Hawk, *Pembroke College in Brown University: The First Seventy-five Years, 1891–1966* (Providence: Brown University, 1967), 10.

46. Bronson, *The History of Brown University*, 449–50. In 1783, Yale examined a twelve-year-old girl, Lucinda Foote, and found her "fully qualified, except in regard to sex"; Rosemary Pierrel, "O, Why Should a Woman Not Get a Degree?" *Brown Alumni Monthly,* May 1965, 35.

47. Salitan and Perera, *Virtuous Lives*, 35. Prentice soon after became an important editor of the *Louisville Courier-Journal*, from 1830 to 1870, including the vital war years, when it was desperately important to Abraham Lincoln to keep Kentucky in the Union. Chace wrote admiringly that "he battled royally" for the Union cause.

48. Julia Ward Howe was married to one Brown alumnus (Samuel Gridley Howe), and was the granddaughter of another (Samuel Ward, class of 1771). Her great-grandfather, also named Samuel Ward, was a governor of Rhode

Island in the 1760s and a trustee of the infant Rhode Island College from 1764 to 1776; he was a prominent member of the party trying to lure the college to Newport in 1769–70.

49. Other early pioneers in women's education included Georgia Female College, Mary Sharp College in Tennessee, and Elmira College in New York. See Pierrel, "O, Why Should a Woman Not Get a Degree?" 34–38.

50. Ibid., 35.

51. *The Brunonian,* April 1869, 123.

52. Karen J. Blair, "The Women's Club Movement Creates and Defines the College," in ed. Polly Welts Kaufman, *The Search for Equity: Women at Brown University, 1891–1991* (Hanover, NH: Brown University, 1991) 31, 33. Elizabeth Buffum Chace resigned from the Rhode Island Women's Club when it refused to allow women of color. Ibid., 33–34.

53. Hawk, *Pembroke College in Brown University*, 9.

54. Salitan and Perera, *Virtuous Lives*, 159.

55. Hawk, *Pembroke College in Brown University*, 18.

56. Bronson, *The History of Brown University*, 451.

57. Ibid.

58. Pierrel, "O, Why Should a Woman Not Get a Degree?" 35.

59. Bronson, *The History of Brown University*, 452.

60. Hawk, *Pembroke College in Brown University*, 4; Barry and Mitchell, *A Tale of Two Centuries*, 78.

61. Karen J. Blair, "The Women's Club Movement Creates and Defines the Women's College," 30.

62. Hawk, *Pembroke College in Brown University*, 18.

63. Margaret B. Stillwell, speech delivered at the installation of Dean Nancy Duke Lewis (September 19, 1950, Brown University Archives).

64. Hawk, *Pembroke College in Brown University*, 3; Karen J. Blair, "The Women's Club Movement Creates and Defines the Women's College," 28.

65. Mary Woolley, "After Fifty Years" (manuscript, n.d., Brown University Archives), 3.

66. Hawk, *Pembroke College in Brown University*, 46; Bronson, *The History of Brown University*, 454, 457.

67. Woolley, "After Fifty Years," 6.

68. Stillwell, speech delivered at installation of Dean Nancy Duke Lewis.

69. Hawk, *Pembroke College in Brown University*, 27; Karen J. Blair, "The Women's Club Movement Creates and Defines the Women's College," 29, 45.

70. Raymond P. Rhinehart, *Brown University: An Architectural Tour* (New York: Princeton Architectural Books, 2014), 138.

71. Hawk, *Pembroke College in Brown University*, 29.

72. Ibid., 44. I'm grateful to Ruth Ekstrom for her close study of discrepancies between the courses available to men and women in 1916–1917.

73. Hawk, *Pembroke College in Brown University*, 12.

74. Ibid., 47.

75. *Life*, August 26, 1897. For a superb reading of Andrews and the resistance he encountered from Brown's governing bodies, see Theresa Ross, "'The Lengthened Shadow of One Man': E. Benjamin Andrews and Brown University, 1889–1898," *Rhode Island History* 65, no. 1 (Winter/Spring 2007), 3–28. Andrews was an advocate of free trade, international bimetallism, and the free coinage of silver (at a ratio of sixteen to one of gold), an economic policy that placed him to the left of the Corporation and probably hindered his fundraising ability. Such views also touched upon the presidential election of 1896, when the free coinage of silver was a dominant issue and placed the statements of President Andrews in a more public position than intended. See Bronson, *The History of Brown University*, 462–63. http://www.brown.edu/about/administration/president/andrews

76. "Elisha Benjamin Andrews," in Mitchell, *Encyclopedia Brunoniana*. In a 1958 speech at Pembroke, Brown's president, Barnaby Keeney, praised Andrews and his 1892 report as determining the course of the University for the next sixty-five years, and claimed "We have not departed today in any essential respect from the policies which he laid down there" (typescript, Brown University Archives).

77. Polly Welts Kaufman, ed., introduction to *The Search for Equity*, 18; Bronson, *The History of Brown University*, 428.

78. Bronson, *The History of Brown University*, 428–29; Barry and Mitchell, *A Tale of Two Centuries*, 78, 101.

79. Hawk, *Pembroke College in Brown University*, 46. Under President Ezekiel Robinson, new professorships were established in physiology, agricultural zoology, botany, geology, and astronomy; Barry and Mitchell, *A Tale of Two Centuries*, 60.

80. Young Rockefeller was part of a Brown tradition already; he led a Bible class at the Fifth Avenue Baptist Church, where Faunce was the minister, and where, until recently, the class had been led by Charles Evans Hughes. Robert M. Miller, *Harry Emerson Fosdick: Preacher, Pastor, Prophet* (New York: Oxford University Press, 1985), 152.

81. Raymond B. Fosdick, *John D. Rockefeller, Jr.: A Portrait* (New York: Harper and Brothers, 1956), 48.

82. Raymond B. Fosdick, "The Student Years of Johnny Rock," *Brown Alumni Monthly,* May 1956, 10. The game was described by the *New York World* as

"the most savage contest between brawn and brain that modern athletic days have seen." Fosdick, *John D. Rockefeller, Jr.*, 72.

83. Fosdick, "The Student Years of Johnny Rock," 11. A letter he wrote on February 2, 1896, expresses this sense of change: "One sees all sorts and conditions of men here viewing life, duty, pleasure and the hereafter, so differently. My ideas and opinions change I find, in many ways. I would stickle less for the letter of the law, now, more for the spirit." Fosdick, *John D. Rockefeller, Jr.*, 75.

84. The Goddard home occupies Brown Street between Charlesfield and Power Streets.

85. Senator Aldrich received an honorary degree from Brown in 1892.

86. After his wife died in 1948, Rockefeller remarried in 1951 to Martha Baird Allen, the widow of a Brown classmate and close friend, Arthur Allen.

87. Fosdick, *John D. Rockefeller, Jr.*, 102.

88. Ibid., 80. Even after graduating, he wrote, "About a week after commencement I visited the old college once more and walked through the deserted campus and among the lonely buildings with a heavy heart" (81).

89. Ibid., 44. This is the second stanza of Horatio Bonar's "The Truest Teaching," published in *Life and Health: The National Health Magazine* 23, no. 10 (October 1908), 453.

90. "The Rockefellers: John D. Rockefeller, Junior, 1874–1960," Rockefeller Archive Center (September 1977).

91. The Riverside Church was the descendant of the Fifth Avenue Baptist Church, where Rockefeller, Faunce, and Hughes worshipped in the nineteenth century. On Rockefeller's support for the liberal wing of the Baptists and his clashes with fundamentalists, see Miller, *Harry Emerson Fosdick*, 153–58. In 1922, the liberal Baptists organized a fellowship named after Roger Williams (157).

92. "The Rockefellers: John D. Rockefeller, Junior, 1874–1960."

93. Fosdick, "The Student Years of Johnny Rock," 11.

94. David Rockefeller, "Father and Brown," *Brown Alumni Monthly,* December 1964, 6–7.

CHAPTER 4. DANCE OF THE BROWNIES

1. Faunce wrote an interesting essay about Roger Williams, praising him for his "tremendous conviction" and quoting John Cotton effectively on Williams's strengths ("conscientiously contentious") and weaknesses ("a haberdasher of small questions"); he embraced Cotton's ultimate verdict

that "the roote of the matter abode in him"; William H. P. Faunce, "Roger Williams and His Doctrine of Soul Liberty," in *Pioneers of Religious Liberty in America: Being the Great and Thursday Lectures Delivered in Boston in nineteen hundred and three* (Boston: American Unitarian Association, 1903), 56, 77.

2. "Dance of the Brownies," *The Brunonian* 28, no. 6 (September 22, 1894), 77.

3. Major military conflicts coincided with all of Brown's earlier anniversaries—those of 1814 (the War of 1812), 1864 (the Civil War), 1914 (the First World War), and 1964 (Vietnam). 2014, while not free of conflict, has been calm in comparison.

4. *Providence Journal*, June 17, 1913. See Jonathan Bateman, "Three Anniversaries and a University: The Meaning of Brown's Celebrations in 1864, 1914, and 1964," Brown University honors thesis (2013), 46–47.

5. Perhaps in response, Brown awarded an honorary degree to Wilson's opponent in the last election, William Howard Taft (other degrees were presented to Andrew Carnegie and John D. Rockefeller Jr., among others).

6. 150th Anniversary Files (Brown University Archives). Another glacier in Antarctica was named "Brunonia"; "They Put Brown On the Map," *Brown Alumni Monthly,* May 1965, 58–61. A planet was also named "Brunonia" in 1954.

7. There had been one previous football game, considered the first Rose Bowl, in 1902.

8. John M. Carroll, *Fritz Pollard: Pioneer in Racial Advancement* (Urbana, IL: University of Illinois Press, 1992), 60.

9. Ibid., 45–46.

10. Sheila Tully Boyle and Andrew Bunie, *Paul Robeson: The Years of Promise and Achievement* (Amherst: University of Massachusetts Press, 2001), 51. Carroll, *Fritz Pollard* (60–61, 65) depicts other examples of racist hazing endured by Pollard.

11. Carroll, *Fritz Pollard*, 103.

12. Ibid., 176.

13. Ibid., 174.

14. Ibid., 45.

15. Boyle and Bunie, *Paul Robeson*, 57–58, 60.

16. Ibid., 81–82, 277; Lloyd Brown, *The Young Paul Robeson: "On My Journey Now"* (Boulder: Westview Press, 1997), 84, 92, 111–12; Carroll, *Fritz Pollard*, 189; Jay Barry, "Fritz," *Brown Alumni Monthly,* October 1970, 30–33.

17. Hughes, *Autobiographical Notes*, 37–38.

18. Ibid., 38.

19. Ibid., 42.

20. Wriston, *Wriston Speaking*, 125; James F. Simon, *FDR and Chief Justice Hughes: The President, the Supreme Court, and the Epic Battle over the New Deal.* (New York: Simon and Schuster, 2012), 19–20.

21. Simon, *FDR and Chief Justice Hughes*, 25.

22. Ibid., 100.

23. Ibid., 101.

24. Ibid., 103.

25. Ibid., 101.

26. Wilson won New Hampshire by only 56 votes; overall, the national margin was a thin 594,188 votes for Wilson.

27. James Brown Scott, introduction to eds. James Brown Scott et al., 18 vols., *The American Secretaries of State and Their Diplomacy* vol. 1 (New York: Cooper Square Publishers, 1963), 221–401.

28. Charles Evans Hughes, "Remarks of Chief Justice Hughes" (typescript, June 21, 1937, Brown University Archives).

29. Hughes is remembered on the Brown campus by the Hughes Court in Wriston Quad. His name also endures in Antarctica, attached to the mountains known as the Hughes Range.

30. *Brown Alumni Monthly,* April 1917, 8–9.

31. Three ambulances were donated by Brown alumni.

32. "The First Brown Man to Fall in the War," *Brown Alumni Monthly,* June 1917, 2. Price had joined the Black Watch of the 5th Royal Highlanders of Canada; see "The Story of Florence Price," *Brown Alumni Monthly,* March 1919, 158–160.

33. William H. P. Faunce, *Annual Report of the President to the Corporation of Brown University* (Providence: Brown University, October 1917), 5.

34. Ibid., 6 and 7–8.

35. Ibid., 8.

36. William H. P. Faunce, *Annual Report of the President to the Corporation of Brown University* (Providence: Brown University, October 1919), 6; "The War-Time College," *Brown Alumni Monthly,* October 1918, 45–46; "The New Brown," *Brown Alumni Monthly,* November 1918, 68–72. The letters of a pilot killed in action, Joseph B. Bowen of the class of 1915, were collected in "A Brown Aviator," *Brown Alumni Monthly,* December 1918, 97–100.

37. Faunce, *Annual Report of the President to the Corporation of Brown University* (October 1919), 5–6.

38. Ibid., 9.

39. Ibid., 7.

40. Ibid., 8.

41. *Brown Alumni Monthly,* May 1919, 199.

42. William H. P. Faunce, "Brown in the War," *Brown Alumni Monthly,* July 1918, 33.

43. "To Brown Men in the Nation's Service," typescript letter, dated March 21, 1918. Brown University Archives.

44. Faunce, *Annual Report of the President to the Corporation of Brown University* (October 1919), 8.

45. It ultimately brought in $210,000, $50,000 of which came from John D. Rockefeller Jr.

46. 1,469 served in the Army, 448 in the Navy, 12 in the Marines, 13 in foreign armies, and 32 in militarized service. For a full list of the World War I Honor Roll, see *Brown Alumni Monthly,* January 1919, 112–13; and *Brown Alumni Monthly,* February 1919, 150.

47. William H. P. Faunce, "Baccalaureate Address," *Brown Alumni Monthly,* July 1917, 26.

48. Zechariah Chafee Jr., *Freedom of Speech* (New York: Harcourt, Brace and Company, 1920), 376.

49. Zechariah Chafee Jr., *Freedom of Speech and Press* (New York: Carrie Chapman Catt Memorial Fund, 1955), 355.

50. William H. P. Faunce, *Annual Report of the President to the Corporation of Brown University* (Providence: Brown University, 1924), 17–18.

51. Jerome Karabel, *The Chosen: The Hidden History of Admission and Exclusion at Harvard, Yale, and Princeton* (Boston: Houghton Mifflin, 2005), 2, 51, 75, 81, 109, 115; Marion Meade, *Lonelyhearts: The Screwball World of Nathanael West and Eileen McKenney* (Boston: Houghton Mifflin Harcourt, 2010), 48.

52. "On the Hill," *Brown Alumni Monthly,* November 1922, 97–98.

53. Faunce, *Annual Report of the President to the Corporation of Brown University* (1924), 9–10.

54. Amy Sohn, "Probing Brown's Dark History," Forward.com (November 10, 2006). Many institutions at the time justified quotas or limited admissions in terms of "character," and an Admissions Report from 1931 followed that logic: "It must be our purpose to bring to Brown men who can make the most effective use of the educational facilities which the University has to offer. In choosing men who will meet this qualification, intellectual ability must be recognized as one of the primary considerations, but we must also take into account character, personality, and other factors related to a man's prospective success in an after-college world in which personal relationships are of vital importance. We must recognize our position as an institution with national educational interests and at the same time fulfill our obligation as a New England institution located in the state of Rhode Island. We must

see to it that our student body is representative of young American manhood." "Report of the Committee on Admissions," in *Bulletin of Brown University: Report of the President to the Corporation* 28 (October 1931), 47.

55. Dorothy Herrmann, *S. J. Perelman: A Life* (New York: Putnam, 1986), 28–29.

56. Faunce, *Annual Report of the President to the Corporation of Brown University* (1924), 17–18.

57. On Faunce's work against fundamentalists and his alliance with John D. Rockefeller Jr., see Miller, *Harry Emerson Fosdick*, 152, 158.

58. *Brown Daily Herald*, Homecoming Issue, November 15, 1975.

59. *Pembroke Record,* October 2, 1929.

60. In October 1930, a report called for Brown's rapid evolution from a typical New England college into something grander, worthy of a large city; "Report of the Survey Committee," *Brown University Bulletin*, vol. 27 (October 1930).

61. "Diary of a Brown Girl 2500 A.D." *Sepiad* 5, no. 1 (December 1904), 17.

62. Katharine Hinds, "The Minkins Sisters," *Brown Alumni Monthly,* April 1982, 23–24, 41.

63. http://news.brown.edu/features/2011/02/fisher.

64. Boyle and Bunie, *Paul Robeson*, 81–82. Eubie Blake sang with them as well (135).

65. On the experience of Jewish women at Pembroke, see Karen M. Lamoree, "Why Not a Jewish Girl? The Jewish Experience at Pembroke College in Brown University," in eds. George M. Goodwin and Ellen Smith, *The Jews of Rhode Island* (Waltham: Brandeis University Press, 2004), 139–46. Lamoree identifies the first as Clara Gomberg, class of 1897. In the *Encyclopedia Brunoniana*, Mitchell identified Israel Strauss (class of 1894) as the first Jewish student at Brown in the modern era. Mitchell also did valuable research on Brown's earliest Asians, including Sau-Abrah from Burma (class of 1877), Heita Okada from Japan (class of 1895), and a group of five Chinese students who attended Brown in 1906 but did not graduate. A helpful chronology is given at http://www.brown.edu/campus-life/support/students-of-color/history. Ethel Robinson (class of 1905) was Pembroke's first African American woman.

66. Not every writer in Rhode Island could sharpen his or her pen at Brown. Some did their work in the penumbra of the university, such as H. P. Lovecraft, the great horror writer. As a young teenager, he stared at the heavens through the telescope at the Ladd Observatory, at the invitation of Professor Winslow Upton, and his earliest writings were about astronomy. He always expected to someday attend Brown, and nearly did in 1908, but

poverty and a nervous constitution intervened, and he spent most of his life near, but not actually at Brown. One of his final dwellings was at 66 College Street, on the site of the List Art Building—in fact, Brown was Lovecraft's landlord. For more information, see S. T. Joshi, *A Dreamer and a Visionary: H. P. Lovecraft in His Time* (Liverpool: Liverpool University Press, 2001); H. P. Lovecraft, *Lord of a Visible World: An Autobiography in Letters*, eds. S. T. Joshi and David E. Schultz (Athens, OH: Ohio University Press, 2000). Lovecraft wrote (89) that he "liked the cloistral hush of the Brown University campus, especially the inner quadrangle, where in the deserted twilight there seemed to brood the spirit of the dead generations."

67. Tom Teicholz, ed., *Conversations with S. J. Perelman* (Jackson, MS: University Press of Mississippi, 1995), 48.

68. Herrmann, *S. J. Perelman: A Life*, 24

69. Years later he found one of the books he had taken out from the library and recognized "the very smear of chicken fat that my greasy fingers had imprisoned on the flyleaf." Teicholz, *Conversations with S. J. Perelman*, 48.

70. The same professor, Benjamin Crocker Clough, would help conceive of Josiah Carberry.

71. Teicholz, *Conversations with S. J. Perelman*, 29.

72. Laurence B. Chase, "S. J. Perelman and Nathanael West: Two for the Hee Haw or Tender is the Blight," *Brown Alumni Monthly,* February 1971, 12–17.

73. Teicholz, *Conversations with S. J. Perelman*, 66; Herrmann, *S. J. Perelman: A Life*, 26. Herrmann uses the year 1916 to describe Perelman's early encounter with the Marx Brothers, but this seems unlikely; he was only twelve at the time.

74. Teicholz, *Conversations with S. J. Perelman*, 72.

75. Herrmann, *S. J. Perelman: A Life*, 28, 31, 39–40.

76. Ibid., 41.

77. Ibid., 40.

78. Ibid., 44.

79. Teicholz, *Conversations with S. J. Perelman*, 50.

80. Herrmann, *S. J. Perelman: A Life*, 49.

81. Ibid., 32. A Brown classmate, Quentin Reynolds, wrote, "Pep was perhaps the most inappropriate nickname ever given to a man, for Weinstein was slow-talking, slow-moving and proudly lazy. He was tall, stoop shouldered, he took part in absolutely no Campus activities, and he studied just enough to get by." "When Pep Was a Ghost," *Brown Alumni Monthly,* December 1957, 8.

82. Meade, *Lonelyhearts*, 47.

83. Ibid., 50–51.

84. Teicholz, *Conversations with S. J. Perelman*, 69.

85. Reynolds, "When Pep Was a Ghost," 8–9

86. S. J. Perelman, "Nathanael West: A Portrait," in Jay Martin, *Nathanael West: The Art of His Life* (New York: Farrar, Straus and Giroux, 1970), 12.

87. Herrmann, *S. J. Perelman: A Life*, 49, 56.

88. Ibid., 54.

89. Thomas J. Watson Jr. and Peter Petre, *Father, Son & Co.: My Life at IBM and Beyond* (New York: Bantam Books, 1990), 38.

90. Ibid., 41.

91. Jeff Shesol, *Supreme Power: Franklin Roosevelt vs. the Supreme Court* (New York: W. W. Norton, 2010), 28.

92. Chafee, *Freedom of Speech and Press*, 54–55. For a full assessment of Hughes, see Shesol, *Supreme Power*; Simon, *FDR and Chief Justice Hughes*. On the *Chambers* decision, see Simon, *FDR and Chief Justice Hughes*, 373. In 1937, Hughes came back to campus to reassert the freedoms upon which Brown had been founded, in a language not entirely unfamiliar to Franklin D. Roosevelt (who would assert the Four Freedoms in 1941), but he also praised the "self-restraint" that ought to accompany it; Hughes, "Remarks of Chief Justice Hughes."

93. Miller, *Harry Emerson Fosdick*, 152.

94. S. J. Perelman, *The Last Laugh* (New York: Simon and Schuster, 1981), 158.

95. A long and prescient article about Hitler appeared in the *Brown Daily Herald,* November 4, 1930.

96. *Pembroke Record*, April 28, 1938, 3.

97. *Brown Daily Herald*, October 23, 1939.

98. *Brown Alumni Monthly,* October 1942, 67.

99. http://www.jhmc.com.ph/knowledgebase/cjh-history/

100. *Brown Alumni Monthly*, October 1942, 70.

101. *Brown Alumni Monthly*, June 1942, 3.

102. *Brown Alumni Monthl,* Summer 1942, 32.

103. Brown's wartime transformation was described in the *Brown Alumni Monthly*, January–February 1943; April 1943; July 1943; a roll of the war dead was offered in *Brown Alumni Monthly,* July-August 1946, 2, 34–35.

104. Elizabeth Zwick, "The Pembroke Class of 1945: A Wartime Generation of College Women" (Brown University honors thesis, May 1982), 25, 27, 30, 33, 38; Hawk, *Pembroke College in Brown University*, 183–95.

105. *Brown Alumni Monthly*, Summer 1942, 37.

106. *Pembroke Record*, December 17, 1941.

107. *Brown Alumni Monthly,* Summer 1942, 33.

108. *Brown Alumni Monthly*, November–December 1945, 54.

109. *Brown Alumni Monthly*, January–February 1944, 138.

110. *Brown Daily Herald*, June 1, 1945.

111. Jessica Rotondi, "Navy Blue and Brown: World War Two Comes to College Hill," Brown University senior thesis (2007), 133.

112. "An Unprecedented A.M.," *Brown Alumni Monthly*, March 1950, 10.

113. *Brown Alumni Monthly*, July–August 1946.

114. Rotondi, "Navy Blue and Brown," 7, 102; *Brown Alumni Monthly,* September–October 1945, 46.

115. *Brown Alumni Monthly,* February 1943, 170.

116. *Brown Alumni Monthly*, May 1965, 67–68.

117. *Brown Alumni Monthly,* March 1943, 199. Another adviser to General Stilwell was a former Brown football star, Colonel Parker Tenney, class of 1915, who in addition to his military duties gathered more than 1,100 plant specimens for the Smithsonian. *Brown Alumni Monthly*, April 1943, 225.

118. "Eleven Missionaries, Boy, 9, Beheaded by Japs on Panay, Baptist Foreign Mission Reveals Atrocities," *Evening Independent* (St. Petersburg, FL), June 1, 1945. The settlement may also have been called Hopevale. Remarkably, one of daughters of the martyrs chose to work for a Japanese relocation center in Colorado, to express her belief in peace. The story of her forgiveness so impressed the Japanese that the architect of the Pearl Harbor attack ultimately converted to Christianity. See Lynn Belluscio, "The Story of Forgiveness," *Le Roy Pennysaver*, June 12, 2011, and Yuka Ibuki, Toshimi Kumai, and Susan Fertig-Dykes, "2011 Dialogue on the Hopevale Martyrdom Panay in 1943: A Japanese Veteran Inspired by Daughter of American Guerilla Officer."

119. Henry M. Wriston, 1943 Commencement Speech (Brown University Archives).

120. "Meiklejohn, Alexander," from Mitchell, *Encyclopedia Brunoniana*; "The Militancy of Alexander Meiklejohn," *Brown Alumni Monthly,* March 1965, 12–15. Meiklejohn was also partly responsible for bringing hockey to the United States and helped arrange the first intercollegiate game, between Brown and Harvard ("Hockey Pioneers," *Brown Alumni Monthly*, April 1951).

121. Wriston, *Wriston Speaking*, 146.

122. *Brown Alumni Monthly,* September–October 1945, 28–29; January 1957, 15, 24. A former Brown student named Charles Flick received notoriety for joining the Nazis; *Brown Alumni Monthly*, July 1943, 39.

123. *Brown Alumni Monthly*, June 1942, 4.

124. Janet M. Phillips, *Brown University: A Short History* (1992; Providence: Office of Public Affairs and University Relations, 2000) 74.

125. Wriston, *Wriston Speaking*, 209.

126. Chafee, *Freedom of Speech and Press*, 6. Chafee worked for the United Nations in 1947–48 as a member of Subcommittee on Freedom of Information and of the Press. In March 1948, he was one of five U.S. delegates to the UN World Conference on Freedom of Information at Geneva.

127. "The Refectory is designed for table service, with all the students seated at one time instead of eating in shifts; the room is arranged so that table conversation is possible," Wriston, *Wriston Speaking*, 93. Andrews Hall, built in 1947, served that function for Pembroke.

CHAPTER 5. THE BROWN DECADES

1. Lewis Mumford, *The Brown Decades: A Study of the Arts of America, 1865–1895* (1931; New York: Dover Publications, 1955), 4.

2. According to Mumford, the book germinated with a visit to the Experimental College of the University of Wisconsin, created by Brown's former dean, the educational innovator Alexander Meiklejohn. Mumford, *The Brown Decades* (1955), v.

3. James T. Patterson, *Grand Expectations: The United States, 1945–1974* (New York: Oxford University Press, 1996), 68 and 313, n. 6.

4. "Veterans College," from Mitchell, *Encyclopedia Brunoniana*.

5. Allen Dulles spoke at Commencement on June 16, 1947, at the beginning of the Cold War.

6. "Keeney, Barnaby C.," from Mitchell, *Encyclopedia Brunoniana*.

7. Ibid.

8. Aided by John D. Rockefeller Jr. in the purchase, Brown named the fields "Aldrich-Dexter," to honor his wife's Rhode Island family, along with the older name.

9. "Computing Laboratory," in Mitchell, *Encyclopedia Brunoniana*; Rhinehart, *Brown University*, 203.

10. Barnaby C. Keeney, "The Humanities and the Arts on the Verge of a Revolution," *Brown Alumni Monthly*, April 1965, 9–11.

11. *Brown Alumni Monthly*, October 1970, 12–17.

12. C. Gerald Fraser, "J. Saunders Redding, 81, Is Dead; Pioneer Black Ivy League Teacher," *New York Times*, March 5, 1988.

13. Beth Schwartzapfel, "The Doctor of Prejudice," *Brown Alumni Magazine*, September–October 2011. See also Augustus A. White III and David Chanoff, *Seeing Patients: Unconscious Bias in Health Care* (Cambridge: Harvard University Press, 2011), 44–49.

14. "African Americans," from Mitchell, *Encyclopedia Brunoniana*. On the loneliness of the tiny African American community at Brown, see J. Saunders Redding, *No Day of Triumph* (New York: Harper and Brothers, 1942), 35–42.

15. Kennedy spoke to forty thousand in what is now Kennedy Plaza, in downtown Providence, on November 7, 1960; *Brown Daily Herald*, November 8, 1960.

16. "The Birth of a New Age," speech delivered in Buffalo, August 11, 1956, in *The Papers of Martin Luther King*, eds. C. Carson et al., vol. 3, *The Birth of a New Age, December 1955–December 1956* (Berkeley: University of California Press, 1997), 340. Derek Chollet and Samantha Power, eds., *The Unquiet American: Richard Holbrooke in the World* (New York: Public Affairs, 2011), 47; *Brown Daily Herald*, November 10, 1960; November 14, 1960; supplement of November 29, 1960.

17. Barnaby Keeney, "President's Report to the Brown University Corporation" (Providence: Brown University, June 4, 1960), 15–16. Barnaby Keeney, "Speech on Magna Carta" (May 2, 1960); "President's Report to the Brown University Corporation" (October 19, 1963). Keeney's report of October 13, 1962, contained an unusually candid assessement of the difficulties African Americans faced in gaining admission to Brown and other universities; see Barnaby Keeney, "President's Report to the Brown University Corporation" (Providence: Brown University, October 13, 1962), 3–4.

18. Barnaby Keeney, "Report of the President," insert to *Brown Alumni Monthly,* December 1961; *Brown Daily Herald*, November 3, 1961; November 13, 1961.

19. http://www.neh.gov/about/history

20. Robert Goldberg and Gerald J. Goldberg, *Citizen Turner: The Wild Rise of an American Tycoon* (New York: Harcourt Brace, 1995), 59, 74; Roger Vaughan, "Ted Turner: 'I Didn't Fail College; College Failed Me,'" *Brown Alumni Monthly,* September 1975, 10–17. Turner would recall his Brown education in blunt terms: "I learned mainly about drinking and sex, and I could have gotten that for less than $3000 a year." But one suspects that it went deeper than that.

21. *Brown Alumni Monthly*, September 1975. The letter Turner's anguished father wrote to him, upon learning of his decision to major in classics, is a classic in its own right and easily available online.

22. Margaret Mead, convocation speech, October 22, 1959 (Brown University Archives).

23. *Brown Daily Herald*, November 10, 1960; November 14, 1960; supplement November 29, 1960.

24. *Pembroke Record*, May 8, 1964.

25. *Brown Daily Herald*, October 1, 1964. For more on racial attitudes at Brown in the mid-1960s, see the *Brown Alumni Monthly*'s profiles of fraternities and race (February 1965) and town/gown issues (May 1965).

26. James T. Patterson, *The Eve of Destruction: How 1965 Transformed America* (New York: Basic Books, 2012), xiii–xiv.

27. Chollet and Power, *The Unquiet American*, 46.

28. Ibid.

29. "The Amazing Story of the Black Muslims," *Brown Daily Herald*, supplement February 21, 1961. This well-reported story profiled a local temple of the Black Muslims on Chalkstone Avenue.

30. Chollet and Power, *The Unquiet American*, 47; *Brown Daily Herald*, May 10, 1961; May 12, 1961. The exact quote reported was "Get Martin Luther King to stand on a platform with me at Brown University and I'll pay his expenses." The audiotape of the talk (May 11, 1961) is available in the Brown University Archives.

31. Richard Holbrooke, audiotape recording of Ogden Lecture, May 25, 1997 (Brown University Archives).

32. Audiotape of Malcolm X lecture, May 11, 1961 (Brown University Archives).

33. Chollet and Power, *The Unquiet American*, 23, 77.

34. Undersecretary of State Nicholas Katzenbach wrote that "his ebullience is like a breath of fresh air in a world in which too few of us have retained the excitement and earnestness which we once enjoyed." Chollet and Power, *Unquiet American*, 4.

35. Chollet and Power, *The Unquiet American*, 33.

36. By coincidence, Brown's Alexander Meiklejohn, long a champion of student expression, died in Berkeley as students were protesting; *Brown Alumni Monthly,* March 1965.

37. There was some synchronicity—Berkeley was named after the Yale College of that name, which in turn was named after the Anglo-Irish philosopher who had come to Rhode Island in the eighteenth century and dreamed of an innovative new kind of university. See Wills, *Mr. Jefferson's University*, 47.

38. David Rockefeller, "Father and Brown."

39. *Brown Alumni Monthly*, April 1965; Johnson's remarks are recorded in the *Congressional Record* (October 15, 1964), A5353.

40. Patterson, *The Eve of Destruction*, 1.

41. *Brown Daily Herald*, September 30, 1964.

42. Nancy L. Buc, personal communication (December 9, 2013).

43. The *Brown Daily Herald* reviewed the show ecstatically: "There was Janis. Hunching, jumping, lunging at the microphone, stamping, clawing the air, the Blue-Eyed Soul Sister electrified an audience she huskily called 'groovy.' Janis was fresh from a show at MIT, where ironically enough, there were technical difficulties with the sound system; and she seemed as appreciative of the mammoth, undulating crowd as it was of her." *Brown Daily Herald*, April 28, 1969. A guidebook to Brown Spring Weekend proclaimed, "Repent! Repent, for judgment is at hand" (Brown University Archives).

44. Jonathan R. Cole, *The Great American University: Its Rise to Preeminence, Its Indispensable National Role, Why It Must Be Protected* (New York: Public Affairs, 2009), 145.

45. Tom Hayden, *The Port Huron Statement: The Visionary Call of the 1960s Revolution* (New York: Thunder's Mouth Press, 2005), 165–166. The Port Huron Statement was developed by Students for a Democratic Society, based on an early draft by Hayden.

46. Patterson, *The Eve of Destruction*, xiv; Nick Lemann, *The Big Test: The Secret History of the American Meritocracy* (New York: Farrar, Straus and Giroux, 1999), 167–69.

47. *Brown Alumni Monthly*, November 1968, 8.

48. *Brown Alumni Monthly*, November 1968. The Grad Center was dedicated October 12, 1968.

49. Curfews ended for juniors and seniors at Brown and Pembroke in September 1967. See *Brown Daily Herald*, September 13, 1967.

50. *Brown Daily Herald*, June 2, 1967.

51. Stuart Crump, "Folksingers Don't Eat Enough Mushrooms," *Brown Daily Herald*, April 27, 1964.

52. http://www.rirocks.net/Band%20Articles/Bob%20Dylan%201964%20 04.24%20-%20Meehan%20Aud.%20Brown%20Univ..htm

53. The two Rhode Islanders were Irving Fain and Lawrence Durgin. Anthony Walton, "The Tougaloo Connection," *Brown Alumni Monthly*, September 1997.

54. *Brown Daily Herald*, October 11, 1967; *Pembroke Record,* November 6, 1964; *Brown Alumni Monthly*, September 1997; Stanley Aronson, "One of the Righteous Few," *Brown Alumni Magazine*, January–February 2003; *Brown Alumni Monthly*, January 2013. Michael Gross, class of 1964, became a civil

rights lawyer for the Navajo tribe after his time at Tougaloo, and won important cases before the Supreme Court; Stephen Rae Brown, "Righting Wrongs," *Brown Alumni Magazine*, January–February 2013.

55. *Brown Daily Herald*, April 24, 1985.

56. *Brown Daily Herald*, April 30, 1968; Robert A. Reichley, "The Painful Birth of Afro-American Studies," *Brown Alumni Monthly*, April 1970, 30–35.

57. These seismic changes, and the experience of living through them, are eloquently captured by Spencer R. Crew, "Creating Change: Black at Brown in the 1960s," in ed. Judy Sternlight, *The Brown Reader* (New York: Simon and Schuster, 2014), 234–40. James Brown performed on April 27, 1968, on the eve of releasing "Say It Loud—I'm Black and I'm Proud." History 166 was announced in the *Brown Daily Herald*, April 30, 1968. For more background, see "African Americans," from Mitchell, *Encyclopedia Brunoniana*.

58. Kwame Anthony Appiah and Henry Louis Gates Jr., eds., *Civil Rights: An A–Z Reference of the Movement that Changed America* (Philadelphia: Running Press, 2004), 233.

59. *Brown Daily Herald*, April 24, 1967.

60. *Brown Daily Herald*, May 2, 1967. The editorial had been rejected by the *Providence Journal*, giving it all the more force in the Providence community.

61. Cole, *The Great American University*, 149.

62. Wendy Strothman, letter to Mary Ann and Walter Strothman, December 1969. Personal correspondence of Wendy Strothman.

63. *Brown Alumni Monthly,* March 1969, 2–5; July 1969. A moving profile of two wounded veterans, Alan Vaskas, class of 1967 and Thomas Coakley, class of 1968, recovering in Walter Reed Hospital, appeared in the *Brown Alumni Monthly*, January 1970, 8–13.

64. Abbott Gleason wrote, "There were four presidents in four years." Abbott Gleason, *A Liberal Education* (Cambridge: TidePool Press, 2010), 288.

65. *Brown Daily Herald*, March 14, 1969; *Pembroke Record*, May 3, 1968.

66. *Brown Alumni Monthly*, November 1969; WBRU is the oldest college radio station in the country, tracing its origins to a wire strung between rooms in Slater Hall in the 1930s.

67. Rhode Island Rocks website (rirocks.net), edited by Paul Fernandes. A roadie later remembered the show in four short but vivid sentences: "The crowd came in, everybody was drunk, a few fights broke out, there were no cops. We told the promoter that the group wouldn't play unless he got some security, which he did. The Experience did their show, which went down very well. Jimi smashed up an old Stratocaster, everybody went mad." Ibid.

68. Paine's comments at a press conference in Houston on December 27, 1968, were widely reported over the following days. They are quoted in *Brown Alumni Monthly*, April 1969.

69. To be fair, Harvard allowed some free choice, and Virginia more, under the influence of Thomas Jefferson, who wrote, "We shall . . . allow them uncontrolled choice in the lectures they shall choose to attend." Bronson, *The History of Brown University*, 271. In 1868, the *Providence Press* wrote, "Brown has always been known as the college where the instruction is of the best nature, and where the buildings are almost the poorest that could be devised." Rhinehart, *Brown University*, 28.

70. Guild, *The Life, Times, and Correspondence of James Manning*, 105.

71. *Brown Alumni Monthly*, March 1965.

72. John Rowe Workman, a Brown professor of classics, wrote a detailed history of the IC program, in which he offered the prevailing ideas each department brought into the program—it remains an interesting barometer of mid-twentieth-century thinking on what each discipline considered essential; John Rowe Workman, *New Horizons of Education: Innovation and Experimentation at Brown University* (Washington, DC: Public Affairs Press, 1959), 3, 12–13, 27–28, 51–52.

73. *Brown Daily Herald*, May 9, 1969. See also Ira C. Magaziner, "Talkin' 'Bout My Generation," in Sternlight, *The Brown Reader*, 224–33.

74. *Interim Report and Recommendations by the Special Committee on Educational Principles* (typescript, April 10, 1969, Brown University Archives), 41.

75. *Brown Alumni Monthly,* February 1969; March 1969; May 1969; July 1969; *Brown Daily Herald*, May 1–13, 1969.

76. Magaziner was profiled as a leader of the new generation, alongside Hillary Rodham of Wellesley College, in the June 20, 1969, issue of *Life* magazine.

77. Jay Barry, *Gentlemen under the Elms* (Providence: Brown University, 1982), 270; Gleason, *A Liberal Education*, 287.

78. *Brown Daily Herald*, April 12, 1975; the strike's dual purpose was to raise awareness of the war and end racial repression. See daily coverage, *Brown Daily Herald*, May 5–7, 1970; see also *Brown Alumni Monthly*, July 1970. In other theatrical protests, students held up bananas when the ambassador to Guatemala received an honorary degree, and held mock funerals for "Sacco and Vanzetti" and "Etcetera."

79. Before the Immigration Act of 1965, only 2,990 Asians a year came to the United States; after, 1.5 million came in 1970, and 7 million in 1990. Nick Lemann, *The Big Test*, 241–42.

80. The *Brown Daily Herald*, December 10, 1969, describes students mobilizing to fight pollution. A subsequent exposé describes Brown's dumping of trash along the Seekonk River; *Brown Daily Herald*, April 9, 1970.

81. "Gay Liberation Comes of Age," *Brown Daily Herald*, October 30, 1973; "Homosexuality: Does Anyone Care?" *Brown Daily Herald*, March 20, 1974; history of LGBT students at Brown by Raymond Butti, document shared by permission. A letter to the *Brown Daily Herald* recalled anti-gay hazing as far back as 1963.

82. Thomas Mallon, "The Year of Thinking Dangerously," *Brown Alumni Magazine*, May 1998, 48–53.

83. *Brown Daily Herald*, March 18, 1969; Rhinehart, *Brown University*, 44–46. Rhinehart indicates the striking degree to which John Nicholas Brown—who might have been a staunch defender of conservatism—was an avatar of modernism, and guided Philip Johnson through a difficult design process. Once again, it was Old Brown and New Brown.

84. Mallon, "The Year of Thinking Dangerously," 48–53.

85. Ibid.

86. *Brown Daily Herald*, March 21, 1969; *Brown Alumni Monthly,* April 1969.

87. *Brown Alumni Monthly,* March 1969, 10; "The Making of a Medical School" (The Warren Alpert Medical School of Brown University).

88. *Brown Daily Herald*, January 29, 1970. The final issue of the *Pembroke Record*, announcing its own demise, appeared May 5, 1970.

89. The first Women's Studies courses were given by Anne Fausto-Sterling and Louise Lamphere; Elizabeth Weed, "Notes on Pembroke Center's History, 1981–2011" (Providence: Pembroke Center for Teaching and Research on Women, 2011), 4.

90. Ibid.; Lyde Cullen Sizer, "A Place for a Good Woman: The Development of Women Faculty at Brown," in Kaufman, *The Search for Equity*, 184.

91. Hornig letter to Brown community, May 1, 1975.

92. *Brown Daily Herald*, April 12, April 16, April 24–26, June 1, 1975; April 24, 1985.

93. The John Carter Brown Library and the *Brown Alumni Monthly* published a book of essays in honor of the Bicentennial, *Liberty's Impact: The World Views 1776* (Providence: Brown Alumni Monthly and John Carter Brown Library, 1976).

94. Howard Swearer obituary, *New York Times*, October 21, 1991.

95. Weed, "Notes on Pembroke Center's History," 4. By 1992, it was determined that Brown was in full compliance; Vartan Gregorian, *The Road to Home: My Life and Times* (New York: Simon and Schuster, 2003), 323–24.

96. Richard Perez-Pena, "Don't Call Me a Boomer," *New York Times*, January 12, 2014.

97. I thank Raymond Butti for these statistics.

98. Irene Chen, "TWC Turns Thirty Years Old," *Brown Daily Herald*, May 23, 2007.

99. Gleason, *A Liberal Education*, 268.

100. Bob Marley played at Meehan Auditorium on September 17, 1980, four days before collapsing while jogging in Central Park; he died on May 11, 1981.

101. Jeffrey Eugenides, *The Marriage Plot* (New York: Farrar, Straus and Giroux, 2011), 4.

102. I am grateful to Karen Sibley and Alyssa Frezza for their help with the history of what is now the School of Professional Studies.

103. Leon Cooper shared the 1972 Nobel Prize in Physics; Gordon Wood won the Pulitzer Prize for History in 1993.

104. Gregorian, *The Road to Home*, 315–16. Trillin's poem is worth reprinting, in part:

> *And now he is Rhode Island bound*
> *In Providence he thinks he's found*
> *A tranquil place—a place where he*
> *Can write about philosophy.*
> *As he presides as chief Brown bear,*
> *And brings a little culture there,*
> *And talks of Plato, such as that,*
> *And eats the food of Ararat.*
> *It sounds so good.*
> *But what he'll find in several weeks*
> *Is Brown has roofs, and roofs have leaks.*
> *And Brown has books, and books get old.*
> *Their temperature must be controlled.*
> *He may find walls decaying or*
> *Curriculum in need of core.*
> *He'll have the usual on his plate.*
> *So Socrates will have to wait.*

Calvin Trillin, "The Man Who Saved the Library: An Ode to Vartan Gregorian," *Brown Alumni Monthly*, March 1989, 32–33. Reprinted with permission from *The New York Times Book Review*, February 5, 1989. ©1989 by the New York Times Company.

105. Francis Fukuyama's essay "The End of History?" appeared in *The National Interest* (Summer 1989).

106. Gregorian, *The Road to Home*, 310.

107. Ibid., 318–19, 325.

108. Ibid., 322.

109. The Annenberg Institute for School Reform was dedicated in 1993, the Watson Institute was officially named, and a residential quad was named after Gregorian. Gregorian, *The Road to Home*, 324.

110. *Brown Daily Herald*, January 22, 1997.

111. Gregorian, *The Road to Home*, 321.

112. *Brown Daily Herald*, January 22, 1997.

113. *Brown Daily Herald*, November 11, 2000.

114. *Brown Daily Herald*, November 16, 2013.

115. "Providence Puts Focus on Making a Home for Knowledge," *New York Times*, December 13, 2011.

116. Ruth J. Simmons, "Address at Touro Synagogue on President Washington's Letter" (Brown University news release, August 19, 2007).

117. Christina Paxson, "Class of 2016 Welcome," Office of the President (Providence: Brown University).

118. *Brown Alumni Monthly*, January–February 1998, 57.

119. *Brown Alumni Monthly*, July–August 2014, 69.

120. Brown admissions applications are up from 12,638 for the class of 1988; in that year, 43 percent of applicants were from New York and New England; that figure is now 24 percent. *Brown Daily Herald*, March 3, 2014.

121. I'm grateful to James Miller and the Admissions Office for helping me calculate this figure.

122. *The Adams Papers*, *Adams Family Correspondence*, vol. 2, *June 1776–March 1778*, ed. L. H. Butterfield (Cambridge: Harvard University Press, 1963), 31.

123. Williams, *A Key into the Language of America*, xiv. On Curiosity, see "Ralph Milliken: Curiosity's Mission on Mars" (Brown University news release, August 2, 2012).

BIBLIOGRAPHY

Aldrich, Nelson W., Jr. *Old Money: The Mythology of America's Upper Class*. New York: Alfred A. Knopf, 1988.

Angell, James B. *The Reminiscences of James Burrill Angell*. New York: Longmans, Green, 1912.

Appiah, Kwame Anthony, and Henry Louis Gates, Jr., eds. *Civil Rights: An A–Z Reference of the Movement that Changed America*. Philadelphia: Running Press, 2004.

Appleton, Marguerite. *A Portrait Album of Four Great Rhode Island Leaders*. Providence: Rhode Island Historical Society, 1978.

Aronson, Stanley. "One of the Righteous Few." *Brown Alumni Magazine*, January–February 2003.

Backus, Isaac, *The Diary of Isaac Backus*. 3 vols., edited by William G. McLoughlin. Providence: Brown University, 1979.

Bailyn, Bernard. *The Peopling of British North America: An Introduction*. New York: Knopf, 1986.

———. *Voyagers to the West: A Passage in the Peopling of America on the Eve of the Revolution*. New York: Knopf, 1986.

Barry, Jay. *Gentlemen under the Elms*. Providence: Brown Alumni Monthly, 1982.

———. "He Pitched Baseball's First 'Perfect Game.'" *Brown Alumni Monthly*, October 1964.

Barry, Jay, and Martha Mitchell. *A Tale of Two Centuries: A Warm and Richly Pictorial History of Brown University, 1764–1985*. Providence: Brown Alumni Monthly, 1985.

Barry, John M. *Roger Williams and the Creation of the American Soul: Church, State and the Birth of Liberty*. New York: Viking, 2012.

Bateman, Jonathan. "Three Anniversaries and a University: The Meaning of Brown's Celebrations in 1864, 1914, and 1964." Brown University honors thesis, 2013.

Belluscio, Lynne. "The Story of Forgiveness." *Le Roy Pennysaver*, June 12, 2011. http://www.leroyhistoricalsociety.org/assets/061211---the-story-of-forgiveness.pdf.

Bicknell, Thomas Williams. *The History of the State of Rhode Island and Providence Plantations.* New York: American Historical Society, 1920.

Bishop, J. Leander. *A History of American Manufactures from 1608 to 1860.* Philadelphia: E. Young and Company, 1866.

Black, Jeannette D., and William Greene Roelker, eds. *A Rhode Island Chaplain in the Revolution: Letters of Ebenezer David to Nicholas Brown, 1775–1778.* Providence: Rhode Island Society of the Cincinnati, 1949.

Blair, Karen J. "The Women's Club Movement Creates and Defines the College." In *The Search for Equity: Women at Brown University, 1891–1991*, edited by Polly Welts Kaufman. Hanover, NH: Brown University, 1991.

Blau, Joseph L. *American Philosophic Addresses, 1700–1900.* New York: Columbia University Press, 1946.

Boyle, Sheila Tully, and Andrew Bunie. *Paul Robeson: The Years of Promise and Achievement.* Amherst: University of Massachusetts Press, 2001.

Bridenbaugh, Carl. *Cities in Revolt: Urban Life in America, 1743–1776.* New York: Alfred A. Knopf, 1955.

———. *Fat Mutton and Liberty of Conscience: Society in Rhode Island, 1636–1690.* Providence: Brown University Press, 1974.

———. "Newport's Graceful Gestures." *Brown Alumni Monthly*, October 1964.

———. *Peter Harrison: First American Architect.* Chapel Hill: University of North Carolina Press, 1949.

Bronson, Walter C. *The History of Brown University, 1764–1914.* Providence: The University, 1914.

Brown Alumni Monthly / Brown Alumni Magazine. Providence: Brown University.

Brown, Cynthia Stokes. *Alexander Meiklejohn: Teacher of Freedom.* Berkeley, CA: Meiklejohn Civil Liberties Institute, 1981.

Brown Daily Herald. Providence: Brown University.

Brown, John Nicholas. "The Story of Brown's Amazing Charter." *Brown Alumni Monthly*, April 1964.

Brown, Lloyd. *The Young Paul Robeson: "On My Journey Now."* Boulder: Westview Press, 1997.

Brown, Marion E., ed. "Solomon Drowne, Student: His Papers and Journals, 1753–1774." Brown University master's thesis, 1954.

Brown, Robert Perkins, Henry Robinson Palmer, Harry Lyman Thompson, and Clarence Saunders Brigham, eds. *Memories of Brown: Traditions and Recollections Gathered from Many Sources.* Providence: Brown Alumni Magazine, 1909.

Brown, Sharon. *Two Centuries of Brown Verse, 1764–1964.* Providence, Brown University Bicentennial Publications Committee, 1964.

Brown, Stephen Rae. "Righting Wrongs." *Brown Alumni Magazine*, January–February 2013.

Brown University in the War. Providence: War Records Committee of Brown University, May 1919.

Brown, William J. *The Life of William J. Brown, of Providence, R.I., with Personal Recollections of Incidents in Rhode Island*. Providence: Angell & Co., 1883. Reprint, Durham, NH: University of New Hampshire Press, 2006.

Burlingame, Edwin A. *Plat of the Rhode Island College Property of 1770, and Plats of the Succeeding Brown University Properties in 1870, 1904 and 1938: Together with an Abridged History of These Properties*. Providence: The University, 1938.

Burrage, Henry S., ed. *Brown University in the Civil War: A Memorial*. Providence: Providence Press Company, 1868.

———. "The College During the Civil War." In *Memories of Brown: Traditions and Recollections Gathered from Many Sources*, edited by Robert Perkins Brown, Henry Robinson Palmer, Harry Lyman Thompson, and Clarence Saunders Brigham. Providence: Brown Alumni Magazine, 1909.

———, ed. *Civil War Record of Brown University*. Providence, 1920.

Butterfield, L. H., ed. *The Adams Papers* (34 vols.), *Adams Family Correspondence* (9 vols.), editor of vol. 1 (December 1761–May 1776) & vol. 2 (June 1776–March 1778). Cambridge: Harvard University Press, 1963.

Carroll, John M. *Fritz Pollard: Pioneer in Racial Advancement*. Urbana, IL: University of Illinois Press, 1992.

———. *Celebration of the One Hundredth Anniversary of the Founding of Brown University*, September 6th, 1864. Providence: S. S. Rider, 1865.

Chafee, Zechariah, Jr. *Freedom of Speech*. New York: Harcourt, Brace and Company, 1920.

———. *Freedom of Speech and Press*. New York: Carrie Chapman Catt Memorial Fund, 1955.

Chaput, Erik. *The People's Martyr: Thomas Wilson Dorr and His 1842 Rhode Island Rebellion*. Lawrence, KS: University Press of Kansas, 2013.

Chase, Jeremy. "Francis Wayland: A Uniting Force in an Era of Disunion." Brown University bachelor's thesis, 2006.

Chase, Laurence B. "S. J. Perelman and Nathanael West: Two for the Hee Haw or Tender is the Blight." *Brown Alumni Monthly*, February 1971.

Chen, Irene. "TWC Turns Thirty Years Old. " *Brown Daily Herald*, May 23, 2007.

Chollet, Derek, and Samantha Power, eds. *The Unquiet American: Richard Holbrooke in the World*. New York: Public Affairs, 2011.

Clark-Pujara, Christy. "The Business of Slavery and Anti-Slavery Sentiment:

The Case of Rowland Gibson Hazard—An Antislavery 'Negro Cloth' Dealer," *Rhode Island History* 71, no. 2 (Summer/Fall 2013).

Cole, Jonathan R. *The Great American University: Its Rise to Preeminence, Its Indispensable National Role, Why It Must Be Protected.* New York: Public Affairs, 2009.

Coleman, Peter J. *The Transformation of Rhode Island, 1790–1860.* Providence: Brown University Press, 1963. Reprint, Westport, CT: Greenwood Press, 1985.

Commager, Henry Steele, ed. *Lester Ward and the Welfare State.* Indianapolis: Bobbs-Merrill, 1967.

Conley, Patrick. "The War of 1812 and Rhode Island: A Bicentennial Bust," *Rhode Island History* 72, no. 1 Winter/Spring 2014.

Coughtry, Jay. *The Notorious Triangle: Rhode Island and the African Slave Trade, 1700–1807.* Philadelphia: Temple University Press, 1981.

Cremin, Lawrence, ed. *The Republic and the School: Horace Mann on the Education of Free Men.* New York: Teachers College of Columbia University, 1957.

Crew, Spencer R. "Creating Change: Black at Brown in the 1960s." In *The Brown Reader,* edited by Judy Sternlight. New York: Simon and Schuster, 2014.

Crump, Stuart. "Folksingers Don't Eat Enough Mushrooms." *Brown Daily Herald,* April 27, 1964.

Curran, Kathleen, ed. *Thomas Alexander Tefft: American Architecture in Transition, 1845–1860.* Providence: Department of Art, Brown University, 1988.

David, Leroy. "John Hope at Brown University: The Black Man Who Refused to Pass for White." *The Journal of Blacks in Higher Education* 22 (Winter 1998–1999).

Delbanco, Andrew. *College: What It Was, and Should Be.* Princeton: Princeton University Press, 2012.

Downing, Antoinette F. *The Architectural Heritage of Newport, Rhode Island, 1640–1915.* Cambridge: Harvard University Press, 1952.

Dunwell, Steve. *The Run of the Mill: A Pictorial Narrative of the Expansion, Dominion, Decline and Enduring Impact of the New England Textile Industry.* Boston: David R. Godine, 1978.

Edwards, Morgan. *Materials for a History of the Baptists in Pennsylvania.* Philadelphia: Printed by Joseph Crukshank and Isaac Collins, 1770.

———. *Materials for a History of the Baptists in Rhode Island.* Manuscript, 1771, Rhode Island Historical Society. Photocopy, Brown University Library.

Ellison, Ralph. *The Collected Essays of Ralph Ellison.* Edited by John F. Callahan. New York: Modern Library, 1995.

———. *Invisible Man.* New York: Random House, 1952. Reprint, New York: Penguin, 1965.

———. "Portrait of Inman Page." *The Carleton Miscellany* 18, no. 3 (Winter 1980). Reprinted in Ralph Ellison, *Going to the Territory*. New York: Modern Library, 1995.

Emlen, Robert P. "Slave Labor at the College Edifice: Building Brown University's University Hall in 1770." *Rhode Island History* 66, no. 2 (Summer 2008).

———. "Picturing Brown: The First Views of the College." http://library.brown.edu/cds/images_of_brown/emlen/

Eugenides, Jeffrey. *The Marriage Plot*. New York: Farrar, Straus and Giroux, 2011.

Faunce, William H. P. *Annual Report of the President to the Corporation of Brown University*. Providence: Brown University, October, 1917.

———. *Annual Report of the President to the Corporation of Brown University*. Providence: Brown University, October, 1919.

———. *Annual Report of the President to the Corporation of Brown University*. Providence: Brown University, 1924.

———. "Baccalaureate Address," *Brown Alumni Monthly*, July 1917.

———. "Brown in the War," *Brown Alumni Monthly*, July 1918.

———. "Roger Williams and His Doctrine of Soul Liberty." In *Pioneers of Religious Liberty in America: Being the Great and Thursday Lectures Delivered in Boston in nineteen hundred and three*, 49–82. Boston: American Unitarian Association, 1903.

Filler, Louis, ed. *Horace Mann on the Crisis in Education*. Yellow Springs, OH: Antioch Press, 1965.

Fleming, Donald. *Science and Technology in Providence, 1760–1914: An Essay in the History of Brown University in the Metropolitan Community*. Providence: Brown University, 1952.

Folsom, Mitchell Brewster, and Steven D. Lubar. *The Philosophy of Manufactures: Early Debates over Industrialization in the United States*. Cambridge: MIT Press, 1982.

Fosdick, Raymond B. *John D. Rockefeller, Jr.: A Portrait*. New York: Harper and Brothers, 1956.

———. "The Student Years of Johnny Rock." *Brown Alumni Monthly*, May 1956.

Fountain, Henry. "A Lost World Is Resurrected at Brown." *New York Times*, July 28, 2014.

Franklin, Benjamin. *Writings*. New York: Library of America, 1987.

Fraser, C. Gerald. "J. Saunders Redding, 81, Is Dead; Pioneer Black Ivy League Teacher." *New York Times*, March 5, 1988.

Fukuyama, Francis. "The End of History?" *The National Interest*, Summer 1989.

Gale, Steven H. *S. J. Perelman: A Critical Study*. New York: Greenwood Press, 1987.

Garland, Joseph E. *To Meet These Wants: The Story of Rhode Island Hospital, 1863–1988*. Providence: Rhode Island Hospital, 1988.

Gaustad, Edwin S. *George Berkeley in America*. New Haven: Yale University Press, 1979.

George, Robert H. *Brown University on the Eve of the Civil War. Brunonians in Confederate Ranks, 1861–1865*. Providence: Brown University, 1965.

Gettleman, Marvin E. *The Dorr Rebellion: A Study in American Radicalism, 1833–1849*. New York: Random House, 1973.

Gleason, Abbott. *A Liberal Education*. Cambridge: TidePool Press, 2010.

Goldberg, Robert, and Gerald J. Goldberg. *Citizen Turner: The Wild Rise of an American Tycoon*. New York: Harcourt Brace, 1995.

Greene, Lorenzo J. "Some Observations on the Black Regiment of Rhode Island in the American Revolution," *Journal of Negro History* 37 (April 1952).

Gregorian, Vartan. *The Road to Home: My Life and Times*. New York: Simon and Schuster, 2003.

Guild, Reuben Aldridge. *A Biographical Introduction to Roger Williams*. Providence: Publications of the Narragansett Club, 1866.

———. *The Early History of Brown University, Including the Life, Times and Correspondence of President Manning, 1756–1791*. Providence: Snow and Farnham, 1896.

———. *Footprints of Roger Williams*. Providence: Tibbits and Preston, 1886.

———. *Historical Sketch of Brown University*. Providence: Snow and Greene, 1858.

———. *Historical Sketch of the Library of Brown University, with Regulations*. New Haven: Tuttle, Morehouse and Taylor, 1861.

———. *History of Brown University, with Illustrative Documents*. Providence: Providence Press Company, 1867.

———. *Life, Times, and Correspondence of James Manning, and the Early History of Brown University*. Boston: Gould and Lincoln, 1864.

Hamlin, Talbot. *Greek Revival Architecture in America*. New York: Oxford University Press, 1944.

Hanlon, John, and David Philips. *Ever True: The History of Brown Football*. Providence: Brown University Sports Foundation, 2003.

Hawk, Grace. *Pembroke College in Brown University: The First Seventy-five Years, 1891–1966*. Providence: Brown University, 1967.

Hay, John. *The Life and Works of John Hay, 1838–1905*. Providence: Brown University Library, 1961.

Hayden, Tom. *The Port Huron Statement: The Visionary Call of the 1960s Revolution*. New York: Thunder's Mouth Press, 2005.

Hedges, James B. *The Browns of Providence Plantations: Colonial Years.* Providence: Harvard University Press, 1952.

————. *The Browns of Providence Plantations: The Nineteenth Century.* Providence: Brown University Press, 1968.

Heimert, Alan. *Religion and the American Mind: From the Great Awakening to the Revolution.* Cambridge: Harvard University Press, 1966.

Herbst, Jurgen. *From Crisis to Crisis: American College Government, 1636–1819.* Cambridge: Harvard University Press, 1982.

Herrmann, Dorothy. *S. J. Perelman: A Life.* New York: Putnam, 1986.

Hinds, Katharine. "The Minkins Sisters," *Brown Alumni Monthly*, April 1982.

Historical Catalogue of Brown University, 1764–1904. Providence: The University, 1905.

Historical Catalogue of Brown University, 1924: The Women's College. Providence: The University, 1924.

Holbrooke, Richard. Audiotape recording of Ogden Lecture, May 25, 1997. Brown University Archives.

Hopkins, Stephen. *The Rights of Colonies Examined.* Providence: William Goddard, 1765. Reprint, edited by Paul Campbell. Providence: Rhode Island Bicentennial Foundation, 1974.

Horwitz, Tony. *Midnight Rising: John Brown and the Raid that Sparked the Civil War.* New York: Henry Holt, 2011.

Hughes, Charles Evans. *The Autobiographical Notes of Charles Evans Hughes.* Edited by David J. Danelski and Joseph S. Tulchin. Cambridge: Harvard University Press, 1973.

————. "The Historical Address." In *A Century of Scholars: Rhode Island Alpha of Phi Beta Kappa, 1830–1930*, edited by William T. Hastings. Providence: D. B. Updike, The Merrymount Press, 1943.

————. "Remarks of Chief Justice Hughes." Typescript, June 21, 1937, Brown University Archives

Hühner, Leon. "Jews in Connection with the Colleges of the Thirteen Original States Prior to 1800." *Publications of the American Jewish Historical Society*, 1910.

Ibuki, Yuka, Toshimi Kumai, and Susan Fertig-Dykes. "2011 Dialogue on the Hopevale Martyrdom Panay in 1943: A Japanese Veteran Inspired by Daughter of American Guerilla Officer." http://www.us-japandialogueonpows.org/Ibuki%20Kumai.htm.

Interim Report and Recommendations by the Special Committee on Educational Principles, April 10, 1969. Typescript, Brown University Archives.

Jefferson, Thomas. *Notes on the State of Virginia.* Edited by William Peden. Chapel Hill: University of North Carolina Press, 1955. Reprint, 1982.

Jeremy, David J. "Innovation in American Textile Technology During the Early Nineteenth Century." *Technology and Culture* 14 (January 1973).

Jones, Howard Mumford. "Horace Mann's Crusade." In *America in Crisis: Fourteen Crucial Episodes in American History*, edited by Daniel Aaron. New York: Knopf, 1952.

Joshi, S. T. *A Dreamer and a Visionary: H. P. Lovecraft in His Time*. Liverpool: Liverpool University Press, 2001.

Joukowsky, Artemis, Harold Ambler, David Philips, Christian Albert, and Marcia Hooper. *Ever True: The History of Brown Crew*. Providence: Brown University Sports Foundation, 2010.

Kaminer, April. "New Contenders Emerge in Quest to Identify Yale's First African-American Graduate." *New York Times*, March 16, 2014.

Karabel, Jerome. *The Chosen: The Hidden History of Admission and Exclusion at Harvard, Yale and Princeton*. Boston: Houghton Mifflin, 2005.

Kaufman, Polly Welts, ed. *The Search for Equity: Women at Brown University, 1891–1991*. Hanover, NH: Brown University, 1991.

Keen, William Williams. *The Early Years of Brown University, 1764–1770*. Address delivered in the Baptist Church at Warren, October 13, 1914. [Boston: D. B. Updike, Merrymount Press, 1915].

———. "The Early Years of Brown University (1764–1770) While Located in Warren, Rhode Island." Typescript, 1914. 150th Anniversary Files, Brown University Archives.

Keeney, Barnaby C. "The Humanities and the Arts on the Verge of a Revolution." *Brown Alumni Monthly*, April 1965.

———. "President's Report to the Brown University Corporation." Providence: Brown University, June 4, 1960.

———. "President's Report to the Brown University Corporation." Providence: Brown University, October 13, 1962.

———. "President's Report to the Brown University Corporation." Providence: Brown University, October 19, 1963.

———. "Report of the President." Insert to *Brown Alumni Monthly*, December 1961.

———. "Speech at Pembroke, 1958." Typescript, Brown University Archives.

———. "Speech on Magna Carta." May 2, 1960.

Kenny, Robert W. *Town and Gown in Wartime*. Providence: University Relations Office of Brown University, 1976.

Kesack, Robert A. "The Old Brick School House (1769)." Providence: The Providence Preservation Society, 2013. http://www.ppsri.org/documents/brick-school-house-history-report-for-web-pdf.pdf.

Kimball, Gertrude Selwyn. *Pictures of Rhode Island in the Past, 1643–1833.* Providence: Preston and Rounds Company, 1900.

———. *Providence in Colonial Times.* Boston: Houghton Mifflin, 1912.

Kulik, Gary, Roger Parks, and Theodore Z. Penn, eds. *The New England Mill Village, 1790–1860.* Cambridge, MIT Press, 1982.

Lamoree, Karen M. "Why Not a Jewish Girl? The Jewish Experience at Pembroke College in Brown University." In *The Jews of Rhode Island*, edited by George M. Goodwin and Ellen Smith. Waltham: Brandeis University Press, 2004.

Lee, Maureen D. "Rhode Island's Star Soprano: Sissieretta Jones." *Rhode Island History* 72, no. 2 (Summer/Fall 2014).

Lemann, Nicholas. *The Big Test: The Secret History of the American Meritocracy.* New York: Farrar, Straus and Giroux, 1999.

Lemons, J. Stanley. *The First Baptist Church in America.* Providence: Charitable Baptist Society, 1988.

Long, Robert Emmet. *Nathanael West.* New York: Ungar, 1985.

Lovecraft, H. P. *The Case of Charles Dexter Ward.* 1943; New York: Ballantine, 1971.

———. *Lord of a Visible World: An Autobiography in Letters.* Edited by S. T. Joshi and David E. Schultz. Athens, OH: Ohio University Press, 2000.

MacDonald, William. "Address." In *Exercises Commemorating the Restoration of University Hall.* Providence: Standard Printing Company, 1905.

Magaziner, Ira C. "Talkin' 'Bout My Generation." In *The Brown Reader*, edited by Judy Sternlight. New York: Simon and Schuster, 2014.

Mallon, Thomas. "The Year of Thinking Dangerously." *Brown Alumni Magazine*, May 1998.

Marcus Aurelius, *Meditations*, in *Marcus Aurelius and His Times: The Transition from Paganism to Christianity.* Roslyn, NY: W. J. Black, 1945.

Maring, Norman H. *Baptists in New Jersey: A Study in Transition.* Valley Forge, PA: Judson Press, 1964.

Marks, Percy. *Nathanael West: A Collection of Critical Essays.* Englewood Cliffs, NJ: Prentice-Hall, 1971.

———. *The Plastic Age.* New York: Century Co., 1924.

McLachlan, John, ed. *Princetonians, 1748–1768: A Biographical Dictionary.* Princeton: Princeton University Press, 1976.

McLoughlin, William G. *Isaac Backus and the American Pietistic Tradition.* Boston: Little-Brown, 1967.

———. *New England Dissent, 1630–1833: The Baptists and the Separation of Church and State.* Cambridge: Harvard University Press, 1971.

———. *Rhode Island: A History.* New York: W. W. Norton, 1978. Reprint, 1986.

———. *Soul Liberty: The Baptists' Struggle in New England, 1630–1833*. Hanover, NH: University Press of New England, 1991.

Mead, Margaret. Convocation speech, October 22, 1959. Brown University Archives.

Meade, Marion. *Lonelyhearts: The Screwball World of Nathanael West and Eileen McKenney*. Boston: Houghton Mifflin Harcourt, 2010.

Meiklejohn, Alexander. *Education between Two Worlds*. New York: Harper and Brothers, 1942.

———. *The Experimental College*. New York: Harper and Brothers, 1932.

———. *Free Speech and Its Relation to Self-Government*. New York: Harper, 1948.

———. *What Does America Mean?* New York: W. W. Norton, 1935.

Menand, Louis. *The Marketplace of Ideas: Reform and Resistance in the American University*. New York: W. W. Norton, 2010.

Miller, Robert M. *Harry Emerson Fosdick: Preacher, Pastor, Prophet*. New York: Oxford University Press, 1985.

Mitchell, Martha. *Encyclopedia Brunoniana*. Providence: Brown University Library, 1993. http://www.brown.edu/Administration/News_Bureau/Databases/Encyclopedia/

Moore, Donald K., ed., *Liberty's Impact: The World Views 1776*. Providence: Brown Alumni Monthly and John Carter Brown Library, 1976.

Morgan, Edmund S. *The Gentle Puritan: A Life of Ezra Stiles, 1727–1795*. New Haven: Yale University Press, 1962.

Mumford, Lewis. *The Brown Decades: A Study of the Arts of America, 1865–1895*. New York: Harcourt, Brace and Company, 1931. Reprint, New York: Dover Publications, 1955.

Munro, Walter Lee. *The Old Back Campus at Brown*. Providence: Haley and Sykes, 1929.

Okrent, Daniel. *Great Fortune: The Epic of Rockefeller Center*. New York: Penguin, 2003.

Parsons, Charles W. *The Medical School Formerly Existing at Brown University, Its Professors and Graduates*. Providence: S. S. Rider, 1881.

———. *Memoir of Usher Parsons, M.D., of Providence, Rhode Island*. Providence: Hammond, Angell and Company, 1870.

Parsons, Usher. *Battle of Lake Erie: Discourse before the Rhode Island Historical Society*. Providence: B. T. Albro, 1854.

———. *Indian Names of Places in Rhode-Island*. Providence: Knowles, Anthony and Co., 1861.

———. *Sketches of Rhode Island Physicians, Deceased Prior to 1850*. Providence: Knowles, Anthony and Co., 1859.

Pastore, Christopher L. *Between Land and Sea: The Atlantic Coast and the Transformation of New England.* Cambridge: Harvard University Press, 2014.

Patterson, James T. *The Eve of Destruction: How 1965 Transformed America.* New York: Basic Books, 2012.

———. *Grand Expectations: The United States, 1945–1974.* New York: Oxford University Press, 1996.

Paxson, Christina. "Class of 2016 Welcome." Providence: Office of the President, Brown University, 2012. http://www.brown.edu/about/administration/president/class-of-2016-welcome.

Pembroke Record. Providence: Brown University.

Perelman, S. J. *The Last Laugh.* New York: Simon and Schuster, 1981.

———. "Nathanael West: A Portrait." In Jay Martin, *Nathanael West: The Art of His Life.* New York: Farrar, Straus and Giroux, 1970.

Perez-Pena, Richard. "Don't Call Me a Boomer." *New York Times,* January 12, 2014.

Perry, Amos. *Memorial of Zachariah Allen.* Cambridge: J. Wilson and Son, 1882.

Phillips, Janet M. *Brown University: A Short History.* Providence: Office of University Relations, 1992, Revised edition, Providence: Office of Public Affairs and University Relations, 2000.

Pierrel, Rosemary. "O, Why Should a Woman Not Get a Degree?" *Brown Alumni Monthly,* May 1965.

Piersen, William. *Black Yankees: The Development of an Afro-American Subculture in Eighteenth-century New England.* Amherst: University of Massachusetts Press, 1988.

Pierson, George Wilson. *Tocqueville in America.* Baltimore: Johns Hopkins University Press, 1996. Originally published as *Tocqueville and Beaumont in America.* New York: Oxford University Press, 1938.

Rappleye, Charles. *Sons of Providence: The Brown Brothers, the Slave Trade, and the American Revolution.* New York: Simon and Schuster, 2006.

Redding, J. Saunders, *No Day of Triumph.* New York: Harper and Brothers, 1942.

———. *A Scholar's Conscience: Selected Writings of J. Saunders Redding, 1942–1977.* Edited by Faith Berry. Lexington, KY: University Press of Kentucky, 1992.

Reichley, Robert A. "The Painful Birth of Afro-American Studies." *Brown Alumni Monthly,* April 1970.

Renehan, Edward J., Jr. *The Secret Six: The True Tale of the Men Who Conspired with John Brown.* New York: Crown, 1995.

Reynolds, Quentin. "When Pep Was a Ghost." *Brown Alumni Monthly,* December 1957.

Rhinehart, Raymond P. *Brown University: An Architectural Tour.* New York: Princeton Architectural Books, 2014.

Rhode Island Black Heritage Society. *Creative Survival: The Providence Black Community in the 19th Century*. Providence: Rhode Island Black Heritage Society, 1985.

Rhode Island Rocks website (rirocks.net). Edited by Paul Fernandes. http://www.rirocks.net/Band%20Articles/Jimi%20Hendrix%201968%2003.08%20-%20Marvel%20Gym,%20Brown%20Univ.htm.

Rockefeller Archive Center. "The Rockefellers: John D. Rockefeller, Junior, 1874–1960." September 1997. http://www.rockarch.org/bio/jdrjr.php.

Rockefeller, David. "Father and Brown." *Brown Alumni Monthly*, December 1964.

Roelker, William Greene. "The Browns and Brown University." In *Essays Honoring Lawrence C. Wroth*, edited by Frederick R. Goff. Portland, ME: Anthoensen Press, 1951.

———. "The Browns of Brown University." *Brown Alumni Monthly*, December 1948.

Ross, Theresa. "'The Lengthened Shadow of One Man': E. Benjamin Andrews and Brown University, 1889–1898." *Rhode Island History* 65, no. 1 (Winter/Spring 2007), 3–28.

Rotondi, Jessica. "Navy Blue and Brown: World War Two Comes to College Hill." Brown University senior thesis, 2007.

Salitan, Lucille, and Eve Lewis Perera, eds. *Virtuous Lives: Four Quaker Sisters Remember Family Life, Abolitionism, and Women's Suffrage*. New York: Continuum, 1994.

Sanborn, F. B. *Dr. S. G. Howe, the Philanthropist*. New York: Funk & Wagnalls, 1891.

Sammis, Norman L. "Hockey Was Our Game, Too." *Brown Alumni Monthly*, May 1965.

Schwartzapfel, Beth. "The Doctor of Prejudice." *Brown Alumni Magazine*, September–October 2011. http://www.brownalumnimagazine.com/content/view/2981/40/.

Scott, James Brown. Introduction to volume 1, *The American Secretaries of State and Their Diplomacy* (18 vols.), edited by Samuel Flagg Bemis and Robert H. Ferrell. New York: Cooper Square Publishers, 1963.

Shenk, Joshua Wolf. *Lincoln's Melancholy: How Depression Challenged a President and Fueled his Greatness*. New York: Houghton Mifflin Harcourt, 2005.

Shesol, Jeff. *Supreme Power: Franklin Roosevelt vs. the Supreme Court*. New York: W. W. Norton, 2010.

Slavery and Justice: Report of the Brown University Steering Committee on Slavery and Justice. Providence: Brown University, 2006.

Simmons, Ruth J. "Address at Touro Synagogue on President Washington's Letter." Brown University news release, August 19, 2007. https://news.brown.edu/articles/2007/08/touro-address.

Simon, James F. *FDR and Chief Justice Hughes: The President, the Supreme Court, and the Epic Battle over the New Deal*. New York: Simon and Schuster, 2012.

Sizer, Lyde Cullen. "A Place for a Good Woman: The Development of Women Faculty at Brown." In *The Search for Equity: Women at Brown University, 1891–1991*, edited by Polly Welts Kaufman. Hanover, NH: Brown University, 1991.

Sohn, Amy. "Probing Brown's Dark History." Forward.com, November 10, 2006. http://forward.com/articles/8366/probing-brown-s-dark-history/.

Steinberg, Theodore. *Nature Incorporated: Industrialization and the Waters of New England*. New York: Cambridge University Press, 1991.

Sternlight, Judy, ed. *The Brown Reader: Fifty Writers Remember College Hill*. New York: Simon and Schuster, 2014.

Stillwell, Margaret B. "Speech delivered at the installation of Dean Nancy Duke Lewis." September 19, 1950. Brown University Archives.

Sweet, William Warren. *Religion on the American Frontier: 1783–1850*. New York: H. Holt and Company, 1931.

Taliaferro, John. *All the Great Prizes: The Life of John Hay, from Lincoln to Roosevelt*. New York: Simon and Schuster, 2013.

Taylor, George R. *The Transportation Revolution, 1815–1860*. New York: Rinehart, 1951.

Teicholz, Tom, ed. *Conversations with S. J. Perelman*. Jackson, MS: University Press of Mississippi, 1995.

Thayer, William Roscoe. *The Life and Letters of John Hay*. Boston: Houghton Mifflin, 1908.

Tolman, William Howe. *The History of Higher Education in Rhode Island*. Washington, DC: Government Printing Office, 1894.

Trent, James W., Jr. *The Manliest Man: Samuel G. Howe and the Contours of Nineteenth-century American Reform*. Amherst, MA: University of Massachusetts, 2012.

Tucker, Barbara M. *Samuel Slater and the Origins of the American Textile Industry, 1790–1860*. Ithaca: Cornell University Press, 1984.

Vaughan, Roger. "Ted Turner: 'I Didn't Fail College; College Failed Me,'" *Brown Alumni Monthly*, September 1975.

Waite, Frederick C. "The Third Medical College in New England, That of Brown University (1811–1828)," *New England Journal of Medicine* 207 (1932).

Walton, Anthony. "The Tougaloo Connection." *Brown Alumni Monthly*, September 1997.

Ward, Lester. "Our Better Halves." In *Against the Tide: Pro-Feminist Men in the United States, 1776–1790: A Documentary History*, edited by Michael S. Kimmel and Thomas Mosmiller. 1888; Boston: Beacon Press, 1992.

Ware, Caroline F. *The Early New England Cotton Manufacture: A Study in Industrial Beginnings*. New York: Russell and Russell, 1966.

Watson, Thomas J., Jr., and Peter Petre. *Father, Son & Co.: My Life at IBM and Beyond*. New York: Bantam Books, 1990.

Wayland, Francis. *A Discourse, Delivered at the Dedication of Manning Hall, the Chapel and Library of Brown University, February 4, 1835*. Providence: Marshall, Brown and Co., 1835.

Wayland, Francis, Jr., and H. L. Wayland. *A Memoir of the Life and Labors of Francis Wayland*. New York: Sheldon and Company, 1868.

Weed, Elizabeth. "Notes on Pembroke Center's History, 1981–2011." Providence: Pembroke Center for Teaching and Research on Women, 2011. http://brown.edu/research/pembroke-center/sites/brown.edu.research.pem-broke-center/files/uploads/Notes_PC_History_Final.pdf.

Weeden, William B. *Early Rhode Island: A Social History of the People*. New York: Grafton Press, 1910.

White, Augustus A., III, and David Chanoff. *Seeing Patients: Unconscious Bias in Health Care*. Cambridge: Harvard University Press, 2011.

Widmer, Ted. "1643: A Nearer Neighbor to the Indians." In *A New Literary History of America*, edited by Greil Marcus and Werner Sollors. Cambridge: Harvard University Press, 2009.

Wilder, Craig Steven. *Ebony and Ivy: Race, Slavery and the Troubled History of America's Universities*. New York: Bloomsbury, 2013.

Williams, Roger. *A Key into the Language of America*. London: Gregory Dexter, 1643. Reprint, edited by Howard M. Chapin, Providence: Rhode Island and Providence Plantations Tercentenary Committee, 1936.

Wills, Garry. *Mr. Jefferson's University*. Washington, DC: National Geographic, 2002.

Wilson, J. Walter, and Diana Fane. *Brown University as the Land Grant College of Rhode Island, 1863–1894*. Providence: Brown University, 1966.

Wood, Gordon S. *The Radicalism of the American Revolution*. New York: Knopf, 1992.

Woolley, Mary. "After Fifty Years." Manuscript, n.d., Brown University Archives.

Workman, John Rowe. *New Horizons of Higher Education: Innovation and Experimentation at Brown University*. Washington, DC: Public Affairs Press, 1959.

Wriston, Henry M. *Wriston Speaking: A Selection of Addresses*. Providence: Brown University Press, 1957.

———. Commencement speech, 1943. Brown University Archives.

Wroth, Lawrence C. *The Colonial Printer*. Portland, ME: Southworth-Anthoensen Press, 1938. Reprint, Charlottesville, VA: Dominion Books, 1964.

———. "The Construction of the College Edifice, 1770–1772." Typescript, Brown University Archives

———. *The First Century of the John Carter Brown Library: A History with a Guide to the Collections*. Providence: Associates of the John Carter Brown Library, 1946.

X, Malcolm. Audiotape of lecture, May 11, 1961. Brown University Archives.

Young, Robin. *For Love & Liberty: The Untold Civil War Story of Major Sullivan Ballou & His Famous Love Letter*. New York: Thunder's Mouth Press, 2006.

Zeitz, Joshua. *Lincoln's Boys: John Hay, John Nicolay and the War for Lincoln's Image*. New York: Viking, 2014.

Zwick, Elizabeth. "The Pembroke Class of 1945: A Wartime Generation of College Women." Brown University honors thesis, May 1982.

ACKNOWLEDGMENTS

L IFE ON A UNIVERSITY CAMPUS IS OFTEN COLLABORATIVE, and I benefited immensely from the advice of others while writing this book.

When Christina Paxson, the president of Brown University, asked me to undertake this project, she had a much clearer idea than I did that I was the right person to do it. I'd like to thank her for that confidence.

The act of writing about Brown drew upon a lifetime spent near the university (although I did not actually attend Brown). But it was wonderful to grow up on a campus, attending athletic events, making free use of the libraries, reveling in the medieval carnival of commencement, and experiencing the burst of adrenaline that always attended the return of students in September. That feeling came back as I turned to the task of writing about what makes Brown special. In many ways, I feel privileged to have the memories of an older person, from a childhood running around buildings that no longer exist. I took swimming lessons in the Colgate-Hoyt Pool, next to Lincoln Field (it was so antiquated that it seemed fitting that it was located near the statue of Marcus Aurelius—a kind of Roman bath near the emperor). I ran around the rickety wooden second-floor track of Marvel Gym, and tried to play squash in the freezing courts located in the building's aerie, up endless stairways. Before Brown soccer games (I was a ball boy, with my brother and friends), we sometimes changed in the old field house, which had housed the indigent citizens of Providence in the nineteenth century. I loved visiting the Ladd Observatory, which seemed to be forever poised on the cutting-edge of astronomy, circa 1891. With school groups, I went on field trips to

Brown's distant Bristol campus to sit in King Philip's Seat and gaze out over his former dominions. All of that history came flooding back again as I walked down the old pathways once more.

But when my memories began to sound like those of someone approaching dotage, I was fortunate to work with people who focused. Wendy Strothman was a painstaking reader, who read the manuscript many times and brought a sharp editorial eye to lazy phrases and assumptions. David Ebershoff always brought common sense and literary grace. The Brown 250 office was a model of teamwork, and Eve Ornstedt, Kat Schott, Valerie Taylor, and Raina Fox all stepped in when it came time to convert the manuscript into a book. In the president's office, Kim Roskiewicz was unfailingly helpful, and Heather Goode as well. Marisa Quinn leavened every conversation. Will Balliett and his team at Thames & Hudson were the perfect partners. I'd like to thank Elizabeth Keene, Beth Tondreau, Vittorio Maestro, Neil Mann, and Janice Carapellucci for their first-rate expertise throughout the publishing process.

Brown is fortunate to have battalions of friends and alumni, ready to assist at the drop of a hat. Betsy West and Oren Jacoby, in addition to making a very good film about Brown, read the manuscript and offered valuable suggestions. Norman Boucher also read the manuscript and improved it significantly. Likewise, Luther Spoehr offered invaluable advice and a close reading that stemmed from his own profound understanding of the long history involved. Speaking of long history, it was a pleasure to continue the conversation that began when he let me sneak into a history class he was teaching, more years ago than either of us will want to verify. Similarly, I have never stopped learning from Gordon Wood, who kindly allowed me to take his course on colonial history when I was in high school. In this book, I tried to make the point that a university radiates light and knowledge to many more people than its actual undergraduates, and I was lucky to experience this first hand.

Some of these friendships go back even deeper than memory. Betsy West's father was a close friend of my grandfather's. I can't remember not knowing two professors in the Department of History,

Abbott Gleason and James Patterson, and they have been a constant inspiration, not only for their professional standards, but also for their lifelong dedication to Brown and its students. On certain days, usually around election time, Rhode Island can seem like a petri dish for an experiment gone horribly wrong; but at its best, it's a nurturing environment in which people look after each other, and children run interchangeably from one backyard to another. I was lucky to be able to run into quite a few historians along the way.

I was fortunate also to know two former members of the Department of History. Donald Fleming never lost his attachment to Brown, even after leaving for a university to the north, and his history of science at Brown remains definitive. I benefited from many conversations with him, long ago. Edmund S. Morgan left Brown for a university to the south, but he too remained a friend of the university. His visit to the John Carter Brown Library, at the age of ninety-five, was an unforgettable day. Through him, one could feel as if Ezra Stiles were in the room and it was 1764 all over again.

Many more recent faculty and friends added their considerable knowledge of Brown University. I appreciated early conversations with Jane Lancaster, working on a history of her own. Rob Emlen and Dietrich Neumann were always ready to help make a point more precise. I enjoyed talking about early American universities with Jeremy Mumford. All of the members and staff of the Department of History were congenial. From other departments, I particularly enjoyed interactions with Laurel Bestock, Tricia Rose, and Andre Willis.

This book simply would not have been possible without the care that generations of librarians and archivists have brought to the preservation of Brown's past. Nothing forces one to appreciate sources more than losing access to them, and for a long stretch of the writing of this book, during the renovation of the John Hay Library, it was almost impossible to find what I needed. To the extent that I could, I'm grateful to Brown's superb team, including Raymond Butti and Jennifer Betts in the Archives, and Ann Morgan Dodge, Holly Snyder, Kathleen Brooks, James Moul, and Alison Bundy at the Hay. I also want to thank Harriette Hemmasi, the head of the Brown University Library.

I will always be grateful to the Board of Governors of the John Carter Brown Library for inviting me to work in a place where history is so elegantly preserved, and so palpably alive. Well known as a shrine for the study of the early history of the Americas, the JCB, following the strong interests of its founder, also holds essential records relating to the history of Rhode Island, Brown University, and the Browns themselves. I learned a great deal about those topics and all facets of early American history while there, with much of the learning coming from the visiting scholars and fellows whom we were ostensibly there to help. In this way, wonderfully, the quest for knowledge produces a genuine community of friendship. I also want to thank the Governors for their collegiality as we all did our bit to advance work on "the great subject," as John Carter Brown called it. Fred Ballou, Arte Joukowsky, David Rumsey, Clint Smullyan, and Bill Twaddell were particularly delightful companions and conscientious stewards of the past. In addition, I want to acknowledge the friendship of a former librarian, the late Thomas R. Adams, who always went out of his way to be helpful. Maureen O'Donnell's indefatigable efforts to support the work of the library still amaze me, years after the fact. She is one of the institution's greatest treasures.

It would surely delight the eighteenth-century Browns to know that this hill had become the home for an institution of such hemispheric scope. I also want to express special thanks to the members of the Brown family, who still do a great deal to enrich the community at the John Carter Brown Library and the university—Angela Brown Fischer and Edwin Fischer, Captain Nicholas and Diane Brown, Sylvia Brown, and the younger members of the family who, it can be hoped, will someday feel a connection of their own. I only met the late J. Carter Brown on one occasion, in Washington, but it was a memorable meeting, and I appreciated his advice.

Throughout my life of proximity to Brown, I have known many friends who were either students, or alumni, or, increasingly, parents of students. One group of Brown alumni was especially important to me—the brilliant young editors who gathered around John F.

Kennedy Jr. as he started *George* magazine. That experiment turned out to be anything but short-lived, for it gave me a lifelong desire to write up to the standards that John set. I will always be grateful for the chance that he and his colleagues gave me to approach history in a new way. Years later I met another alumnus, Tony Horwitz; his independent, participatory way of writing history struck me as very much in the spirit of Brown, and I was delighted when we could formally recognize that fact, during his time as a visiting scholar at the John Carter Brown Library. I appreciated his insightful reading of this manuscript. Another history-minded alumnus, Thomas Mallon, helped me both by reading this manuscript and by writing so perceptively about Brown in the pages of the *Brown Alumni Magazine.*

Two current students, Zeyna Tabbaa and David Kaufman, performed valuable research for this history, and the history classes that I was teaching also provided a forum for lively digressions into Brown history. I'm grateful to the Department of History for that opportunity. Another young person was essential for keeping the production line moving along—my son Freddy, who patiently endured history lectures from which there was no escape. He took a lovely photograph for the book.

I also want to acknowledge a group that cannot hear me. On every page I have been deeply informed by the work of earlier historians. Brown's nineteenth-century librarian and historian Reuben A. Guild set a high standard near the beginning, meticulously gathering and interpreting the university's early documents, and writing prolifically and well on a variety of topics relating to Brown and Rhode Island. The twentieth century brought a quickening of interest. In 1905, a detailed *Historical Catalogue of Brown University* was issued, listing everyone who ever received a degree (a similar work for Pembroke was issued in 1924). A 1909 volume, *Memories of Brown*, is rich in anecdotal material relating to early student life. In 1914, for the 150th anniversary, Walter C. Bronson of the Department of English wrote a beautifully researched book, *The History of Brown University: 1764–1914*, that remains essential. That same year, a number of historical addresses were given, one of which I found especially informative, W. W. Keen's "The Early Years of Brown University (1764–1770), While Located in Warren, Rhode Island." In 1952, Donald Fleming wrote an important booklet, *Science and Technology in Providence, 1760–1914: An Essay in the History of Brown University in the Metropolitan Community.*

The 1964 Bicentennial also produced a plethora of historical writings, in pamphlet form as well as in the pages of the *Brown Alumni Monthly.* Pembroke College did not make it to a centennial, but two works cover its eighty-year run: Grace Hawk's *Pembroke College* (1967), and a collection of essays issued in 1991, *The Search for Equity: Women at Brown University, 1891–1991.* From the 1960s to the 1980s, a Brown professor of history, William McLoughlin, wrote a series of insightful books on the Baptists and other religious dissenters in the eighteenth century, and anyone seeking a thorough understanding of Brown's theological origins ought to wrestle with this complex but rewarding topic. In 1985, Jay Barry and Martha Mitchell issued an entertaining, well-illustrated history, *A Tale of Two Centuries.* I did not know Mitchell, but her work compiling the *Encyclopedia Brunoniana* was a boon to all future historians of the university. In 1991, Janet M. Phillips wrote a helpful short history, republished in 2000. The *Slavery and Justice* report of 2006 was, in addition to addressing its main focus, another compelling work on the subject of Brown's origins.

I mentioned earlier that I did not attend Brown University. But like John Hay, I had a grandfather who did, my mother's father, Edward M. Read III of the class of 1931. He found employment in the John Hay Library as an undergraduate, the same place where I did much of the research for this book. His mother, Harriet Louise Campbell, Pembroke class of 1905, worked in the Providence Athenaeum, just down the hill. (At times, it feels as if we are a family of hobbits, staying close to the Shire.) My great-uncle Bradford C. Read was a member of the class of 1933. I am grateful for their example and long lives of loyalty to Brown, Pembroke, and Rhode Island.

When I was a child, my father was a member of the Department of Asian History (the Department of History had rejected Asia as unworthy of its attention). It was a particular joy to see the university's ups and downs through his eyes, especially as things began to go better for Brown. He later served as Brown's first Dean of Student Life, and then as Dean of Admissions and Financial Aid, and in each of those positions he communicated a sense of what an honor it is to belong to a university community. He remains connected to it, not only as the parent of this author, but as a faculty spouse, courtesy of Meera Viswanathan of the Department of Comparative Literature. Marcus Aurelius urges us to pass through our short time here "conformably to nature," reaching our end like an olive that falls when ripe, "thanking the tree on which it grew." With this book, I tried to do that. Every page was improved by his careful reading. I would also like to thank Loui's Family Restaurant for giving us a place to hold our editorial conferences. Figuring out where to place that apostrophe was a challenge; I commend the proofreaders for accepting that Rhode Island sometimes makes its own rules.

I begin the book standing before the Van Wickle Gates. To one side, there is a lovely inscription from Cicero, chosen in 1905 by Professor Albert Harkness. It reads, "*Haec studia adulescentiam alunt, senectutem oblectant, secundas res ornant, adversis perfugium ac solacium praebent*," which translates as, "These studies fortify one's youth, delight one's old age; amid success they are an ornament, in failure they are a refuge and a comfort." I hope this book will serve a similar set of restorative purposes for the many individuals, in all of their diversity, who constitute the Brown community.

INDEX

PICTURE CREDITS